I0816192

Déjà BLUE

A Sportswriter Reflects on 41 Seasons of Kentucky Basketball

by

JERRY TIPTON

Acclaim Press
MORLEY, MISSOURI

P.O. Box 238
Morley, MO 63767
(573) 472-9800
www.acclaimpress.com

Book & Cover Design: Frene Melton
Cover photos by Mark Cornelison

ISBN: 978-1-956027-68-6 | 1-956027-68-8
Library of Congress Control Number: 2023944967

Second Printing: 2024
Printed in the United States of America
10 9 8 7 6 5 4 3 2

Contents

Dedication

To the four people who would be on my personal Mount Rushmore. My grandmother, Ella Agnes Mason, who gave me the love any child needs; to an uncle, Charles "Bo" Basham, who steered me to sportswriting; to my last sports editor at the *Huntington Herald-Dispatch*, Mike Connell, who enhanced my appreciation for treating sports as news; to my wife, Paula Anderson, who brought color to my black-and-white life.

Acknowledgments

By definition, a memoir is a personal history written by the author. But I've never been comfortable being in the public eye. Fortunately, the reporting job means gathering facts and opinions from others.

With 41 seasons of University of Kentucky men's basketball as the focus, I wanted to get memories and insights of others in order to form a quasi-historical remembrance.

The former UK players who kindly shared their memories were Sam Bowie, Kenny Walker, Richie Farmer, Tyler Ulis, Tayshaun Prince, Kellan Grady, Wayne Turner, Dan Issel, Rex Chapman, Scott Padgett, Dwane Casey, Tony Delk, John Pelphrey and Jeff Sheppard.

I also spoke to Kentucky Coach John Calipari and former UK Coach Tubby Smith. Other coaching perspectives came from former Eddie Sutton assistant Doug Barnes, former Rick Pitino assistant Jim O'Brien and former John Calipari assistant Joel Justus. Kentucky Director of Athletics Mitch Barnhart shared his thoughts. Thanks also to two Hall of Famers: former Arkansas Coach Nolan Richardson and Michgan State Coach Tom Izzo. And Martin Newton answered questions about his father, Charles Martin (C.M.) Newton, being UK's Director of Athletics.

From the journalism world, there's many people to thank. I appreciated the guidance and support from former *Huntington Herald-Dispatch* sports editor Mike Connell. My sports editors at the *Herald-Leader* – Mike Johnson, Gene Abell and Mat Graf – did the same. All four generously shared their thoughts on my time covering Kentucky. Former *Herald-Leader* executive editors John Carroll, Tim Kelly and Rufus Friday inspired a journalistic approach to covering Kentucky basketball.

Colleagues in the world of sports coverage who provided friendship and expertise include Mark Bradley, Jimmy Hyams, David Cloninger, Parrish Alford, Scott Rabalais, Sheldon Mickles, Glenn Guilbeau, Chip Towers, Chris Harry, Mike Strange, Wally Hall, Bob Holt, Ron Higgins, Rick Bozich, Billy Reed, Mike Embry, Gary Graves, David Climer, Joe Biddle and Cecil Hurt.

Friends and colleagues at the *Herald-Leader* who made my time at the newspaper so enjoyable included John Clay, Mike Fields, Angela Duerson, Merlene Davis, Deedra Lawhead, Tina Croley, Ben Roberts, Mark Sonka, Franklin Renfro, Chip Cosby, Jennifer Smith, Rob Kandt, Chuck Culpepper, D.G. FitzMaurice, Johnny McGill, Bill Pinkston, Maryjean Wall and Tony Wilson.

LuAnn Farrar, who was Director of News Research at the *Herald-Leader*, provided invaluable help in terms of navigating the *Herald-Leader* archives. And former *Herald-Leader* photographers Mark Cornelison and Charles Bertram kindly agreed to provide photos for this book.

I owe sincere gratitude to long-time administrative assistant Marta McMackin and the walking/talking UK athletics history book that is Jim Host.

Marsha Poe was always fun to talk to at the fan campouts for tickets to Big Blue Madness.

This book inspired me to contact childhood friend Mike Lapkewych. It was fun going down memory lane with him. The same was true of David Byrd, a college friend and roommate who shared his memories of the Marshall football team plane crash.

An aunt, Patty Noe, reminded me of family history. She and Uncle Cliff gave the insecure boy that was me reason to believe things could work out.

I'll be forever grateful for the insights on fans shared by Dan Wann, a psychology professor at Murray State University. He made writing a chapter on Kentucky fans a lot of fun.

In terms of sportswriting, I always sought to venture out from the predictable or routine. Those who gave this book that quality were Frank X Walker (professor in UK's English department and the state's Poet Laureate from 2013 to 2015), former *Herald-Leader* colleague Paul Prather (now the pastor at Bethesda Church in Mt. Sterling), Gene Strange (former pastor at St. Luke Church in Lexington), Linda Buch (store manager for Kentucky Branded, which sells I Still Hate Laettner shirts) and Joe Mattingly (long-time attorney in Lebanon, Ky., who worked for *The Cats Pause* as a UK student).

Foreword

I started at the *Lexington Herald* in 1981 when sports editor Mike Johnson hired me for the summer while the newspaper searched for a new University of Kentucky sports beat writer. At the end of that search, the *Herald* hired Jerry Tipton.

We became colleagues and friends, but it wasn't until 2000 when I was fortunate enough to be named sports columnist that we became travel partners. That's when I got to know the real Jerry Tipton.

Over the past two decades — not counting the pandemic — we logged a countless number of miles together covering Kentucky basketball. We flew together. We drove together. We ate together. We shared the same flights, the same hotels, the same restaurants, the same press rooms, the same press boxes, the same bad press food. We complained together, celebrated together, second-guessed together, sweated deadlines together.

Over the last few years, we did a lot of driving to games together. In all those trips, we rarely listened to the radio. I remember once picking Jerry up at his house and when he got in the car he immediately turned off the radio. This was during the overtime of a basketball game I was following. "Hey, I was listening to that," I said.

But the reason we rarely listened to the radio is because we were too busy talking. We talked basketball, family, newsroom gossip, writing, referees, music, movies, football, baseball, books, politics, the state of journalism, technology and newspapers.

Here's the thing: over all those years, in all those airports, in all those rental cars, at all those games, what I admired most about Jerry was his tremendous work ethic. If you traveled with Jerry, you were going to be the first one at the arena and the last one to leave the arena. He always made that one extra phone call to talk to that one extra person to get that one extra fact to make his story that one bit better.

True story: Jerry once missed his flight out of Maui because he waited to talk to Tubby Smith one more time for a story. When he finally made it back to the states, he ended up spending the night in the Atlanta airport. If you don't believe me, ask his very good friend Ralph Hacker. He found Jerry sleeping at his gate, and left him a note at his feet.

Jerry was never afraid to ask the tough questions, a trait that didn't always win him friends among fans. But it did win him the respect of his colleagues, competitors and readers, those who admired his peerless reporting skills. That's why Jerry is in not one but three Hall of Fames — the Kentucky Journalism Hall of Fame, the US Basketball Writers Hall of Fame and the Marshall Journalism Hall of Fame. For my money, he was the best basketball beat reporter in the country.

And that's what Jerry has done here. Instead of merely writing a memoir about his days covering the Wildcats, he has done reporting, as well. Even after retiring from the newspaper, it's a habit he just can't kick. To that, I say thank goodness, because it makes his book an entertaining and enlightening read.

John Clay
Herald-Leader sports columnist

A Sportswriter Reflects on 41 Seasons of Kentucky Basketball

God Has a Special Place

As I became acquainted with journalism, I came to understand that friction between a reporter and people he or she is covering is all but inevitable. To borrow a well-worn cliché, the truth can hurt.

The sportswriter-coach relationship is no exception to this rule. There are different agendas at play. The coach wants to win. The reporter wants to tell the reader/view/listener what's going on or add perspective. And sometimes making the public more fully aware of what's going on can hinder the chances of winning, complicate recruiting and/or merely annoy the coach.

Of course, the coach is conditioned to be the authority figure. Often during my newspaper career, it seemed that the coach expected to all but dictate the storyline. During the coronavirus pandemic, I did a story on how coaches reacted to losing control because of COVID-19.

"We're all control freaks," Michigan State Coach Tom Izzo said. "If you're successful, that's almost part of the deal. . . . If you don't control (the players) on a daily basis, I think it gets out of control quickly."

Doug Barnes, an assistant coach on Eddie Sutton's Kentucky staff in the late 1980s, recalled Sutton's controlling nature.

"It was almost like during basketball season, he wanted to know where you were, what you were doing, yada, yada," Barnes said in my July, 2020 story on how COVID lessened the control coaches wanted.

Rex Chapman, the leading scorer on Sutton's teams in his two seasons of college basketball, spoke publicly of Sutton wanting to control his dating life.

"The reason they have so many practices, so many meetings is because basically they're kind of controlling what these young people do as much as they can," Barnes said. "One of the reasons I think they're control freaks is there are so many 'uncontrollables:' Injuries. Illness. Personality conflicts. Fans' expectations."

Control of the media seemed merely part of this desire (perceived necessity?) to control. There can be a transactional aspect to covering a sports beat. If the reporter will help promote the team, the program, the coach or a player, he or she can gain greater access or be given scoops. I could not do that because I knew a "negative story" would likely arise at some point. I did not want to be compromised.

When I wrote a story perceived as "negative," I could be accused of violating the unspoken agreement or being disloyal. My loyalty was to the newspaper I worked for, to the readers and to journalism.

With the reporter intent on being objective, rooting for or against a team or player has nothing to do with it. On a radio show relatively late in my time covering Kentucky basketball, host Woody Paige, then with *The Denver Post*, asked me if I had a rooting interest when covering a game. I said I only rooted for a good storyline to come to mind and an ability to execute that storyline. He chuckled knowingly.

For example, say a Kentucky player had been struggling, but seemed to be snapping out of a slump in a game. I would be thinking that if he hit a key shot late in the game that would help the story.

Otherwise, winning and losing were in the province of the players and coaches. Neither affected my mood. How I executed the story regularly brightened or darkened my mood.

The goal is objectivity, which can be misconstrued as rooting against a team. I had reasons to hope Kentucky made a deep run in the NCAA Tournament. The postseason brought the most fun. New locales. Seeing in person players from different parts of the country for the first time. The win-or-go-home factor heightens the drama.

The idea of not rooting against Kentucky hit home for me during the 2011 Final Four. UK had not played in a Final Four since 1998. That made for the longest drought in the history of the ever-proud program.

The 2011 Final Four was played in Houston. I remember sitting in the media workroom on Thursday, the day before news conferences previewing Saturday's national semifinals. As I did research and collected notes to use that weekend, I suddenly realized I was smiling broadly . . . and I couldn't stop smiling. And I tried to stop. But I was so happy to be back at college basketball's grandest stage and be amongst noted sportswriters. Kentucky basketball had returned me there and I was happy about it.

But I knew I had to be objective and not let this happiness prevent me from doing my job.

This dynamic of not considering any news beat an exception to the rule of objectivity regularly came to mind in my 41 seasons covering Kentucky basketball. UK basketball evokes reverence. But irreverence rules in newspaper newsrooms.

This was especially true when Joe B. Hall was Kentucky's coach. My first four seasons covering UK basketball were his last four seasons as coach. He seemed to not look favorably upon the *Herald-Leader*. One story I heard about involved a *H-L* reporter sitting near the UK bench during a game and writing about Hall's coarse language.

Even though this story was published years before I came to Lexington, it seemed that I represented the *Herald-Leader* and therefore bore the brunt of Hall's unhappiness.

In those days, the media could attend practices. So, interaction between coach and reporter occurred regularly. I remember a casual post-practice conversation turning bad when I innocently suggested that a coach — not necessarily Hall — could feint a public image that differed from his or her true self. Perhaps this reminded Hall of the *Herald-Leader* story about his in-game language. He did not react kindly. In making the case for being genuine, he said his dear mother would not allow cursing, and he would never want to disappoint her. As he grew emotional in making his case, Hall began sprinkling expletives into his argument. I thought it best not to point this out.

Upon later reflection, I linked his response to the *H-L* story about his coarse language during games and the inference in our center-court conversation that I was suggesting that the "real" Hall differed from the public Hall.

Lexington businessman and Hall confidant Jim Host said this was merely the UK coach's sense of humor on display.

When told of Hall cursing while saying his mother would not allow foul language, Dwane Casey, who played for Hall in the late 1970s, suggested this was not an offhand remark by the coach.

"He was tough," Casey said in 2023. "But everything was calculated, I came to find out. Everything he said, everything he did was all calculated. . . . I think he would say things contrary to what you were saying just to debate or stimulate conversation."

In those younger days, I did not shave every day. I might go a day or three without shaving. At one point, Hall told me a person looked like a bum if he did not shave daily.

Casey likened this to when he coached the Toronto Raptors and received calls from Hall in which the former Kentucky coach offered — shall we say — constructive criticism.

"'When are you going to get your players to play some defense?'" Casey recalled Hall saying. "'You know how to play defense better than that.'

"Just stuff to (spur) you a little bit. To keep you going."

On another occasion when he was Kentucky coach, Hall changed his routine of speaking to reporters after practice. He said he would not answer questions if I was in the group. I don't remember what prompted this, but I backed off so other reporters could ask questions.

Mike Embry, who was working for The Associated Press at the time, kindly agreed to share Hall's quotes with me afterwards. With Embry's help and listening ever more attentively to Hall's weekly radio and television shows, I was able to continue writing stories that included his quotes.

Within a week or two, Hall said I could rejoin the group sessions after practices.

Happily, my relationship with Hall improved after he retired in the spring of 1985. Thereafter, if the story could be helped with his perspective, I'd call him. Sometimes we met for lunch, then we'd do an interview after eating.

Alas, more than once, Joe brought up stories I had written that he still found objectionable. Once, he took his wallet out, reached in and pulled out a newspaper clipping of a story of mine that he continued to dislike. I don't remember what the story was, but I remember feeling sad — not mad — that Hall had saved the story. As I recall, I sat quietly as he voiced his continuing objection to the story.

At another of our quasi working lunches, he surprised me with a pointed question: Did I realize that I would someday meet my Maker and have to explain the stories I had written?

Not knowing if this was his playful sense of humor on display or an attempt to make a point about divine judgment, I did not respond.

A few minutes later, Joe again asked the same question. I smiled as if to acknowledge the point he seemed to be making while wondering if I needed to respond.

When he asked a third time about me someday having to explain what He — and by inference, God – saw as the error of my ways, I responded with my own question.

"Did Joe ever think that God had a special place reserved for sportswriters?"

To which, Joe said enthusiastically, "He does! He does!" as he motioned downward with a thumb.

I again smiled and decided that this was an example of Hall's sense of humor.

The memory of my at-times contentious relationship with Hall came to mind again in the summer of 2011 when then UK Coach John Calipari would be coaching the Dominican Republic national team in the FIBA Americas Championship. Perhaps not so coincidentally, the mother of coveted recruit Karl-Anthony Towns was a native of the Dominican Republic.

A media event to mark Calipari's new coaching assignment — and recruiting tactic (?) — was set up at a downtown Lexington restaurant near Rupp Arena. Reporters could talk to people attending the gathering as they walked onto a blue carpet outside the restaurant.

Calipari, who throughout his coaching career has shown a soft spot for former coaches, invited Hall. This was no surprise. Calipari had repeatedly credited Hall with helping him adjust to being Kentucky coach and rallying support. As he arrived, Hall was in a jovial mood. Reporters laughed repeatedly at his quips. I had been told that this was the Hall persona reporters knew when he was an assistant coach for Adolph Rupp. Following a legend as the coach of a program that already involved suffocating scrutiny put Hall permanently on the defensive. That the legend, Adolph Rupp, second-guessed him publicly on a weekly television show as I was told after I came to Lexington only made the challenge of being the next Kentucky coach exponentially more difficult.

At one point as media members and Hall shared another laugh outside the Lexington restaurant, a young reporter turned to me and asked if Joe B. had been this funny and engaging when he was Kentucky's coach.

"Uh, no," I answered. Reporters young and not so young laughed.

Hall was not the only Kentucky coach I covered who voiced objections to stories or questions. It was a common occurrence.

I did not take this personally. Insults, a cold shoulder, feeding stories to a competitor and other acts of retribution were part of the job. I did not think complaining about someone or wishing them bad luck was a healthy way to live. There was also a fear that animosity toward a coach would somehow creep into stories.

So, I always tried to find something to like or admire about the Kentucky coach. When strains in the relationships emerged, I'd remind myself of these attractive attributes. This helped to roll with the psychic punches.

It wasn't hard to think of admirable qualities or alluring aspects of a coach's biography or personality.

For Hall, it was charming to think of him as someone who grew up in Cynthiana, Ky., (about 30 miles north of Lexington) as a Kentucky fan who bought into the program's the-regular-rules-don't-apply ethos. And now, he led the program he had loved since childhood.

Next came Eddie Sutton. His success as Arkansas coach made him a popular choice to succeed Hall. Despite fans second-guessing repeatedly (for instance he didn't move to a house in Lexington fast enough, they said; his playing style was too slow), Sutton maintained a friendly tone. Even with his program imploding in his fourth and final season as UK coach because of a NCAA investigation, Sutton was available to the media on almost a daily basis.

Rick Pitino radiated a can-do intelligence. He also flashed a sense of humor. I remember a small media gathering in a meeting room near the coaches' offices. Pitino spoke about fans who were upset about a loss or a call or something. Such a fan could gain perspective, he said, by joining his wife for a romantic dinner, then "putting on the Chairman of the Board." The rest was left to our imaginations. The reference to Frank Sinatra and the seeming inference to love making drew a hearty laugh.

The humanity of Tubby Smith leavened any possible grousing. Any reporter's thoughts of ill will would be quickly followed by the expectation of regret. He seemed to recognize that the other person — even the lowly sportswriter — had feelings and responsibilities. He credited his father with instilling this magnanimous approach to life. If he turned down my interview request, I learned to adopt a hangdog look. Almost always, Smith then agreed to answer a few questions.

Of course, Billy Gillispie was only Kentucky's coach for two seasons. There was talk about how disagreeable he could be. But that wasn't how he struck me. He seemed ill-suited for the job, so I had sympathy for someone trying to make it work while seemingly destined for failure.

Like Pitino, John Calipari radiated an intelligence that could take the form of comedy. He also seemed to like witty repartee. I tried to engage him this way while keeping in mind that a post-game news conference following a defeat would not be the best time for a battle of wits.

I also found it amazing — and unprecedented? — the success Calipari had as UMass coach. The UMass program's rise from nonentity to a No. 1 ranking and a Final Four appearance in the 1990s was impossible to resist. Admiration for what he did at UMass made any friction between Calipari and me seem merely temporary.

I accepted criticism from coaches, players, referees, fans, fellow reporters and anyone else as part of the job. I was my biggest critic. I second-guessed many things. I remembered that my last sports editor at the *Huntington (W.Va.) Herald-Dispatch*, Mike Connell, had said that a reporter reaches a key point in his or her development when a story can be improved with each reading. As a result, I looked upon every story as lacking in some way.

The second-guessing, if that's the right term, included interactions with people in the course of reporting and writing. I was likely to think later about how I could have better responded or asked a better question.

One example with Calipari came when someone mentioned hockey at a news conference. He playfully questioned whether I knew anything about hockey. I said I knew what icing was. This did not win the exchange.

After thinking about it, I wish I had said "I grew up in Detroit. Also known as 'Hockey Town.' That's 'check' and 'mate.'"

Kentucky Basketball from Afar

Surely every newspaper reporter wants to cover a beat that draws intense interest from readers.

Given the history of achievement, Kentucky basketball has been likened to the New York Yankees. As a sports fan, it's difficult, if not impossible, to be nonchalant. A fan might feel compelled to root for or against such a dynastic program.

Before every home game, public address announcer Patrick Whitmer welcomed fans to Rupp Arena by saying the downtown Lexington landmark is "home to the greatest tradition in the history of college basketball!" Scott Stricklin, then UK"s Associate Athletic Director/Media Relations, suggested this claim of unrivaled superiority be included in welcoming remarks before every home game, Whitmer said.

The crowd always cheered.

Blending in — or even suggesting that Kentucky reigns as only one member of an exclusive club of so-called blue-blood programs — is viewed as too big of a concession.

With UCLA having won 11 national championships to Kentucky's eight, and Kansas surpassing Kentucky in the 2021-22 season for most all-time victories, I jokingly suggested to the public address announcer that he could still proclaim Rupp Arena as home to the second-greatest tradition. Whitmer laughed, but demurred.

However difficult, objectivity is the reporter's goal. After all, there are two teams on the court, thus doubling the chances of an attention-getting angle to the story. I took that too far in my first few seasons covering Kentucky basketball. If the other team's storyline was more compelling, that's what drove my game story (or "gamer" in newspaper parlance).

I believe not growing up in what's known as the Big Blue Nation helped make objectivity more achievable.

I was born and raised in Michigan. It was not until my early teens that I first linked Kentucky with basketball. That happened in the 1963-64 season. An uncle, Charles "Bo" Basham, had given me a subscription to *Sports Illustrated* as a Christmas present. I remember seeing Cotton Nash wearing a Kentucky uniform on the cover. Hmmm, Kentucky has a basketball team, I thought.

I grew up in Hamtramck, Mich., which takes some explaining. Hamtramck is one of two independent towns within the Detroit city limits. A French Canadian soldier, Jean Francois Hamtramck, founded the town in 1798.

I considered it like living in a small town (the population was about 25,000 when I was growing up in the 1950s and 1960s) while surrounded by a major metropolitan city (Detroit was the fifth most populated U.S. city at the time).

I came to think of Hamtramck as an example of the United States being a melting pot. The auto industry sparked this coming together of a diverse population. There was a Dodge plant in Hamtramck. There was also a Chevrolet plant on the Detroit side of Hamtramck's western boundary.

Jobs in the auto industry drew White and Black people from the South to Hamtramck. I remember Dwane Casey, who integrated his Kentucky elementary school as a third grader, being surprised when I told him Hamtramck schools were fully integrated when I entered kindergarten in 1956. If you lived in the district, that was the school you attended. One of my classmates was Betty Lou Henson, who as an adult became an actor and appeared in the movie "Kindergarten Cop".

Black and white families lived on the same streets, sometimes next-door neighbors.

A large population from eastern Europe — primarily from Poland and Ukraine — also came to Hamtramck for work.

Motown Records made Detroit notable in popular music. Because of its majority Polish population, Hamtramck was playfully dubbed Po-town. Incidentally, Hamtramck's middle school (which was called a junior high school) was named for Nicolaus Copernicus, a Polish astronomer who proposed that Earth and other planets orbited around the sun about 70 years before Galileo. That explains Hamtramck High School's nickname being the Cosmos.

My grandmother, Ella Agnes Smith, came to Hamtramck from West Virginia during World War II. My mother, Gloria Faye, followed Aggie, as she was called, to Michigan after completing her education at the West Virginia School for the Deaf. The scarlet fever she contracted as a two-year-old robbed her of a good bit of her hearing. She read lips, which could lead to confusion. For example, as a teenager I told her about my musical tastes and mentioned funk. She recoiled because she thought I had dropped a F-bomb. I learned some sign language, but mostly spelled out words with my fingers if I wanted to make sure she understood.

My mother met my father, Sidney Tipton, in Hamtramck. I was told that he came from Terre Haute, Ind., to work in the auto industry after serving in the U.S. Army for two decades. They married in 1950. I was born the next year.

My father died in a car accident when I was two years old. I have no memory of him. Only many decades later did I learn that his father was from Owingsville, Ky.

My thoughts about Kentucky were positively glowing. That's because of a neighbor who had come to Hamtramck from Benton, Ky. Evalee Dutcher — or "Aunt Evalee" as I called her — seemed to be a warm, welcoming auntie for everyone. If you had a problem, you could seek advice or a solution from Evalee. Once after finishing college, I drove to Hamtramck for a visit. Upon learning that I was driving back the next day, Evalee surprised me by packing a lunch for me to take on the trip. Uncle Bo, who did not pass out compliments easily, said Evalee was "a saint."

The first house I remember living in was a boarding house for auto workers that my grandmother ran. My mother and I moved there after my father died. Evalee lived two houses down Alice Street. A Hispanic family lived next door. A Black family lived down the street.

The Chevy plant was within easy walking distance. I remember the plant's forging hammer causing the ground to vibrate. And you would hear a whistle signaling the end of a work shift.

Hamtramck was a sports minded town. Hamtramck High School was a tennis dynasty. Between 1949 and 1969, HHS teams won 18 state championships in boys tennis. HHS players also won 16 singles and 13 doubles titles.

The coaches were Jean Hoxie, who was of Polish descent, and her husband, Jerry Hoxie.

I remember Jean Hoxie, who was inducted into the Michigan Sports Hall of Fame in 1965, bringing players to the elementary school I attended and putting on a tennis exhibition. I also recall her insisting that people say they were from Hamtramck, and not round it off by saying Detroit.

Arguably her most famous player was Jane "Peaches" Bartkowicz, who won the Junior Wimbledon championship one year.

Art "Pinky" Deras was another local youth sports icon. He led Hamtramck to the 1959 Little League World Series championship. It remained the only time a team from Michigan won that championship until 2021.

Two years later, Deras led Hamtramck to the Pony League World Series championship.

My sports accomplishments did not compare. Our team, the Red Sox, won the 1962 Hamtramck Little League title. Being left handed, I was typecast as a first baseman.

Mostly, I played pickup softball, touch football, basketball and hockey with neighborhood friends. We dubbed ourselves the "Schoolfield Gang" because we played on a paved expanse across the street from Holbrook Elementary School.

"That was kind of the glue that melted everyone together," a childhood friend, Mike Lapkewych, recalled in 2023.

We imagined ourselves a "gang" in a non-threatening sense. I recall the gang members liking the movie *West Side Story.* Lapkewych remembered decades later how older members of our group spray painted the words "Sharks" and "Jets" on the playground pavement.

Maybe most importantly, the Schoolfield Gang gave me a sense of belonging.

"I don't think there was anyone that was shunned," Lapkewych said. "If they came to play, they came to play."

Hamtramck's city leaders seemed intent on keeping young people occupied and out of trouble. There was an ice skating rink at the city park. That's where I learned to skate, although the Schoolfield Gang's pickup hockey games were played on snow that we tamped down to a smoother surface. Rather than a puck, we used a frozen tennis ball.

In the summer, Hamtramck's elementary schools were converted into recreation centers. You could check out a basketball to play on a basket Lapkewych and a friend hung on the three-tier fence bordering the school field. You could check out a checkerboard. In the winter, the school gyms were opened to kids.

I clearly remember my introduction to basketball. I was in the third or fourth grade. Friends said they were going to the school gym. I did not know about the gym being available. Growing up as the only sports fan in the house, I was unaware of basketball. Baseball was my first sporting love, then came football and then hockey.

Another discovery came before we actually played my first basketball game: the layup line. Friends told me to try to bounce the ball off the box over the basket. The ball should then deflect into the basket, they said. I succeeded on the first try. Being unacquainted with immediate athletic success, I became a basketball devotee. Shooting a basketball was an irresistible pleasure and a skill that could be easily practiced. I later thought of it having a therapeutic quality. If I was sad or anxious about something, making basketball shots eased my worried mind.

This love affair further bloomed when I was in the eighth grade. Friends asked if I wanted to come along to the Hamtramck High School game that evening. Huh? I was only faintly aware that high schools had teams. For me, the pros were sports and brought out the fan in me. My favorite teams were the Detroit Tigers, Detroit Lions, Detroit Red Wings and the Boston Celtics.

The Pistons were OK. I especially liked Dave Bing. But . . .

Representing Detroit was usually enough to make me a fan. But the Celtics grabbed me with their distinctive qualities: the parquet floor, the black shoes, celebrated Sixth Man John Havlicek (I later learned that Kentuckian Frank Ramsey was the original Sixth Man), champion of champions Bill Russell and, of course, the winning.

I remember being transfixed the first time I saw the Celtics play. Near the end of the game with victory assured, Coach Red Auerbach appeared on the television screen lighting a victory cigar.

I was a goner.

I was always drawn to other teams or players that were distinctive. Another example was the Montreal Canadiens. I liked that the team was known as "the Flying Frenchmen." Because we got a Canadian television station — CKLW — I watched Hockey Night in Canada on Saturdays. Usually, it was a game in Toronto. But on occasion, it was a Montreal home game. If the game was in Montreal, I'd hear another distinction: the public address announcements were made in French as well as English.

That first Hamtramck High School basketball game left me enthralled. The pep band, which was on a balcony behind a baseline, played "Sweet Georgia Brown" during warmups. The fans were enthusiastic. The star player that 1964-65 season was compelling: John Brisker, a future ABA and NBA player who I quickly learned had the reputation of not being someone to mess with. He saw himself as preeminent on the basketball court and wanted others to also see him that way.

A junior on the team was future Hall of Famer Rudy Tomjanovich. That season he was a rebounder, rim protector and glorified sidekick to Brisker.

The next season Tomjanovich was the star. He had a court presence as a big man (6-foot-8). But he was a forerunner to what is now known as a "stretch four:" a big man with a soft and accurate shooting touch from the perimeter. When the All-Suburban team was to be announced for the 1965-66 season, the Schoolfield Gang was concerned that "our Rudy" would not get his due. The headline on the newspaper story announcing the All-Suburban team eased our worried minds. It read: "Tomjanovich is Great."

Tomjanovich signed with Michigan. His first college game was against . . . Kentucky. By that opening game of the 1967-68 season, I knew Kentucky was an elite program. So, I saw a game against Kentucky as a way to judge whether Rudy could be a productive college player. Though Kentucky won 96-79, Rudy had 17 points and 27 rebounds. I was reassured.

"He played great," Dan Issel recalled more than 50 years later. Issel, who also made his college debut in that game, scored 18 points and grabbed 15 rebounds.

It was also the first game in Michigan's then new Crisler Arena, Issel recalled.

The following season, UK beat Michigan in Memorial Coliseum. This time, Rudy had 26 points and 17 rebounds. Issel scored 34 points and grabbed 12 rebounds. UK won 112-104.

I also remember the Schoolfield Gang talking about Adolph Rupp being an elite coach. I thought they were saying the name was "Rump," a word I was familiar with. When I mentioned Coach Rump, they laughed as they corrected my innocent mistake.

In the 1965-66 season, I was enthralled with Rupp's Runts. Their David-and-Goliath component was impossible to resist. Plus, the Runts played as a unit. Many years later, I told Larry Conley that the Runts looked like five guys playing with one mind. Larry liked that description.

True confession: I rooted for Texas Western in the famous 1966 national championship game. This was not because of an anti-Kentucky sentiment. It was just that Texas Western guard Bobby Joe Hill, whose two first-half steals set a tone in the game, was from the other independent town inside the Detroit city limits: Highland Park. Hill was (relatively) little (5-foot-11) and left handed. I was little and left handed.

The pros always remained what ignited my rooting interest in sports. I considered college sports an attractive form of entertainment rather than an emotional roller coaster that evoked ecstasy or despair.

No doubt this helped me maintain a professional distance when my journalism life moved to Lexington in 1981.

Introduction to Journalism

When I graduated from Hamtramck High School in 1969, the options for the immediate future seemed to be college or Vietnam. A nightmare about the Viet Cong infiltrating my bedroom made me feel all the more ill-equipped to serve in the U.S. Army. Plus, I remember a high school teacher in a social studies class asking students why the United States was fighting in *Viet Nam*. The room was silent until a student innocently guessed to make Vietnam a state. That drew a laugh.

Going to Canada was a plausible option since Windsor, Ontario, was about a seven-mile drive from Hamtramck through downtown Detroit and then across the Detroit River on the Ambassador Bridge to Canada. But I knew no one in Canada nor did I have any clue on how Canadians helped U.S. citizens avoid the draft.

This further cemented the already seemingly obvious decision to attend college. I had done well academically in high school (94.28 grade-point average). But what college?

Detroit Mercy (then known as the University of Detroit) and Wayne State University were nearby. But I had no clue how to proceed.

An uncle, Charles "Bo" Basham, came to my rescue.

Uncle Bo was a Marshall University graduate and was working as a stock broker/financial advisor in its college town of Huntington, W.Va. In what was one of many times he acted as a surrogate father, he reached out to me and asked about my interest in attending Marshall. On family visits, I had walked by the front of the Marshall campus. I remembered small green metal fencing bordering the side of campus that included the administration building. So, there was a bit of familiarity. Otherwise, a move to Huntington and attending Marshall was a mystery.

Bo sent me the admission application, which I completed and returned to him. He took it from there. He also arranged a bank loan to help pay tuition and housing. Plus he arranged for me to be eligible for what was known as a work-study job on campus to provide spending money.

I was accepted to Marshall and told I would have a dormitory room in what was then known as South Hall.

In the late summer of 1969, I remember my mother and grandmother seeing me off at the train station in downtown Detroit.

Early in the trip, I got teary eyed. Leaving my friends and everything familiar in my hometown was difficult. But, of course, I knew that starting a new life could be part of the college experience. Seemingly the only alternative — Vietnam — bolstered my courage to proceed as a Marshall student.

I got off the train in Ashland, Ky., where another aunt and uncle (Patty and Cliff Noe) lived and met me at the station. Bo drove the 15 miles from Huntington to Ashland the next day and took me to Marshall.

Bo asked me what my major would be. I said math. A high school math teacher, Carl Aardema, had made a positive impression. One day in class he mentioned how well the Detroit Tigers had played in the previous night's game. And I had done well academically in high school math. I remember the class taking a test. Students around me seemed stumped, so they passed around my completed test paper. If the teacher noticed this subterfuge, it was not called out.

When I told my uncle I planned to be a high school math teacher, he frowned and shook his head slightly. I noted his negative reaction, but I embarked on what I thought would be a teaching career.

Bo checked on me regularly. About mid-way through the fall semester of my freshman year, I told him I needed to change majors. I was merely getting by in an introductory math class. Plus, the instructor spoke with a heavy Greek accent that I found hard to understand.

Bo asked what I thought would be a new major.

I said I did not know.

"What about being a sportswriter?" he asked.

I was intrigued. Bo knew I shared with him a love of sports. Bo was a Marshall fan and a friend of several staffers in the sports department of Huntington's newspapers: the morning *Huntington Herald-Dispatch* and the afternoon paper, *The Huntington Advertiser*.

My uncle probably did not know that I always liked the sound of words and learning new words. In elementary school, "curiosity" was a favorite new word. I remember my playground friends teasing me when I dropped an unusual word into the conversation. The word play in Marx Brothers movies, led by Groucho, made me a fan.

I did not work for the high school student newspaper, but I had been intrigued by its existence. And I had long been a regular reader of the Detroit newspapers — at various times the *The Detroit Times*, the *Free Press* or the *The Detroit News* — and Hamtramck's weekly newspaper, *The Citizen*. For a while, Hamtramck's newspaper had a contest for readers to submit an example of wit. I was thrilled to win the contest once.

So, I decided to change my major to journalism.

A week or so later, I was walking on campus to the South Hall dormitory with a friend. We were having a similar conversation. I need to change majors. What are you going to change to? I said, journalism.

My friend recoiled. "Oh no," he said. "You don't want to do that."

I asked with a bit of anxiety, "Why not?"

"Because you'll have to do a lot of writing," he said.

I knew almost nothing about what I was getting myself into. But I knew that. It was right there in the job title I would aspire to attain: sportsWRITER.

Bo had signed me up for an on-campus job in Marshall's work study program. Knowing my interest in sports, Bo recommended a job in Marshall's athletic department. I worked in the "cage," handing out towels and other items that athletes and coaches requested.

Another sports moment came early that fall semester of my freshman year. While in the student union, I noticed a poster of Hal Greer on the wall. Huh? Why was a poster of the Philadelphia 76er guard on display? Belatedly, it dawned on me. He played collegiately for Marshall! I later learned that Greer was the first Black scholarship player at a public college in West Virginia. Years later, the name of the street bordering the front of the Marshall campus was changed from 16th Street to Hal Greer Boulevard. By then, I was well aware of the connection.

The student union was the site of another sports-inspired moment during my college days. I happened to be there one day in my sophomore or junior year and ran into a student friend. He was anxious because he was in charge of finding speakers for what Marshall called its Impact program that school year. He was looking for ideas on whom to invite. I said I'd like to hear Bill Russell speak. The Celtic great had retired after the 1968-69 season. He had led the Celtics to 11 championships in his 13-year career.

And I admired him off the court as well as on. I had read his first two books — *Go Up for Glory* and *Second Wind* — and knew he was active in the civil rights movement.

A month or two later, the list of speakers coming that school year was announced. Bill Russell was on the list.

Of course, I was in the audience at the Memorial Student Center's Multipurpose Room to hear Russell speak.

After being introduced, he began by saying it had always been his dream to come to Huntington, W.Va. This was met with silence. Surely I wasn't the only person in the audience who wondered if Russell had said what it sounded like he said.

Then Russell erupted in his famous cackle of a laugh. Then we all laughed.

"Thinking and participating in society" was the theme of Russell's 90-minute talk.

"The only way we go about solving the problems in our society — racism, poverty, pollution and war — is by working together to solve them," he said.

A story in Marshall's student newspaper, *The Parthenon*, noted that Russell received several rounds of applause. The loudest came when he shared his opinion of athletic dorms.

"The saddest thing I've seen is an athletic dorm," he said. "No school should admit any student who does not wish to fully participate in all aspects of campus life."

Becoming a journalism major led to a new work study job my sophomore year. I was sort of an all-purpose assistant in Marshall's journalism department. One task was to get the mail each morning and put it in the appropriate boxes.

I never asked, but I've wondered if this job helped me make more of an impression on the professors — Ralph Turner, in particular — than my journalism skills could display at that early stage of development.

My naiveté became apparent immediately. The introductory class, Journalism 101, consisted of guest speakers. One I especially looked forward to hearing late in the semester was George Rorrer, a Marshall graduate who at the time covered the Thundering Herd for the *Huntington Herald-Dispatch*. He later worked for the *Louisville Times* and the *Courier-Journal*.

The students were to write a story on each speaker. The instructor said that there was a 100-word limit on each of our stories.

Not knowing any better, I thought that was a minimum. Surely, each story had to be at least 100 words. So, I wrote . . . and wrote . . . about what the first speaker said. I felt good about what I had written, and when our papers were about to be returned with a grade, I was prepared to take a bow.

Alas, I had received a F. One hundred words was the maximum limit.

Lesson learned. In the days long before social media and websites, stories were limited by the space available in the daily newspaper, so getting to the point was important. I quickly came to learn about the "inverted pyramid" style of stories: lead with the most important element, then write the second-most important, etc., etc.

During that first semester, I also heard students and professors speak of picas. Huh? I had to learn this was a unit of type size.

And I remember a professor saying that if a reporter was the subject of the story, this was bad. I did not fully understand this, but I came to live by that creed. This also fits my personality, which has always valued blending in rather than standing out.

The need for humility was helped by learning that no matter how accomplished, a Marshall journalism student could never claim to be the most noted product of the department. That distinction belongs to Soupy Sales, who earned a master's degree in journalism from Marshall before becoming a comedian. As a child, I was a big fan of Soupy. I regularly watched his television shows based in Detroit.

Soupy — real name Milton Supman — was born in North Carolina, but the family moved to Huntington, where he went to high school and then college.

When I worked for the Huntington *Herald-Dispatch*, I learned that the sports columnist, Ernie Salvatore, was a classmate of Sales and remained a friend. During a reunion weekend, Ernie put me on the phone with Sales. I'm afraid I was too awestruck to make much conversation.

I fairly quickly noticed that becoming a sportswriter would require a personality adjustment. The star journalism students at Marshall had outgoing personalities. They were engaging people. I was quiet, especially around people I did not know. I had to learn how to be more personable in order to speak to players, coaches and other subjects of stories.

It took me time to appreciate that the reporter should not become the story. That rule—for reporters to avoid being the subject of a story—helped reinforce the need for just-the-facts objectivity throughout my career.

In speaking to readers, I've noticed that they sometimes do not differentiate the roles of reporter and columnist. The latter has the license, if not the obligation, to offer an opinion. The reporter does not.

I liked to have fun with stories as long as light-heartedness was appropriate to the topic. But as for forming an opinion, I always tried to keep an open mind about new information altering an opinion. So whatever opinion I might have, I tried to keep to myself.

But if I discovered facts that contradicted someone else's opinion, that could help broaden a story.

Marshall Plane Crash

The biggest sports story during my 50-plus years in journalism came when I was still wearing diapers in terms of reporting experience. For this I feel fortunate. Because I can't imagine another story being more consequential and needing a wealth of reporting experience. By comparison, a national championship would seem relatively routine.

As a college sophomore, I was wholly unprepared to be part of the coverage of the plane crash that killed 37 Marshall football players, eight coaches and 25 boosters from the Huntington area. Counting the flight crew, 75 people died in the crash of Southern Airways Flight 932 returning the Marshall team from a 17-14 loss at East Carolina on Nov. 14, 1970. Among the dead was Jeff Nathan, the sports editor of the Marshall student newspaper, *The Parthenon*.

At the time, I was in my second semester as a journalism major. The beginning reporting class involved such basics as students interviewing each other and writing trial stories. We did no actual reporting, so I played no part in the coverage of the plane crash.

Actual reporting for the student newspaper would come in the spring semester of 1971.

I wrote stories for the *Lexington Herald-Leader* on the 20th anniversary of the crash and then again in 2006. The first story tried to put the crash in context. The second was a remembrance of a student manager who was not on the plane. Later, he and I were roommates.

"Until that night of misty rain and fog, it was widely believed that Marshall University football could not get any worse," I wrote in the 1990 story. That was the conventional wisdom in Huntington when I arrived as a freshman in the fall of 1969. The team had gone winless the previous two seasons. The only non-loss was a 7-7 tie against Morehead State University in 1968. With the team having not won 27 straight games, the national record for futility, then 28 straight games, loomed. "Stop the streak" was the theme for the homecoming game in 1969. A sign bearing those words was hung on my dorm, then known as South Hall.

The Herd did stop the streak, beating Bowling Green 21-16 to make for a happy homecoming.

Yet, the Marshall football program remained synonymous with embarrassing futility.

Perry Moss, whose coaching resume would later include two stints as a University of Kentucky assistant, had been Marshall's coach in 1968. His efforts led to an NCAA probation in the spring of 1969. More than 120 rule violations prompted the unusual step of expulsion from the Mid-American Conference that same year.

It was assumed that it could not get any worse for Marshall football.

That assumption was wrong.

The 1970 season began with promise. The roster had only eight seniors. The younger players were considered a notch or two better than the Marshall standard. Marshall beating Kentucky in a freshman game a year or two earlier fueled optimism.

By hook or, more likely, by crook, Moss had recruited a squad which, with experience, could win regularly. The first nine games of the 1970 season reinforced that belief. The Thundering Herd won three. Four of the losses were by a combined 14 points.

But on Nov. 14, 1970, the plane carrying the upwardly mobile Marshall team home from East Carolina University came in too low in its approach to landing, clipped trees and crashed short of the Tri-State Airport. There were no survivors.

The National Transportation Safety Board cited improper use of cockpit instrumentation data or an altimetry systems error as the cause of the crash at 7:36 p.m.

That Saturday night, I was in my room in South Hall trying to write a term paper on an electric typewriter. This probably says something about my social life — or lack thereof — at the time.

A friend from down the hall stuck his head in the open door and said the team plane had crashed. My immediate reaction was to laugh. The previous month, Oct. 2 to be exact, one of two planes carrying Wichita State's football team crashed. The head coach, an assistant coach and 14 players were killed.

Now the Marshall plane crashed? This had to be my friend's attempt at dark humor. Such a thing could not happen twice in about six weeks.

We turned on the radio. It was true. There was no more laughter for days. We rushed to the student lounge on the dorm's top floor. The television there showed reporters repeating again and again what they could confirm: The Marshall plane had crashed. There were no survivors.

A good friend, an engineering student named David Byrd, lived down the hall. He was a manager on the team. I kept wondering if he had been on the plane. Of course, this was decades before cell phones and text messaging. We could only wait to learn if David had been a passenger on the plane. If we saw him Sunday, we would know he wasn't. But if we didn't see him . . .

The list of those killed that appeared in the *Huntington Herald-Dispatch* the next morning included David's name. By the time I saw this, I knew David was not on the plane.

In 2022, I asked David if this was like reading his own obituary.

"At the time, I didn't think much about it," he said. "But looking back on it and seeing that, it kind of hit home more about how close I came to being on that plane, and wondering how that would have affected my family and my friends."

David had ridden to the game with equipment manager John Hagan. Carrying the team's equipment on the round trip that covered 900-plus miles, David acted as navigator as the equipment manager drove.

The talk then was that Hagan was superstitious. He refused to fly on the only flights of the season because the plane had taken off from Huntington the day before, which was Friday the 13th.

David did not recall superstition being a factor. Usually, the equipment was loaded on the bus that took the team to away games. With the rarity of a flight, it was decided to use a truck.

Those of us in the dorm did not know this. A friend and I decided to walk the six blocks or so into town. We had no particular destination in mind. We just could no longer sit there helplessly watching the television. We had to do something.

We paid little attention to the fog and misty rain except to speculate on how the conditions probably contributed to the crash.

Later, we learned the pilot, Capt. Frank Abbott, had never landed a plane at Tri-State Airport.

In contrast to Saturday night's gloom, Sunday was bright and sunny. Looking out a window, you had to almost avert your eyes from the bright light. This stark change from the night before added to the surreal feeling of that weekend and fueled my wishful thinking: Surely, the plane had not really crashed. Any second now, we'd wake up from this collective nightmare.

Reality hit hard Monday.

I clearly remember opening my dorm room that morning and being startled by the sight. Across the hall, where two football players had lived, their parents were in the room quietly packing their sons' belongings. A walk down the hall where four other players had lived revealed other parents doing the same.

That ended my wishful thinking.

Byrd, who would be my roommate the following school year, and Hagan learned of the Marshall crash as they rode somewhere in Virginia. They were listening to a football game on the radio.

Suddenly, silence.

"Right at a critical juncture of the game, they cut off," Byrd recalled in the 2006 interview. "I thought, what the heck is this interrupting the game?"

A news bulletin: *The plane carrying the Marshall team has crashed.*

Within 15 or 20 minutes, the two stopped at a gas station and called their families to let them know they were not on the plane. Byrd said he did not know if his family knew he was not on the plane.

"They didn't request that I keep them aware of every little thing that I did when I was at school," he said in 2022. "I probably should have kept them more informed on what was going on."

As Byrd and Hagan continued the long drive home in the rain, they listened on the radio for updates.

As they arrived in Huntington an hour or so past midnight, Hagan and Byrd still did not know the extent of the tragedy. They drove straight to Tri-State Airport (which serves eastern Kentucky, southern Ohio and southwestern West Virginia) to see what, if anything, they could do to help.

In the years since the crash, Byrd hasn't spoken much of that night. Until at least 2006, he had told only his wife about what happened next.

Hagan and Byrd were directed to a hangar that rescue workers had converted into a makeshift morgue. Remains transported from the crash site needed to be identified.

"This is the part that David doesn't like to talk about," his wife, Sharon, said in 2006.

As a manager, Byrd wasn't, as he put it, "everyday chums" with the players. But in those days before athletic dormitories, he and fellow students lived in the same dorm with players, ate in the same cafeteria as players and watched television with players in a top-floor lounge. We "regular" students got a sense of the players as people. Sometimes friendships were formed.

"They were there as students, too," Byrd said in 2022 when asked about the players living amongst "regular" students. "They were supposed to associate with the students and have that part of their personality shaped. That they weren't better than anybody else. They were just part of everybody else."

The top floor of South Hall was a gathering place for all residents. There was a television, couches and a ping pong table. You got a hint of what kind of person a football player was.

Fred Wilson was a gentle giant of a tight end. His size shouted football player, but his demeanor featured a friendly smile and welcoming manner.

I remember years later thinking of Fred Wilson. As almost an involuntary reflex, I smiled and wondered how he was doing. Then I remembered what happened on Nov. 14, 1970.

Trying in 2006 to coax the memory of identifying bodies, Sharon reminded her husband, "When they zipped open a bag, it wasn't what you thought it would be."

Clearly uncomfortable, Byrd nodded when asked if he was able to make any identifications.

After a pause, he said, "The bodies were pretty beat up from the fire or from the crash."

In a halting voice, Byrd said he could identify the bodies by facial features. Then he corrected himself.

"Hair, mostly, I think," he said. "I just knew the hair style or the color of their hair, if that was identifiable."

Byrd, then 21, tried to identify remains for only a few minutes before growing physically ill. He said he rushed out of the hangar and vomited. Then he turned around and faced a television reporter asking for a comment.

In 2022, Byrd recalled that Hagan had told him not to speak to reporters.

One thought he did not share with television viewers: a lighthearted exchange he overheard after the game as players boarded the bus that would take them to the plane at the Greenville, N.C., airport for the flight home.

Defensive end Larry Brown was a team leader with a witty comment frequently at the ready. The strength of his personality inspired the nickname "The Gov." Brown dressed well on road trips, but for this special occasion, the only flying trip the team took in Byrd's four seasons as manager, "The Gov" wore a three-piece suit.

"Hey, Gov," a teammate said. "What are you dressed up for?"

"My funeral," Brown said in jest.

That exchange flashed through Byrd's mind soon after he learned about the crash.

Now retired after a career in the West Virginia Department of Environmental Protection, Byrd hasn't changed much from the dorm buddy of yesteryear. He remains a reserved, self-effacing man who quietly rolls with life's punches.

In 2006, he apologized for sounding selfish as he confessed to "a little bone of contention" with his alma mater.

"Marshall didn't reach out or help me in any way," Byrd said, "or offer any type of counseling."

He credited his family, his friends in a church group for college students and his dorm buddies for helping him carry on, unknowingly in many cases, simply by returning him to the everyday rhythms of his life as a Marshall student.

Byrd recalled his family coming unannounced to the dorm the following weekend to be with him.

It sounds melodramatic to ask if he thinks God spared the student manager as part of some cosmic plan.

"It's not melodramatic to me," Byrd said. "It's real."

The son of a Methodist minister, Byrd believes in a God who takes an active role in this world. He calls the crash "a defining moment" in his life.

Byrd came to understand a divine message in the crash and his survival.

"I should be more ready to accept what He has for me, take on the task He has given me," he said in 2006. "At any time we can be taken out of this world. It means we have to enjoy the life we have and the time we have together. And it means we shouldn't waste that time.

"That's the most it's meant to me."

Byrd echoed that sentiment in an interview with a reporter from The Charleston (W.Va.) *Daily News* later that year.

"My father was a Methodist minister," he said, "and I remember him telling me that life is short and can change in an instant. His words rang true that day."

Though there were calls to end the football program, Marshall decided to continue it. The team the following season was dubbed The Young Thundering Herd. It was composed mostly of freshmen, plus three veteran players who had not made the trip to East Carolina.

The movie titled "We are Marshall" told the story of the crash and the program's revival.

I was in the stands for Marshall's first home game of the 1971 season. After losing the opening game, the Herd played Xavier. What happened contained the sense of Hollywood storytelling.

On the game's final play, quarterback Reggie Oliver rolled right, then threw a pass to Terry Gardner on the left. Gardner ran 13 yards for the winning touchdown. Marshall won 15-13.

Novice in the Newsroom

I considered the late Ralph Turner, a professor of journalism at Marshall University for 32 years, my guardian angel. For whatever reason, and I regret never speaking to him about it, he seemed to be looking out for me. He repeatedly gave me much needed guidance in trying to progress in the world of journalism.

Surely Turner saw I needed all the help I could get. I was a novice. My only connection to journalism was being a newspaper reader growing up. This began with the Detroit daily newspapers and Hamtramck's weekly, *The Citizen*, then *Sports Illustrated*. My initial goal was to be a sportswriter, but I had no idea what that meant. Journalism was a mystery to me. One day the advisor to the student newspaper said I would be given the beat covering Marshall's Veterans Club. I pointed out that I knew nothing about this student organization. The advisor noted that learning about the beat was part of the journalism process.

Maybe a connection with the professor was made when my work-study job changed from the athletic cage to the journalism department as a sophomore. I was an all-purpose student assistant. The work shift always began with getting the mail and putting it in the proper boxes.

Whatever the reason, I've always shuddered at the thought of trying to achieve a career in journalism without Turner's guidance.

Early in the fall semester of 1971, I happened to be walking in the hallway outside the Marshall journalism offices. Turner got my attention and said he wanted to speak with me. He said the *Herald-Dispatch* was looking for MU students to work part-time in the sports department. He asked if I was interested?

"Yes," I immediately said. For one thing, I had never been in a newspaper newsroom except for the Marshall student paper. I wanted to get a better idea of what I was getting myself into.

It was arranged for me to *visit their office*, which was six blocks from the Marshall campus, and meet the sports editor. Almost from the start, the newsroom atmosphere gave me a feeling that this could be my place in the world. I was found acceptable and joined three other students on the staff.

Our job was to answer the phone on the nights high school games were played. In the fall, there would be someone at a high school football game calling in the result and statistics. In the winter, the calls would come from high school basketball games.

With the statistics, we would write two or three paragraphs on the game. These mini summaries appeared in the newspaper as part of a roundup of high school games.

Of course, there were no computers in the 1971 newsroom. We typed on manual typewriters. When the just-the-basics "story" was done, you pulled the paper from the typewriter and took it to the layout man's desk.

When I completed my first mini story, the layout man happened to be walking by my desk. So, I handed him the sheet of paper. He stopped and read it, then crumpled it up into a ball and threw it in a waste basket. Then he walked to his desk without saying a word.

If I had been by myself, I might have cried. I fought back tears. Was I that terrible? Would I need to change majors again? If so, what would it be?

I found out later in the evening that my paragraphs on the game were acceptable. The problem? When I handed the sheet of paper to the layout man, it was past the deadline for the schools involved. Whew! That was a relief.

I tried to get as much information on the high school games as I could. Who were the coaches? What were the school nicknames? Anything that could move the mini story beyond the bare basics would be helpful.

I remember a game involving Ceredo-Kenova High School, which was just west of Huntington near the border with Kentucky. Kenova was a combination of Kentucky, Ohio and West Virginia. I asked for the name of the C-K coach. This astonished the caller. In 1971, Carl Ward was on his way to leading C-K to its fourth state championship in a nine-year period. His teams would win 10 state titles in football, two in basketball and one in track.

This was all new to a boy from Michigan. But I remembered the name Carl Ward going forward. This served as an unneeded reminder that I had a lot to learn.

During the high school basketball season of 1971-72, I won the approval of my fellow part-timers by writing that a player "tickled the twine to the tune" of 20-some points. That got a chuckle from my peers. From the beginning, I sought to have fun writing about sports. Yes, readers cared passionately about teams. But, maybe sparked by reading *Sports Illustrated* as a teenager, I thought a comedic touch could enhance stories.

The *Herald-Dispatch* circulation area extended across the Big Sandy River in eastern Kentucky and across the Ohio River in southern Ohio. So, the learning curve included three states.

Ralph Turner served as my guardian angel again in the spring semester of 1972. Once more I was walking in the hallway outside the journalism department. This time, he stopped me to say the *Charleston Gazette* was looking to have an intern work for its sports department during the upcoming summer. Was I interested? Yes, again. This would give me the chance to be a sportswriter in a fuller sense. Beyond the brief summaries of high school games, my experience to that point was limited to fill-up-the-space stories for the Marshall student newspaper.

Charleston was only about 50 miles east of Huntington. I had been to the state capital a few times. Once I went there to watch the annual tournament for smaller colleges in West Virginia. It was noted for being a paradise for basketball lovers. First-round games on opening day began at about 9 in the morning and continued until about midnight. I learned that Fairmont State had an iconic coach. Joe Retton finished with a winning percentage of .836 (478-95). He was also the grand uncle of gymnast Mary Lou Retton, who would win a gold medal at the 1984 Olympics in Los Angeles.

It wasn't long before I learned I had been accepted as an intern at the *Charleston Gazette*. So, after the spring semester, I got on a Greyhound bus and rode to Charleston. Once there, I bought a newspaper and looked in the Want Ads for an apartment. A single bedroom apartment was part of a house about a half mile down Virginia Avenue from the newspaper. That would work.

Upon meeting me, the *Gazette*'s sports editor, Skip Johnson, had a loaded question: "Did I like tennis?" I was going to be agreeable with whatever he said. So, yes, I liked tennis. That was good, he said, because there were a lot of tennis tournaments in Charleston during the summer months. "No one on the staff wanted to cover these tournaments," he said, "so the assignments were given to the student intern."

This was fine with me. The only newspaper stories I'd written to this point were for *The Parthenon*. One on the Marshall track team had been edited down to a single paragraph. So, clearly, I needed more experience with reporting and writing.

One of my first assignments was the Charleston Public Courts Tennis Tournament. When I got there the first day, I realized I knew none of the players. I knew nothing of the tournament's history.

Whatever my story would be (and hopefully I could come up with something), it would need to include a list of the first day's results. So, I decided to hang around the area where results were turned in. While there, I heard staffers talking about one of the players. He was from Colombia, South America. He was a student at West Virginia Tech, which is about 60 miles southeast of Charleston in Beckley, W.Va. He played tennis there. But he broke his two rackets on that first day of the tournament. So, he had to borrow a racket to continue playing, I heard the staffers say.

That sounded like a story to me. So, I asked the staffers what court he was on.

I watched Carlos Chaves win his match. Afterward, we had a friendly interview. Then I returned to the *Gazette* office and wrote about Chaves.

I was so happy with how this had turned out that I practically floated as I started walking to my bedroom apartment. But along the way, I suddenly realized I'd have to return to the tournament the next day and write another story. And it couldn't be about my new friend from Colombia. That brought me down to earth.

Lesson learned. I had to return to the tournament each day and come up with a new story.

Later in the summer, the Girls' 16 National Tennis Championships was played in Charleston. Among the players was Chris Evert's younger sister, Jeannie Evert, who had won the Girls' 14 Championships the previous year and was second-seeded.

Coverage included a quick daily Question-and-Answer exchange with six players. On the first day, I asked the players who they would vote for in November's 1972 presidential election if they were old enough to vote. Five said Richard Nixon.

Another day's question was asking players to react to reports of a romance at Wimbledon between Chris Evert and Jimmy Connors. "I thought it was kind of funny," Jeannie Evert said. "Chris said they exaggerated, but she likes him. They're just two teenagers dating. But he did go to Cleveland after Wimbledon to watch her play."

As for the Sweet 16 tennis tournament, Jeannie Evert lost to top-seeded Marita Redondo 6-4, 6-0 in the singles finals. Evert teamed with Kathy Kuykendall to beat Redondo and Robin Tenney for the doubles title.

Incidentally, the tournament program included pictures of some of the past champions. Jane "Peaches" Bartkowicz of Hamtramck, Mich., won the Girls' 16 National Tennis Championship in 1963, 1964 and 1965.

In an evaluation sheet for interns sent to the Marshall University Department of Journalism, *The Charleston Gazette* gave me an A grade. Sports editor Skip Johnson sent me a two-paragraph note after my summer internship ended. It began with two words: "Come back."

I still had a senior year at Marshall before deciding my journalism future. I would also continue to work part-time at the *Herald-Dispatch*.

Lesson as Side to Tuna Fish Sandwich

Much to my relief, the Huntington *Herald-Dispatch* offered me a full-time position in the sports department soon after I graduated from Marshall with a journalism degree in the summer of 1973. I was happy to immediately accept. I knew the staffers and enjoyed working with them. Plus, it was a relief to know that I wouldn't have to navigate the job market.

No doubt it helped that there were not one but two openings in sports that summer. Maybe it also helped that while home in Michigan during the 1972 Christmas holiday, the phone rang. One of the editors in the *Herald-Dispatch* sports department was calling to ask if I could cut my holiday trip short and return to help work the phones on a high school basketball night later that week. I agreed. My connecting flight in Pittsburgh was delayed. I later learned the editors were annoyed that I still had not arrived when high school games were surely into second halves. But I got there before the first call reporting a high school game rang. So, all was good.

My first daily beat was Ohio high school sports. For a second beat, which would involve only a Sunday notes column, I was given a choice: bowling or outdoors (hunting and fishing). I had never gone hunting. As for my one fishing trip, the only highlight was literally hooking a shoe and pulling it out of the water.

I picked bowling. I had bowled recreationally and occasionally watched professional bowling on television.

On the high school beat, I quickly learned that Ironton was a high school football powerhouse in Ohio. Bob Lutz was the coach. Lutz retired in 2011 after 39 seasons as Ironton coach. His career won-loss record was 381-91-5. He has been inducted into the National High School Federation and Ohio High School Football Coaches Association halls of fame.

Two memories are vivid. In one home game, Ironton played Portsmouth High School. The Portsmouth quarterback, Norm Burrows, threw bullet passes covering 40 or more yards. Until watching Tim Couch play for Leslie County (Ky.), I had seen no other high school quarterback with such an arm. Burrows signed with Ohio State, which puzzled me given that Coach Woody Hayes' offense was dubbed three yards and a cloud of dust given the preference for running the ball. Ohio State listed Burrows as a defensive back.

As for the other memory, I don't remember what team Ironton played. But in those days well before computers, there might not be time to drive back to the office and write the story. The newspaper deadline for stories involving Ohio schools was earlier in the evening than for West Virginia schools. As I recall, Kentucky schools had the earliest deadline.

You had to write from the stadium and dictate the story on a telephone. On this occasion, the phone I was offered was in Lutz's office. He was in the office and could hear me read the story aloud to a typist back at the newspaper.

Ironton's star was named Juan Thomas. He made the decisive plays that enabled the Fighting Tigers to win. In my story, I wrote that Ironton used its "Magic Juan" to win. As I read that, I could not resist looking to see if Lutz would react. He did. He frowned and rolled his eyes.

Later in my eight years as a full-time staffer, I covered West Virginia high schools. A player named Billy Hynus was a diminutive halfback. When he had a starring performance that included punt and kickoff returns that set up scores, my game story noted that "a little Billy Hynus went a long way." Even then, I wanted the stories to have an element of fun.

My playful shadow boxing in the office with other staffers led columnist Ernie Salvatore to recommend that I be assigned to cover a Golden Gloves tournament held in Huntington each year. One of my stories noted that a boxer peppered his opponent's face with punches en route to victory. The opponent was not amused and came to the newspaper office the next day to voice his objection to this description. As he voiced his objections to the sports editor, I chose to listen silently and not point out that his face had several bruises.

This was interesting and amusing. But much to my surprise, the bowling beat introduced me to how reporting the sports news objectively can cause real controversy.

I quickly learned that the bowling community did not consider the sport a recreational activity. Time and effort was put into bowling, which was something of a subculture in Huntington.

Fridays were key in my routine in putting together the Sunday bowling column. I would go to Huntington's three bowling houses (they should not be called "alleys," I was told) and pick up the top scores of the week. The scores at a bowling house in Ashland, Ky., would arrive in Friday's mail. I wrote the bowling notes column during the day on Friday before covering a high school game that night.

In making the bowling rounds, I heard talk of one of the Huntington houses improperly oiling its lanes in order to inflate scores and draw more bowlers. I learned that lanes could be oiled so that the ball is more likely to roll into the desired pocket between the one and three pins (for a right handed bowler). Lanes are oiled in order to reduce friction when the ball is rolled, thus extending the life of the wood, I was told.

The house in question was Ted and Ed's Pro Bowl. Brothers Ted Haun and Ed Haun were the owners. They were known as former professional bowlers who marketed their house as advanced in all things related to teaching bowling and maximizing a bowler's abilities.

I never wrote anything about the possibility of the lanes being oiled improperly. Maybe the teaching at Ted and Ed's was advanced. Maybe professional jealousy caused other houses to question the ethics at Ted and Ed's. I could not write a story based on hearsay.

In picking up the scores of the week on Fridays, my habit was to go to Ted and Ed's Pro Bowl last. By then, it would be late morning and I would buy a quick lunch at the snack bar. If Ted Haun was there and saw me at the snack bar, he would insist on buying my lunch, which was always a tuna fish sandwich. I guess he did so five or six times.

I knew it was not proper to accept gifts from a person you were covering. But naively, a tuna fish sandwich struck me as innocent. Plus, it was only bowling. What ethics question could arise?

Then a bowler bowled a big game or series at Ted and Ed's. As was the custom, the local bowling secretary would check the lanes to make sure all was proper. If so, the secretary would report the big game or series to the national bowling office, which would then send a certificate of recognition to the bowler.

This time I heard that the local secretary judged that the lanes were improperly oiled. Therefore, no recognition.

When I learned of this, I spoke to the secretary who verified that he had not judged the big game or series as legitimate. A followup check at Huntington's three houses showed that bowling averages were significantly higher at Ted and Ed's. I also noted that some bowlers had a markedly higher average at Ted and Ed's Pro Bowl than they did at one of Huntington's other bowling houses.

The following Sunday's notes column began with this story. The big mistake I made was to not get comments from either Ted or Ed. It's embarrassing to admit fear of what the reaction would be played a part in my mistake.

The resulting uproar in the bowling community — where strikes, spares and gutter balls were deemed important — led to a followup meeting at Ted and Ed's Pro Bowl. The sports editor, Mike Brown, and I attended.

My entire focus as I sat and listened was on what errors were in the story. I don't remember anyone citing an error. The tone set was simply that the story shouldn't have been written.

Later in the year, I received an award from the local bowling association for my coverage of the sport.

But I had a more immediate concern after the meeting. I went to Ted Haun and told him there was no personal agenda in doing the story. I was only trying to do my job.

Ted said he did not believe that. "Not after all the tuna fish sandwiches I bought you," he said.

I was taken aback and embarrassed. I realized the mistake I had made in accepting his offer to buy my lunches. A few minutes later, I pulled out some money from my wallet and gave it to Ted to pay for the sandwiches. Now, Ted looked taken aback and embarrassed.

Another lesson learned.

Mike Johnson, the sports editor of the *Herald-Leader* who hired me, recalled in 2023 how the bowling beat was used by some in Lexington as a way to belittle me.

"One of the things that always irritated me when you first took the job and you were covering the team (was) people would get upset about things," Johnson said. "Even the local (media) would say things. Well, he covered bowling."

At this starting point of what I hoped was a career in sportswriting, I needed any and all the experience I could get. I saw nothing embarrassing about covering bowling.

Johnson knew that I covered bowling before hiring me. The sports editor at the Huntington newspaper, Mike Connell, had told him.

"Mike said the thing about Jerry is he will do whatever you need him to do," Johnson said. "He said, for example, he covers Marshall for us. But in Huntington, bowling is a big deal."

Johnson recalled a banquet at a Lexington hotel in which I was introduced as a former bowling writer.

"That made it sound like bowling was the only thing you were covering," Johnson said. "You were covering bowling because you were trying to help the paper out."

Hurray for the *Herald-Dispatch*

After the controversy stirred by my bowling story, I felt the need to step away from sports for a while. There happened to be an opening on the main copy desk. The job was to edit non-sports news stories and write headlines.

I came to believe it was beneficial to work on what was called "the news side." I gained a better appreciation for how words mattered. This lesson hit home when I used the word "lady" in a headline. Another copy editor corrected me. "Lady" carried the inference of an opinion and could be seen as categorizing the person, she said. It was better to use the more neutral word "woman."

Cheering for or against a team is inbred in sports but was absent on the news side. This reminded me of the value of remaining objective.

Although these observations made a lasting impression, my separation from the *Herald-Dispatch* sports department was not long lasting. Within a year or so, I was the person on the news desk assigned to lay out the sports pages. This meant deciding how prominently a story would be displayed in the sports section. I would help write headlines or approve those written by others.

I remember there was a style for cutlines under "head shots," which were photographs of a person's face. The style had two lines: Under the person's name came a brief description. For example, it might read "Robert De Niro . . . Oscar winning actor."

For one story, we had a head shot of Steve Carlton, an accomplished baseball pitcher who beginning in 1974 refused to speak to the media for the rest of his career. He retired in 1989. My cutline for his photo read "Steve Carlton . . . mum's the word."

Although I was technically not part of the Sports Department, my appreciation for including a fun element in my work continued.

The separation from the sports department never seemed permanent. I remained friendly with the sportswriters and editors, and by 1978, I had the job of "Saturday night sports slot," which meant responsibility for laying out the Sunday sports section. That was the largest sports section of the week. Or as my job review that year termed it, "one of the toughest on the news desk."

It was fun trying to bring clarity and playful fun to the section. But one big news story made me realize how much I missed being on the reporting side of sports.

In 1977, Stu Aberdeen moved from being an assistant coach for Tennessee to become head coach at Marshall. As Ray Mears' right-hand man, he had been the lead recruiter for the Vols. Among the players he successfully recruited was future Hall of Famer Bernard King, who along with Ernie Grunfeld formed UT's effective and entertaining tandem known as the "Ernie and Bernie Show."

Although Aberdeen had only a 25-31 record in his first two seasons as Marshall coach, his gift for marketing stirred excitement and anticipation for what was to come.

Then while on vacation in New Smyrna Beach, Fla., in the summer of 1979, Aberdeen suffered a fatal heart attack while jogging. He was 43.

As the sports staffers scrambled to gather information and write the story, I watched from across the *Herald-Dispatch* newsroom with envy.

A few weeks later, there was an opening in the sports department. I expressed an interest and got the job.

The sports editor was Mike Connell. He had been an assistant city editor. He was asked to move to the sports editor job when it became open. He went reluctantly.

When I asked him in 2022 to explain his reluctance, Connell said, "I thought sports was that old toy department. That was not the serious part of the newspaper."

During his career, Connell has worked for newspapers in Morgantown, W.Va., Gainesville, Ga., and Port Huron, Mich., as well as the *National Enquirer*. When asked in 2022 about his late 1970s opinion about sports being a toy department, he attributed that to "arrogance."

But it soon became clear that Connell wanted the sports department to treat the coverage of teams no differently than how a news side might cover, say, city hall or the police beat. There should be no cheering for or against a team. He wanted reporters to just cover their beats fairly and accurately.

I remember Connell saying The Associated Press was "a tip service." This meant that the stories The AP sent to news outlets should be considered a first draft. Further exploration and expansion of a story should be part of the process.

I came to adopt this attitude for press conferences. If time permitted, I'd try to bounce off others what was said from the podium. Time permitting, the press conference was the beginning of the journalistic process, not the end.

Connell also edited stories differently than I was used to. As a young sportswriter, my pride was on the line – or could get in the way? – with almost every word in a story. Unless clearly obvious, any change stung my pride.

But Connell's editing might involve a total rewrite of a story. While stunned and frustrated with this, I had to concede his rewrite improved the story. It was another learning experience.

Somehow I gained Connell's trust and was assigned several enterprise stories (or stories that were not part of a day-to-day beat).

I worked with another sportswriter, Bill Trimble, on a story published in June of

1980 about a Marshall student winning an award for prose writing. His story had the racially charged title "Gray Suits and Big Niggers." The story was a fictional account of an all-White high school basketball team in Raleigh County, W.Va., playing an all-Black team. The all-Black team in the story was led by a 6-foot-11 All-American named Lucious Smith.

A photo of a player Marshall was recruiting, 6-11 Earl Jones, accompanied the short story, which was printed that spring in a collection of short stories and poems written by Marshall students and titled "et cetera."

Jones played three seasons for a high school in Mount Hope, W.Va., before transferring to a school in Washington, DC. Mount Hope is in Fayette County, W. Va., which borders Raleigh County.

Jones' legal guardian, William "Doc" Robinson, told the *Washington Star* that the story depicting racist attitudes written by Marshall student Ken Smith "cemented the situation" with the player's recruiting decision. Jones signed with the University of the District of Columbia, one of the historically Black land-grant universities.

"I'm trying to portray things I've encountered and other people have encountered in southern West Virginia," Smith told the *Herald-Dispatch* in explaining the use of racial slurs. Watching Jones play inspired the short story, Smith said before adding that he did not base the Smith character on Jones.

Marshall's coach at the time, Bob Zuffelato, said the story was "in poor taste." MU school president Robert B. Hayes said "there were a lot of things I didn't like about the story."

Playing for the University of the District of Columbia, Jones scored 2,256 points and grabbed 1,168 rebounds. He was inducted into the Small College Basketball Hall of Fame in 2018.

Another story took me back to the Marshall football plane crash.

Nate Ruffin, a defensive back on Marshall's 1970 team, was the subject of an enterprise story published on Feb. 4, 1981. I wrote a where-are-they-now story that included his memories of the tragedy and how it affected his life.

By then, Ruffin was working as a supervisor of personnel at the Huntington-based Amcar Division of ACF Industries, Inc. He was a husband and father of two daughters. He also worked for the local chapter of the NAACP Action agencies and the Marshall Alumni Association.

Ruffin did not make the ill-fated trip to East Carolina. A preseason injury left his right arm partially paralyzed because of calcium deposits. He played the opening game with the arm in a sling. He suffered several broken ribs in the next game.

Doctors treating the broken ribs noticed the arm injury and recommended Ruffin not play again until after undergoing arm surgery. Marshall officials decided to delay the surgery until after the season.

"I was angry," Ruffin recalled. "We were doing well, coming around. I wanted to be part of it. I'd been through the losses. I wanted some of the wins."

Marshall had a 3-5 record going to East Carolina. "I was going to make the trip," Ruffin said. "I was going to give the team moral support. The coaches called me in and asked if I'd relinquish my seat for a fan. I wanted to go, but I thought, 'Gee, the supporters have been so good.' They helped us a lot back then. Besides, with the coaches away, I could have a blast."

Ruffin listened to the radio broadcast of the game. Then early that evening he went to a movie. Someone came to his seat and whispered that the plane had crashed.

"Everything went blank," Ruffin said. "I walked out of the theater and saw Dickie Carter driving down the street."

Carter, a fullback, had quit the team earlier in the year.

The two rode to the airport.

"The fire was ablaze," Ruffin said. "I'll never forget that sight. There wasn't any moaning. There was just jet fuel burning."

Upon returning to the Marshall campus, Ruffin helped call parents of the players to tell them their sons had died.

"My mom called," he said. "She cried and cried and cried. I kept saying over and over, 'All my friends are gone.'"

The next day Ruffin went to the makeshift morgue at the airport and helped identify bodies. He attended funerals and memorial services.

"For about two months, I'd see them in my sleep," he said. A decade later, he said he still occasionally dreamed of his teammates.

"I'm trying to talk to them," he said of the dreams. "But they're running away. I can't get to them and the sirens go off. I wake up and the sirens are the alarm clock."

Ruffin said he rarely went to Huntington's Spring Hill Cemetery where several players are buried.

"They're not there," he said before pointing to his head and saying, "They're here."

Ruffin died in October of 2001 at age 51.

What prompted another enterprise story was Len Barker pitching a perfect game for Cleveland on May 15, 1981.

Barker was born in Fort Knox, Ky. When he was 18 months old, he and his family moved to Trevose, Pa.

Somehow we found out that a sister, Patricia Grass, and Barker's grandmother, Tokie Lockhart, lived in the Huntington area. In 2022, Connell did not remember how we learned this. But he sent me to interview the Major League pitcher's grandmother.

We sat on her front porch. I like the first quote in any story to make an impression. Tokie came through big time.

"Tell Len I'm proud of him," she said before adding, "I hope he does better the next time."

Of course, it would be impossible to do better than retiring 27 straight batters. At the time, it was only the eighth perfect game in the major leagues since 1900, and the first in 13 years.

Connell remembered the quote as "one of the all-time best lines I've ever read."

Tokie acknowledged not being familiar with baseball. When asked what she knew about baseball, she said, "not a thing. They must be making a lot (of) to-do over him. I guess he's made good."

As for basketball beat reporting, Connell gave me my first college beat. For the 1979-80 season, I was the backup reporter for the coverage of Marshall's basketball team. In the following season, I was the lead reporter for the *Herald-Dispatch.*

The Marshall team rode a bus to away games. After an away game, the players and coaches waited in the bus for me to finish filing my story. After I boarded the bus, we'd start the ride home.

One away game stands out in my memory. I remember boarding the bus more clearly than where the game was played. I believe it was at Appalachian State. Marshall lost a fairly one-sided game.

I figured all were stewing as they waited in the dark for me to get on the bus.

Upon walking into the bus, I did not make eye contact with anyone. The silence was deafening. Keeping my head down, I only glanced side to side looking for an open seat.

When I found one, I sat down and then looked to see who I was next to. It was Huntington's mayor at the time, Harold Frankel. He was an engaging extrovert who might say anything.

After I sat, Frankel turned to me and made a light-hearted putdown of the Marshall team. He said something like "the team played like crap tonight, didn't they?" I thought he said it loud enough to be heard by those in several nearby rows of the bus. I nodded quickly and hoped no one saw it.

On Dec. 28, 1980, Marshall lost 114-89 at Maryland. A personal highlight came before the game. As I stood near an entrance to Cole Field House, who should walk in but Red Auerbach, the Hall of Famer who practically invented the Boston Celtics. I couldn't work up the nerve to speak to him. I presumed he was there to watch Maryland All-American Albert King.

Later that season, an unusual statistical quirk led me to save the clipping of my column published on Feb. 4, 1981. It was a follow-up to Marshall's 82-74 victory over Western Carolina. The Herd had more assists than baskets in the game.

The lead read: Twenty-seven field goals. Twenty-nine assists.

"Impossible," said Jim Wright with a laugh. He was one of two people who compiled basketball statistics for the NCAA at the time.

Actually, it was possible. The NCAA rule book at the time defined an assist as "a pass contributing directly to a field goal or an awarded score of two points."

Marshall defined the awarding of two points as including two made free throws after a foul prevented a basket set up by a pass.

An assist was not limited by the number of dribbles a shooter took before scoring or even who had the ball last before the shooter. A strong outlet pass on a fast break could be interpreted as an assist.

Coincidentally, of Marshall's 408 assists at the time, 287 came in home games. Home games saw an assist credited with 76.3 percent of baskets. The percentage for road games was 45 percent.

I concluded the column by pointing out that sportswriter Rick Nolte called Wright. The sports editor and assistant sports editor, Mike Connell and Bill Trimble, compiled Marshall's assists in home and away games.

The column ended with "give them an assist."

Don Hatfield, the *Herald-Dispatch* executive editor, wrote Connell a note thanking him for "a thoroughly researched column."

The column on assists came in handy decades later. After Joe B. Hall retired as Kentucky coach, he invited me to join him and his friends for lunch at the Roc Cafe, which was behind Lexington's Immanuel Baptist Church.

During one lunch, someone complained about how assists were being counted. I pointed out that assists were a much more subjective statistic than, say, points or rebounds. One person's assist might be another person's routine pass on the perimeter. Hall nodded approval of my comment.

My awareness of University of Kentucky sports strengthened during my time at the *Herald-Dispatch*. With Ashland only 16 miles to the west, Huntington stations were part of the UK television and radio networks. I remember watching Dan Issel and thinking he was machine-like as a low post scorer. Of course, Jack Givens' productive play in the 1978 championship game made a big impression.

While covering Marshall basketball, I started collecting college T-shirts.

One of the news copy editors was Bruce Winges, who as a UK student was editor of the school's student newspaper, *The Kentucky Kernel*. He surprised me by giving me two UK T-shirts.

For those *Herald-Leader* readers who might think my coverage of UK basketball showed a dislike of the Wildcat program, I'd point out that I wore the UK T-shirts Winges gave me so much they wore out.

News reporter Jim Warren was another link to Kentucky. He liked to tell his *Herald-Dispatch* colleagues that he was from "Poosey Ridge." For the uninitiated, that is farmland in the southwestern part of Madison County. Warren liked the reaction the name of his home area got. "Everybody laughed," he said.

Warren later joined the *Herald-Leader* as a news reporter and made for a familiar face when I came to Lexington in 1981.

While we worked at the Huntington *Herald-Dispatch*, Warren introduced me to John Prine. I remember being in the newspaper bar, which at the time was conveniently located across the street from the *Herald-Dispatch*, and listening to Warren sing the praises of Prine's song titled "Paradise." I liked it from the first listen onward. When it came on the jukebox, we sang along.

Decades later, this connection paid off.

Former Kentucky player Reggie Warford was from Drakesboro, Ky., which is about six miles southwest of Paradise.

In one of our telephone conversations, I spoke of how much I liked the John Prine song. I wondered if that would mean anything to Warford. It did. He began singing the song "Paradise," and I joined in to form a player-sportswriter duet.

"And, Daddy, won't you take me back to Muhlenberg County.
"Down by the Green River where Paradise lay.
"Well, I'm sorry my son but you're too late in asking
"Mister Peabody's coal train has hauled it away."

Welcome to Lexington

Throughout my 10 years working for the newspaper in Huntington, W.Va., the *Herald-Dispatch*, I felt fortunate. I tried to learn from watching and listening to such sports staffers as columnist Ernie Salvatore, editors Mike Brown and later Mike Connell, veteran sportswriters Lowell Cade, Bud Perry, Bill Trimble and Tim Massey, plus relative peers like Bob Dehner, Dave Wellman and Gaylen Duskey. All were generous with advice and encouragement.

Getting paid to be a sportswriter for the *Herald-Dispatch* seemed like a bonus. Just being a sportswriter was an ambition realized, but of course that didn't pay the rent. My starting salary in the fall of 1973 was $115 a week. That was the minimum starting pay for reporters. Staffers could get raises every six months. After six months, I met with the executive editor, who told me my pay would be raised to $130. I welcomed the pay increase. But when I returned to my desk and thought about it for a moment, I remembered that during my first six months on the job the minimum pay had been raised to $130. So, I was still making the minimum. Did I really get a raise?

I went back to the executive editor's office and pointed this out. I wasn't upset. I just wanted him to know I was aware. He pointed out that I was free to leave the *Herald-Dispatch* and find a sports reporting job elsewhere. I never considered leaving. I enjoyed working at the Huntington newspaper. The few times I thought of the pay raise that wasn't a pay raise, it made me smile. It made me remember a Marshall journalism professor telling students that if the goal was to be fabulously wealthy, newspaper journalism was not a job to pursue. Money was never the objective. Writing enlightening and/or entertaining stories was.

"That was a great paper for a young reporter," Connell said of The *Herald-Dispatch* when we spoke in 2023. "We were so lucky to hit it when we did. Those were good days for newspapers. It'll never come back the way it was."

News reporter Jim Warren, who preceded me in moving from The *Herald-Dispatch* to the *Lexington Herald-Leader*, echoed that sentiment. He noted the value of The *Herald-Dispatch* as a good place to "get a job and start learning the ropes. Get used to being in a newsroom."

Feedback was plentiful and appreciated. Staff meetings were called regularly to review stories and offer tips on, say, a daily routine of conducting interviews or asking pointed questions.

For a while, the executive editor graded the paper each day and posted his comments on a bulletin board. When John McMillan was editor, he reviewed each day's paper in a staff meeting. He got a laugh at one such meeting when before critiquing a story he asked Warren if his reporting ego was in good shape.

Even more review and assessment often came after work when some editors and staffers would meet at the "newspaper bar" and talk about stories or story ideas between sips of beer. I relished these sessions not because of the alcohol, but to learn from this feedback. And I simply just liked talking about reporting and writing.

Then early in the summer of 1981, I suddenly was asked to interview with the *Akron Beacon Journal*. The job opening was to cover the Cleveland Browns.

The only football I had covered was high schools in southern Ohio during my first stint in H-D sports and later high schools in West Virginia during the second stint. The only college game I ever covered was the 1976 Peach Bowl in which Kentucky beat North Carolina 21-0. The *Herald-Dispatch* circulated into eastern Kentucky, so that's why I was there. Unfortunately, I associated bowl games with warm weather, so I did not dress appropriately for a game in Atlanta that began with the temperature at 32 degrees. As a reporter of secondary importance, my seat was outside the press box. I decided to watch the game on the television inside the press box and go from there.

Because I had never interviewed for a job, I thought it would be good to go to Akron and experience what that was like. I did not expect to get the job covering the Browns. Truth to tell, I did not want it.

I did not interview with the sports editor. I met with the executive editor, Dale Allen, who had come to the *Beacon Journal* the year before and would lead the newspaper to Pulitzer Prizes in 1987 (general local reporting) and 1994 (public service).

The interview seemed perfunctory at best. A low point came when Allen asked me where I attended college. When I said Marshall, he responded after a pause by saying, "well, everyone has to go somewhere."

I did not react. But later in the interview, I asked him where he went to college. He said Missouri Southern (formerly Joplin Junior College). I figured that a point was made and I looked forward to returning to The *Herald-Dispatch*.

Within a few weeks, Connell said that he had recommended me to the *Lexington Herald* for a job covering University of Kentucky football and basketball.

As Connell recalled in 2023, the recommendation came at a gathering of the American Press Institute in Reston, Va. *The Herald* sports editor, Mike Johnson, was at the gathering and asked other sports editors for possible candidates.

"I don't want to lose him, but I've got somebody I can recommend to you," Johnson recalled Connell saying in recommending me.

Johnson offered a word of caution.

"I said, part of this job, it's a pretty demanding job because, first of all, most of the management at the paper is interested in how we're covering UK and how well we're doing," Johnson recalled in 2023. "And then, of course, you have the fans and the coaches who have an interest, but kind of from a different perspective.

"So, I said, how do you feel about Jerry handling that kind of pressure? And he said, it won't bother him. He'll just keep going on."

So, only a few weeks after returning from Akron, I was driving two hours to Lexington to interview for the job. This time it was a job I wanted. Kentucky basketball meant the elite level of the sport. I was glad I had done the interview in Akron. I felt at least somewhat better prepared. For example, I knew executive editor John Carroll had led more than one Pulitzer Prize-winning story or series of stories in his career.

This was intimidating, and when we met in his office during the interview process I braced for another where-did-you-go-to-college putdown. Instead we had a relaxed conversation. When he asked me where I wanted to be professionally in five years, I had practiced a response. But before I could start my rehearsed response, Carroll smiled and said something to the effect that people can make plans, but they have to adjust on the fly. That relaxed me.

Carroll was part of at least 16 Pulitzer Prize-winning efforts in his career. Thirteen came after he left Lexington and was editor of the *Los Angeles Times*. That included a story published five days before a gubernatorial election that reported actor-turned GOP candidate Arnold Schwarzenegger had groped women.

Schwarzenegger won the election and admitted that he had "behaved badly" toward women. Thousands of readers canceled their subscriptions, according to the *Times'* obituary of Carroll, who died in 2015.

Carroll did not flinch.

"One of our goals is to do more investigative reporting," he wrote in a commentary published by the *Los Angeles Times* after the election. "At the risk of offending still more readers, I'll say that if you're put off by investigative reporting, this probably won't be the right newspaper for you in the years to come."

This was the Carroll I grew to know and admire. His view of journalism was inspiring.

When the *Herald* offered me the job of covering UK football and basketball, I knew I had to accept. But there was some hesitation. I thoroughly enjoyed working for Connell. I felt valued and depended upon. An impromptu assignment had been to cover a man threatening to jump off the bridge over the Ohio River connecting Huntington, W.Va., and Chesapeake, Ohio. Fortunately, the man did not jump and I got through the story without it being an embarrassment.

Plus, I liked Connell's approach of treating sports as another news beat. Marshall winning or losing was incidental to coverage of the team.

And if staffers were sitting around in the office chatting about sports like fans at a bar, it wasn't unusual for Connell to hand out assignments that needed immediate attention.

Johnson said his former work stint at *The Daily Independent*, the newspaper based in Ashland, Ky., contributed to my hiring.

"One of the things I had done was cover some Marshall sports," Johnson said in 2023 of his time working for the newspaper in Ashland. "And I knew that in Huntington, Marshall basketball was a big deal. They had (riveting players in the past like) Hal Greer and Mike D'Antoni. So, I knew that was really important in Huntington. And while it was on a smaller scale, I considered it similar to covering UK because I knew in Huntington Marshall basketball was *the* team. And that was really the reason I decided to go that way."

I spoke to an uncle, Charles "Bo" Basham, about the job offer. He did not hesitate to recommend I take the job.

Ultimately, covering Kentucky was a huge step up. So I felt compelled to accept the job while feeling uncomfortable about leaving family and friends. Lexington was a city of strangers.

Fortunately, I felt welcomed by the *Herald-Leader* sports staff. In particular, columnist D.G. FitzMaurice was like an older brother. His welcoming spirit included introducing me to Long Island tea and inviting me to join him one summer on a visit to his parents' home in Sanibel Island, Fla.

But when Fitz, as he was known, introduced me to Kentucky football coach Fran Curci, this set in motion my baptism by fire as the UK beat reporter.

Curci skipped the niceties of "nice to meet you" and "where are you from" chit-chat. He got to the apparent point immediately by asking me which sport I liked better: football or basketball?

As a novice to Kentucky sports coverage, I thought that diplomacy was the best and safest way to respond. So I said, "I like both sports."

This was true, but to be completely honest, I liked basketball more. I had always liked football, too, and had my favorite teams (Detroit Lions, Dallas Texans/Kansas City Chiefs) and players (Mel Farr, Lem Barney, Charlie Sanders, Alex Karas, Len Dawson). But I found basketball more compelling and more relatable. I had played countless pickup basketball games, plus church league, intramural and recreation leagues.

My attempt at diplomacy fell flat. Thus began a contentious first season covering Kentucky football.

Curci's football-or-basketball question came to mind when John Calipari spoke in 2022 of Kentucky being a "basketball school" and not a "football school."

Before coming to Lexington, I had naively thought that all sports on campus were united in representing the same school.

When Curci was fired after the 1981 season, he issued a statement saying this action was unfair. He suggested that he had disciplined players when necessary.

Then he made a pointed comparison. "Let me remind (UK's) ad hoc committee that one of the worst NCAA punishments inflicted on a school was given to (the) UK basketball program for point shaving in the '50s," Curci said in a statement. "UK was not allowed to compete for an entire basketball season."

"Yet they didn't fire Adolf (sic) Rupp or even reprimand him."

Curci also said he had disciplined all eight football players accused of rape, while Rupp was not punished when a basketball player "was convicted of rape and is still in jail."

That was an apparent reference to Tom Payne.

I arrived in Lexington unaware of how hot the proverbial seat that Curci sat on was. I came to think he liked taking out his frustration on reporters.

At one practice, a player went down on all fours and vomited into grass. Curci saw this and reporters standing behind the sideline nearby. Curci turned to the Sports Information Department staffer who stood with the reporters and said that whatever the player had eaten for lunch, he wanted that to be the media meal at the next game.

This drew a laugh.

During that 1981 football season, it was announced that backup quarterback Randy Jenkins would become the starter. I wrote a story in which he talked about how the team with him as quarterback would use passing plays and running plays.

An angry Curci accused me of trying to give away the game plan.

On another occasion, I found myself in the football coaches' locker room. An angry Curci scolded me as assistant coaches sat and watched. I don't remember what irritated Curci this time, but I remember the look on the assistant coaches' faces suggested uneasiness and a wonder about how I might respond. I just took it and left when Curci finished his spiel.

George Rorrer, a Marshall graduate, had a sportswriting resume that included stints at the *Herald-Dispatch*, *Louisville Courier-Journal* and *Louisville Times*. By this time, he was working for a Louisville newspaper. When I saw him at a football practice during that 1981 season, I asked him about covering Kentucky football. I wanted reassurance that I had made the correct career choice. He spoke fondly of his memories of covering Marshall. My heart sank.

One of my later sports editors at the *Herald-Leader*, Gene Abell, remembered when Curci ordered a reporter be kicked out of practice for the sin of wearing a red sweatshirt.

This reporter was Joe Mattingly, who worked for *The Cats' Pause* while a UK student. His offense was wearing red at a practice a few days before a home game against Alabama in that 1981 season.

"It didn't seem funny to me at the time," Mattingly said in 2023. "In retrospect, it was funny."

Mattingly, who practices law in Lebanon, Ky., and had been Marion County attorney for 25 years, said his association with *The Cats' Pause* contributed to his eviction from practice. That summer *The Cats' Pause* had reported that then Kentucky Gov. John Y. Brown wanted Curci fired.

"So not only was Curci ill with all the press, I think he was particularly ill with Oscar (Combs, the founder of *The Cats' Pause*) particularly, and with *The Cats' Pause*."

Mattingly, a native of Marion County, said he wore the sweatshirt because it was cool. Temperatures were in the low 60s and high 50s in the days before the game. He also wore the sweatshirt, which he said had no lettering, to class that day.

"I thought absolutely nothing of it," he said.

As Mattingly recalled, a manager came across the field during practice and asked Mattingly to identify himself. The manager went back across the field and told Curci. Then the manager returned and asked Mattingly what media outlet he worked for. He said *The Cats' Pause*. The manager crossed the field again and told Curci. Then the manager returned and said Mattingly would have to take off the sweatshirt.

Other media members present, including Abell, said he was too cold to take off a sweatshirt. The manager crossed the field, then returned with the coach's demand that Mattingly leave.

Ultimately, Mattingly was escorted off the practice field and told he was banned from attending future practices. This led to a meeting that included then Director of Athletics Cliff Hagan. Mattingly said he was told to be more careful about the colors of his clothing.

"Sometimes people think it's easy," Mattingly recalled of his time covering Kentucky sports. "And it's not. I grew up a Kentucky fan, and was a big Kentucky fan. And I was probably less of a Kentucky fan after you've had a little bit of exposure to coaches and players. It gives you a different perspective."

Many years later, I spoke to Curci for a story. It was a friendly and productive conversation.

But after dealing with Curci in the 1981 football season, UK's basketball coaches seemed like little puddy cats by comparison.

Four Eventful Seasons Covering Joe B. Hall's Teams

My first two seasons covering Kentucky basketball could have been considered a long-running missing person report. Those were the two seasons that Sam Bowie was sidelined because of a stress fracture in his left shinbone.

Upon reflection, a Bruce Springsteen song title captures the dynamic that I unwittingly entered: "From Small Things (Big Things One Day Come)."

In trying to put Bowie's continuing absence into perspective, I wrote a story that began with this: "In its initial stages, a stress fracture doesn't even show up on a common X-ray. The sometimes far-reaching consequences are all too apparent to University of Kentucky basketball fans."

Then UK Coach Joe B. Hall did not like that I spoke to doctors at the universities of Indiana and Pennsylvania to try to give readers a sense of how the medical community viewed stress fractures. I did so because UK's basketball program did not make the doctors treating Bowie available.

As a freshman in the 1979-80 season, Bowie had been the team's second-leading scorer (12.9 ppg). As a sophomore, he was the leading scorer (17.4 ppg). Great expectations gave way to a when-will-it-end waiting game.

The fracture occurred during the spring or summer of 1981, causing Bowie to miss the 1981-82 season.

His first comeback appeared to be progressing nicely as Bowie dominated fellow big man Melvin Turpin and everyone else in spring workouts leading up to Kentucky's 1982 summer tour of Far East Asia. Coach Joe B. Hall could be seen shaking his head in amazement while leaving the practice floor.

But swelling and aching returned to Bowie's leg in Japan.

Surgery was performed on Oct. 20, 1982, causing Bowie to miss a second season.

In 2023, I asked Bowie what it had been like to sit out those two seasons.

"It was extremely tough," he said. "I really felt I'd just be in a cast for six weeks, miss a little conditioning and then my career would go on.

"As time went on, I really started doubting whether or not my career was going to get back on track. I always felt confident. But there comes a point where you're continuously (facing setbacks)."

Again and again, the medical staff removed the cast, checked the stress fracture and then told him it was not yet healed, Bowie said.

In October of 1982, a source told the *Louisville Courier-Journal* that Bowie would be undergoing an additional surgery on his slow-healing left shinbone.

"Physically it was a setback, but mentally there are nights you cry alone in Wildcat Lodge," Bowie said in 2023.

I asked Bowie if he meant he literally cried.

"Yeah," he said. "No shame or ego involved here. When you're seven-foot or you're in the public eye and you play for Kentucky, you have to deal with the general public. There were many times I had to put on a front, saying that I was fine and I'm good mentally.

"Then you go back to Wildcat Lodge and close the door and you let your emotions go."

I never saw this distress. Bowie never betrayed the anxiety he felt when speaking to the media.

As for Bowie the basketball player, I had not seen him play except on television. So, I was eager to see him in action. That chance finally came in my second season of coverage: 1982-83.

UK said that Bowie would be playing in a practice scrimmage. In those days, the media could attend practices. So, I went to Rupp Arena and watched – and judged – if Bowie looked anything like the celebrated star whose absence had been lamented for so long.

To my eye (and to my surprise), Bowie looked like the best player on the court. And this was with players on a team that despite Bowie's absence advanced Kentucky to the Elite 8 round of the 1983 NCAA Tournament.

"To say I was geeked up would be an understatement," Bowie said when asked about the scrimmage. "I needed to prove to myself as well as to all those who had been waiting two years that it was worth the wait."

One of the many benefits of covering Kentucky basketball – and I was always grateful for how many there were – was that every so often you felt like you were part of an event that breathed life into a famous quote by Alan Barth. The longtime editorial writer for *The Washington Post* called journalism the "first rough draft of history."

One of the historical games Bowie missed was when Kentucky played Louisville in the 1983 NCAA Tournament Mideast Region finals. It was dubbed "the Dream Game" in part because the in-state non-rivals hadn't played since the 1959 NCAA Tournament. UK had not played U of L in a regular-season game since 1922.

Hall had cited a "policy" that prevented Kentucky from playing Louisville. Through an Open Records request, I asked for a copy of the policy. The response noted that there was not a written policy.

That bit of history made simply seeing the Kentucky and Louisville teams warming up on the same court a startling sight. Like seeing the Israelis and Palestinians preparing to play, I thought.

Then Kentucky Gov. John Y. Brown famously wore a sports jacket that was half blue and half red. The game that followed made every dribble seem monumental.

"I sat on the bench, and whoo, that was one of the hardest defeats to swallow," Bowie said of Louisville's 80-68 overtime victory at (of all places) Knoxville, Tenn. "And that's where it makes you feel more guilty when you're injured. . . . That's where you just know I let my team down because if I'm on the floor, it's a different result. So, that really hurt."

Bowie recalled how the post-game locker room scene brought no relief.

"I didn't play and I didn't sweat in that game," he said. "But I look around and see my teammates with their heads down, cutting tape off their ankles and pissed off. And they're looked upon as, quote, losers to Louisville."

Coaches, trainers and other people in the locker room tried to encourage Bowie by pointing out that he would play again in the future.

"It's crazy to say, you're getting all this support, but you don't feel like you're part of the team," he said. "At least, I didn't.

"Here I am on the sideline in this environment, and I know this is a historical game. I know I'm young, but I did know this was not a normal ballgame."

My news instinct got a jolt after the game. As I walked toward the room where the post-game press conferences would be conducted, I saw the Kentucky coach's wife, Katharine Hall, talking to Billy Reed in front of the entrance. One of her arms was around Reed's shoulders. I naively thought this was sweet. Reed was consoling her after a bitter defeat.

But the word in the media workroom afterward was that Katharine was scolding Reed because she didn't like how he had repeatedly written columns calling for Kentucky to play Louisville.

Now, I debated internally if I should report this. Would other reporters include it in their stories? Everyone had to see it. But I felt uncomfortable about asking others if they would?

I compromised. I mentioned it deep in a collection of sidebar notes so there would be no eye-catching headline about it.

This decision did not make Hall happy. I found that out a week or so later when I went to Hall's office to interview him for an upcoming story. After I entered the office and sat near his desk, Hall got up and silently walked over and closed the door.

I could feel my body tensing as Hall came and stood over my chair. He then said I could treat him unfairly, but I should keep his wife out of it. I thought it best not to point out that she had injected herself into the coverage.

This was one of several times Hall and/or staffers expressed displeasure about the coverage. This friction was apparent almost immediately. The first game I covered was a home game against Akron to begin the 1981-82 season. This was also the first game Bowie would be sitting out.

The obvious story to preview the game seemed to be about the player who would be filling Bowie's role as Kentucky's big man: sophomore Melvin Turpin, a Lexington native who would be making the first of 95 consecutive starts for Kentucky over three seasons.

The routine was for reporters to make interview requests when practice ended. Barring a conflict with class or some other appointment, the player would return to the court to speak to the reporter.

But instead of Turpin, the person who came onto the court to speak to me was Associate Coach Leonard Hamilton. He was not in a good mood. He scolded me for what he said was the intent to put pressure on Turpin. I had no choice but to write the preview story on the game (aka "the advance") without quotes from Turpin.

A conflict arose on another occasion when a reporter asked Hall to explain the poor shooting in Kentucky's recent home games. Hall responded by pointing out that Rupp Arena was an off-campus facility owned and operated by the Lexington-Fayette Urban County Government. So, Hall explained, the UK team could not practice on its home court as much as teams that practiced and played in on-campus gyms. This meant the players were less accustomed to the shooting environment than most teams playing home games.

In looking to add context to the story, I spoke to Tom Minter, the president and CEO of Lexington Center Corporation. Minter said that Kentucky did not always accept invitations to practice in Rupp Arena because an on-campus gym, Memorial Coliseum, was more convenient.

Hall expressed his irritation about my story including Minter's comments.

Jim Host, a Lexington-based businessman who founded a pioneering collegiate sports marketing company, said he tried to counsel Hall on dealing with the media.

"He wanted to have the fans giving him another excuse if he lost a close one," Host said of Hall's irritation with the story including Minter's comments. "That's all that was. I know Tom worked overboard when he first got there to try to satisfy Joe because it was a new facility."

Hall did not seem shy about expressing his irritation with the media.

For a while one season, Hall repeatedly referred to me as "D.A." I had no idea what he meant. I came to think maybe he meant district attorney as a compliment to what I thought was a diligent work ethic. But I came to believe the initials he cited meant "dumb ass."

"I kept telling him this is part of the job of being the head person," Host said in 2023. "That you put your head down and do the best job you can. And you answer questions from the media fairly and honestly and roll with the punches. If I told him that once, I told him that many, many times."

Hall also clashed with the UK broadcast crew, which was headed by iconic play-by-play announcer Cawood Ledford.

"He would be not abusive, but (he was) not very conversant," Host said. "And he got much better with our broadcast crew as time went on. . . . I think he really matured in the job the further he went along."

Another conflict I had with Hall in the 1983-84 season involved a comment made by Bowie. Kentucky had just finished its non-conference schedule with an unbeaten record (8-0).

"Our goal is to be the best team ever assembled," Bowie said.

Hall endorsed Bowie's statement.

"The potential of this team is unlimited," the UK coach said when asked about Bowie's comment. "This team has more potential than any team we've had."

I wanted to put this goal in context. What was the greatest team ever assembled that Kentucky wanted to surpass? I wondered who I could talk to who could credibly say which team was the greatest ever up until that point. I thought of John Wooden, who had coached UCLA to four of the still only 12 unbeaten teams in the history of Division I basketball.

If I remember correctly, and to my surprise and relief, the UCLA Sports Information office got me Wooden's phone number.

"They haven't looked that good to me," he said in our telephone interview. "Maybe in parts of games, but not consistently."

Wooden said Kentucky had the ingredients to be one of the greatest teams: a dominant big man (Bowie or Turpin), a great forward (Kenny Walker), a zone-busting shooter (Jim Master) and depth (James Blackmon, Winston Bennett, Dickey Beal and Roger Harden).

But intangibles like team chemistry, balance and adapting to different opponents remained unknown, Wooden said before adding that it was too early in the season to be talking about historic greatness as a goal.

"If they think that in December, that would scare me as a coach," Wooden said. "If the players are talking in those terms, they won't be (one of the best). They have no basis for saying it."

Hall, who had acknowledged that it was too early in a season to set such a lofty goal, chastised me for including Wooden's comments in the story.

"Joe didn't care much for John Wooden," Host recalled in 2023. This dislike began when UCLA beat Kentucky in the 1975 national championship game. Hall believed Wooden sought – and gained – a strategic advantage with the referees by announcing the day before that he would be retiring after the game, Host said.

Thinking back almost 40 years, Bowie said he had no problem then or now with Wooden's observations being part of my story.

"That was me because I said it," Bowie told me. "Coach Hall didn't like that. But Sam Bowie made the statement, and you just took off with it. I fess up to it."

Bowie's teammates embraced the goal of being recognized as the best ever.

"The mindset was we were going to do something very, very special that year," Bowie said.

Kenny Walker, who was a sophomore that season, said the players considered Kentucky's 1978 national championship team as the standard to surpass.

"But we were bigger and more athletic and I think a little bit faster" than the 1978 UK team," Walker said. "That was the team we were all hoping to be."

My story ran in the *Herald-Leader* on New Year's Day. On Jan. 13, still undefeated (12-0) Kentucky played at Auburn.

Led by Chuck Person (25 points) and Charles Barkley (21 points and 10 rebounds), Auburn beat Kentucky 82-63.

At that time, there was not necessarily a formal postgame news conference. After Auburn beat Kentucky, reporters formed a semi-circle in front of Hall outside the UK locker room door. Much to my discomfort, I found myself directly in front of Hall, who had still voiced irritation with me including Wooden's comments in the story about Bowie and Kentucky setting a historically high standard for success.

I stood there hoping no one would mention Kentucky's goal of being the greatest team ever assembled. But, alas, a reporter who covered Auburn asked how such a team could not only lose, but lose by 19 points.

Hall pointed at me and said sarcastically, "Ask him. He's the expert on greatest teams."

I did not respond.

On the plus side, this inspired the lead to my game story. It began with Kentucky still having a chance to declare itself "the greatest team ever disassembled."

Four days later, Kentucky lost 69-57 at Florida.

Though not considered the greatest team ever assembled, Kentucky's 1983-84 team did end its season on a historic note. UK won the Southeastern Conference regular-season and tournament championships. Then the Wildcats advanced to the Final Four after beating Louisville and Illinois in the Mideast Region played in Rupp Arena. During the 72-67 victory over Louisville, a fan threw a coin and hit U of L Coach Denny Crum.

A few days before the Mideast Region semifinal games were played, *Herald-Leader* sports editor Mike Johnson had a story idea. We should do a story on two of the four head coaches in the Mideast Region: Hall and Lefty Driesell of Maryland. The story could be about two successful coaches who are under appreciated.

In separate one-on-one interviews, neither Hall nor Driesell warmed to the story idea. Hall's objection included chastising me in front of onlookers in UK's Memorial Coliseum. A one-on-one reprimand I would silently accept. But there being an audience made it harder to accept, so I told Hall to stop. He then challenged me by asking what I was going to do about it. I felt no option other than to take the criticism.

"I felt bad about it because you took all the heat for it, and it was my idea," Johnson said almost 30 years later. "And I thought it was a good idea, and I still do."

By beating Louisville and Illinois, Kentucky advanced to the Final Four. This was the first of nine Final Fours I would cover in which Kentucky played. This was also my first and only time in Seattle. The biggest off-court memory involved a salmon dinner for the media the day before the national semifinals. It was cooked and eaten in the Kingdome, where the games would be played.

I had always liked salmon. My grandmother made salmon cakes regularly. But this salmon was unlike anything I had experienced. It had to be at least four inches thick and delicious.

For Bowie, it was a chance to complete the recovery from the stress fracture with a trip to college basketball's promised land.

Bowie was always friendly, patient and able to show remarkable restraint when asked – for about the billionth time? – how is the leg?

"It doesn't hurt at all," he said the week of the Final Four.

When told that more than 600 members of the media would be in Seattle and would ask that very question, Bowie could manage a sly smile.

"We're ready for those same old questions," he said. "I'd like to say I'm back to 100 percent. I see all the progress I've made since the beginning of the season. But I can't say I'm back to 100 percent. The two-year layoff took a lot more out of me than I first anticipated."

Kentucky played Georgetown the next day in arguably one of the most memorable national semifinal games in history.

As Kentucky fans of a certain age well remember, the Wildcats made only three of 33 shots in the second half in losing to Georgetown 53-40.

"It still haunts me to this day: 9.1 percent," Kenny Walker said in 2023. Walker made one of three shots in the game.

"One of the most disappointing times in my athletic career," Sam Bowie said in 2023. Bowie made three of 10 shots in the game.

Kentucky led 29-22 at halftime. Then UK scored two points in the first 16 minutes of the second half.

In the postgame news conference, Hall struggled to explain three-for-33 shooting.

"I guess it was an extra celestial phenomenon," he said.

Kentucky's three players averaging double-figure points – Turpin, Walker and Bowie – made six of 24 shots in the game.

Almost 40 years later, Walker was still puzzled when asked why he thought Kentucky made only three of 33 shots in the second half.

"That's a crazy question," he said. "We were leading the game at halftime. It's almost like someone put a lid on the basket in the second half. Still to this day, it's probably the most bizarre game that I was ever part of."

Walker recalled Kentucky making only four of 32 three-point shots in losing to West Virginia in the 2010 East Region finals. "But they still shot better than 9.1 percent," he said.

"I remember coming in at halftime, we were all really excited and we were jumping around in the locker room," Walker added. "I remember Coach Hall coming in and saying, 'OK guys, let's just settle down. We have 20 more minutes to go. Georgetown is going to make adjustments. They will be physical. . . . We're in control of the game. Let's just go back out there and we'll finish what we started.'"

From the vantage point of almost 40 years, Walker had second thoughts.

"I almost wish now looking back on it, if he let us continue to jump around and act crazy and be excited because we were loose," Walker said. "I'm thinking that out in the second half, we got off to a slow start and started to miss shots. . . . I think it was one of those things we started thinking about (missed shots) a little bit."

The 1984-85 season was Joe B. Hall's 13th and final season as Kentucky coach.

Kentucky finished tied for third in the SEC with an 11-7 record (16-11 overall). Hall came to the CBS affiliate in Lexington, WKYT, to watch the Selection Sunday show. His reaction to Kentucky being a 12th seed in the West Region proved that a 56-year-old man could be giddy.

"Whew, boy!" he said after turning a smiling face to others in the studio. "That's super."

UK's first-round opponent would be Washington, which was led by two players from Germany, Detlef Schrempf and Christian Welp.

"Maybe they'll defect," Hall quipped.

When 8-seed Auburn advanced from the first round to win the SEC Tournament and its automatic bid to the NCAA Tournament, Kentucky did not expect to be part of Selection Sunday.

"After Auburn won it, I wouldn't give a nickel for our chances," Bret Bearup said the day the NCAA Tournament field was announced.

Hall gave the players the option of returning to Lexington after the SEC Tournament or going home.

Meanwhile, Florida Coach Norm Sloan had a polar opposite reaction when the Gators did not receive a bid. Florida had beaten Kentucky in two of the three games, including in the second round of the SEC Tournament.

"It flashed through my mind that (UK Director of Athletics) Cliff Hagan was strutting his stuff around the (SEC) tournament all week, popping off that they were already in the (NCAA) tournament," Sloan said. "And it looks like he was right. I don't know what you call it, but it's collusion. It's political and it stinks."

For a story 21 years later, Walker agreed that it was good to be Kentucky.

"I'm glad we had that name on our jerseys," he said.

Kentucky validated receiving the bid by beating Washington and UNLV en route to advancing to the Sweet 16 of the West Region. In Denver, Kentucky would play and lose to No. 1 seed St. John's 86-70.

Rumors of Hall's imminent retirement swirled. When I saw him enter McNichols Arena in Denver for the game against St. John's, I suspected the rumors were true. For the first time in a game that I had covered, Hall was wearing a brown suit. This seemed to be a fashion statement given that this had been the trademark attire of Adolph Rupp.

Sure enough, after the game reporters gathered along press row where the UK radio crew was set up for Hall's interview with iconic play-by-play man Cawood Ledford. Hall announced his retirement. After the radio broadcast, reporters were invited to come the next day to Hall's hotel room for another question-and-answer session.

That session went well. Absent was the frequently contentious atmosphere whenever Hall and the media met.

Mike Johnson, the sports editor who hired me to cover Kentucky basketball and football for the *Herald-Leader*, recalled how Hall called one day during my first season or two covering the team and asked for a meeting.

As Johnson recalled, Hall asked, why can't we get positive coverage like other teams in the SEC get?

"I just said, 'Coach, I can't speak for what the other papers do or don't do,'" Johnson remembered replying. "'All I can tell you is our goal isn't to be positive or negative or any other way. Our goal is to just cover the team (and) report what's happening'."

Marta McMackin, who served as Administrative Support Assistant for the Kentucky basketball program from 1976 until 2007, said that paranoia was the staff's defining characteristic during Hall's time as coach.

"One thing I remember about Joe B is that we were all paranoid," she said in 2023. "It was like everybody was out to get us, including internally.

"I don't think I was so paranoid when I started working there. But I surely became paranoid."

Besides wondering if the NCAA and SEC were "out to get us," McMackin recalled Hall wondered about the school administration after asking then UK president Otis Singletary for permission to build an on-campus dorm for the basketball program. Singletary only agreed if Hall could raise the money for construction.

McMackin came to see two Joe B. Halls.

"I always said when he came in with the hat on that said, Joe Hall from Cynthiana, he was the greatest guy in the world," she said. "When he came in with the hat on that said, Joe Hall, head coach at the University of Kentucky, he could be a real hell raiser.

"If you got him away from basketball, he was genuinely a good person."

This was the person John Calipari got to know when he became Kentucky coach in 2009. Hall's unqualified support came as a surprise.

"Nowadays, a guy leaves a program, he wants that program to die," Calipari said in 2023. "He wants it to go in a hole and evaporate and be gone. And, 'no, it could not last without me.'

"I'm going to say 90 percent (of coaches are) out there that way."

Calipari noted Hall's show of support from the beginning.

It was well known that Hall had the inevitable task of following a legend in Adolph Rupp. But Rupp made the job as difficult as possible for his successor. I remember Calipari's eyes widened in disbelief when I told him Rupp publicly second-guessed Hall's coaching.

Calipari helped Hall become a revered figure in Kentucky basketball history. Each year on or near his birthday, Hall would come to center court and do a "Y" to complete a K-E-N-T-U-C-K-Y cheer during a game timeout. Each time the crowd erupted in warm cheers.

When he came to games, Hall's appearance on the Rupp Arena video boards produced more such cheers.

"He left this Earth knowing he was appreciated," Calipari said.

Eddie Sutton Made News On and Off the Court

Marta McMackin worked in the Kentucky basketball office as an administrative assistant from the spring of 1976 to the spring of 2007. The four years that Eddie Sutton was the UK coach stand out . . . for all the wrong reasons.

"It's kind of part of my tenure at UK I've tried to forget . . . ," she said in 2023. "That was the worst four years of my life."

Seemingly from beginning to end, Sutton's time as Kentucky coach was – shall we say – newsy.

Actually, controversy was present before he became Kentucky coach. In Joe B. Hall's final season as coach, *Herald-Leader* reporters Jeffrey Marx and Michael York worked on a series of stories about payments to Kentucky players that won the Pulitzer Prize for investigative reporting in 1986.

My contributions to the series, which was titled "Playing Above the Rules," were minimal. Basically, Marx and/or York might ask me how willing a former player would be to talk about receiving pay for play from Kentucky's program. I would recall for them how outgoing and forthright a player had been during routine interviews.

Ultimately 31 of 33 players Marx and York interviewed acknowledged receiving money while playing for Kentucky.

This cloud hovered over the program when Sutton became Kentucky coach in 1985.

Sutton, who had been the Adolph Rupp of Arkansas basketball, further complicated the situation by saying he would have crawled to Lexington to get the job. This angered Arkansas fans and administrators.

During Kentucky's search for a new coach, which was helped by the Final Four being in Lexington that year, I spoke to a sportswriter from either Oklahoma or Kansas. When I asked about Sutton, the sportswriter mentioned the coach having a drinking problem. That was the first of many, many times over the next four years that I heard that topic raised.

Doug Barnes, an assistant coach in Sutton's first two seasons as Kentucky coach, said he was told by Sutton's wife, Patsy, that alcohol came up in the Kentucky job interview.

During the interview, then UK president Otis Singletary downplayed alcohol as an issue by noting that Rupp enjoyed bourbon, Barnes said he was told.

"And that was all that was said," Barnes said Patsy Sutton had told him. "She didn't think he had any chance of getting the job because they would call Arkansas. They never made any calls to Arkansas, so it was not an issue."

Wally Hall, a sports columnist with the *Arkansas Democrat-Gazette* since 1979, said that Sutton and Arkansas Athletic Director Frank Broyles had been "feuding" during the 1984-85 season.

"Frank wanted him to get help for his drinking," Hall wrote in a 2023 email. "Eddie denied having a problem. I don't think he would have been fired, but they had to sit down and talk things out in Salt Lake City, Utah, at the NCAA Tournament."

Arkansas, the nine-seed in the West Region, lost to one-seed St. John's 68-65 in the second round in Salt Lake City. Incidentally, St. John's beat Kentucky 86-70 in the Sweet 16 round of the West Region, which was Joe B. Hall's final game as Kentucky coach.

During Arkansas' game against St. John's, Sutton left the bench and sat in the stands. It was the second time that season Sutton had done that.

"There were a lot of guys from Kentucky there," Wally Hall recalled. "They were wearing those Kentucky blue blazers. I thought that took him out of the picture."

It did not.

"As far as I know, Frank (Broyles) was never contacted by anyone from Kentucky, and he wasn't happy about it," Wally Hall wrote in the email. "Eddie said he would have crawled to get to Kentucky. He later said he meant he would have crawled to get away from Frank."

Barnes cited heredity as a factor for why Sutton had the disease of alcoholism.

"His father was an alcoholic," the former UK assistant coach said. "That's the reason his mother was so concerned about coach (Sutton). She came a couple times to visit." In addition to Arkansas and Kentucky, Sutton also had alcohol-related issues when he began his NCAA Division I coaching career at Creighton (1969-1974), Barnes said.

I never wrote a story about Sutton's drinking. The thinking was that such a story needed documented proof. It could not be based on hearsay. There was none of the first, but plenty of the second.

Sutton underwent treatment for alcoholism in 1987. But after a recruiting scandal that resulted in NCAA penalties, he was fired in 1989.

Rex Chapman, the leading scorer on Kentucky's teams in the 1986-87 and 1987-88 seasons, became aware early in his freshman season of Sutton's drinking problem. This enlightenment was part of what could be considered the pinnacle of Chapman's time as a Kentucky player: his 26-point starburst that led unranked Kentucky to a 85-51 victory at No. 18 Louisville.

"The thing about that game, I remember well, was Eddie was hammered drunk," Chapman said in 2023.

The hint of this came in early that morning.

"Richard Madison was my roommate on the road," Chapman said. "And Richard had been watching cartoons all night long. And we had an afternoon game. And I just couldn't sleep. So I got up. This was early, like 5:30 (or) six. I just put my sweater on and put my hoodie up because we were in Louisville. I would have been recognized."

Chapman was walking in the hotel, then decided to get on an elevator and return to his room.

"I got on the elevator and my head was down," he said. "And a guy got on the elevator in a trench coat and a bottle clanking in the trench coat. And I looked up and it was Coach (Sutton).

Sutton was "just reeking of vodka," said Chapman, who added that Sutton told him to return to his room.

A victory over Louisville dulled, if not removed, concern about drinking.

In the postgame press conference, a gushing Sutton referred to Chapman as his adopted son. This embarrassed Chapman.

"I was confused and I don't want to get him in trouble," Chapman said. "I'm just figuring out that this is an issue. He had a problem."

Before his freshman season began, Chapman and teammate Reggie Hanson went across the street from Wildcat Lodge to do extra shooting in the Memorial Coliseum gym. There they saw Sutton passed out, Chapman said.

The players called assistant coach Dwane Casey, who rushed to Memorial Coliseum, Chapman said. Another assistant, James Dickey, also came. The coaches told the players not to tell anyone about it.

Combined with what happened the day of the game at Louisville, "now I'm starting to understand what's going on," Chapman said. "We thought he was hurt or had a stroke or something."

Jim Host, the Lexington businessman who practically introduced marketing strategies to college basketball, said Sutton would regularly come to his office early in the morning.

"He smelled like he'd been drinking all night," Host recalled in 2023. "You could smell it many feet away."

Kenny Walker, whose senior season coincided with Sutton's first as Kentucky coach, said he was unaware of the drinking problem. "Winning cures all of that," he said of Sutton's debut season having a 32-4 record that included Southeastern Conference regular-season and tournament championships.

Kentucky was scheduled to play seven games during a tour of Japan and Hong Kong after the season in late June and early July. Walker figured the June 17 NBA Draft (four days before the first game in Japan) made the trip impossible for him.

But Sutton said Walker could go if he got back to Lexington the day after the draft, but Walker would not play in the games because he had not practiced with the team.

"So I went," Walker said. "I just looked at it as a vacation."

After Kentucky struggled to a six-point victory in the fourth game, Sutton said Walker and fellow "vacationing" senior Roger Harden could play in the remaining games. But they would have to practice and obey curfew rules.

"We were, like, coach, why do we have curfew?!" Walker recalled. "What are you going to do? Are you going to kick us off the team?

"Roger and I, we never made curfew."

This led to a telling exchange with Sutton.

"I remember one night we were coming in at about three o'clock in the morning," Walker said.

When the elevator door opened for them to go up to their room, Walker and Harden saw Sutton.

"He had a brown bag in his hand," Walker said.

After asking where the players had been at that hour, Sutton summed up the situation.

"He said, well, you all didn't see me and I didn't see you," Walker said, laughing at the memory. "And you could tell he had had a few."

The newspaper budget at the time allowed me to go on the tour of Japan. It was an experience I'll never forget.

Just walking on the streets of Tokyo and Sendai while looking different from everyone else was interesting.

I noticed how polite and considerate the Japanese were toward other people. This included when stopped at a red light at night. Drivers would dim their lights so as not to shine brightly into the eyes of the driver on the other side of the street. Headlights were turned back on when the traffic lights turned green.

The Japanese also caught the attention of the UK players. Even though the UK players were celebrities in the Big Blue Nation, the cheering and excitement demonstrated by the Japanese upon seeing them brought astonished looks on their faces.

I had an exchange with Sutton during the trip to Japan that brought to mind the speculation of a drinking problem. Because of the time difference, my deadline for stories was about 7 a.m. in Japan or Hong Kong. So after I filed my stories, I would go to the hotel restaurant and have breakfast.

After eating one morning, I went to the cashier to pay for my breakfast. Sutton was in line. He noticed that I noticed he held two bottles of wine in his hands. I did not say anything, but he said he was buying the bottles as gifts to John Carroll, the editor and Vice President of the *Herald-Leader*, and Creed Black, the newspaper publisher.

Sutton asked if I wanted to take the bottles of wine to Carroll and Black, or would I prefer that Sutton take them back to the United States and give them to the newspaper executives?

My playful side kicked in. I said I'd take them. I recalled a slight frown crossing Sutton's face as he agreed.

When I returned home, I gave the bottles to Carroll and Black. They laughed as I told them the story.

During a regular media session in early January sometime during Sutton's four seasons as Kentucky coach, a reporter asked if he had celebrated the New Year with good ole Kentucky bourbon. I wondered how he would answer. Sutton said he had not.

My reporting on a potential recruit drew Sutton's ire in the summer of 1987.

The subject was John Pittman, a 7-footer from Rosenberg, Texas. An issue arose about his academic eligibility as related to NCAA standards then commonly referred to as Proposition 48.

I spoke to the principal at Pittman's school, Terry High School.

"John Pittman does not meet Proposition 48," principal Harry Wright said. "He does not have his 'core' curriculum."

Wright also refuted the rumor that Terry High School would appeal to have the NCAA re-evaluate its "core" curriculum requirement and restore Pittman's eligibility.

However, Rick Evrard of the NCAA's legislative services department said only the University of Kentucky could make such an appeal.

Then UK Director of Athletics Cliff Hagan said the school would not make such an appeal.

I quoted "sources" as saying Pittman had been encouraged to improve his academic standing at a junior college.

At the time, "core" classes required three English classes, two math classes, two social science classes, two physical science classes and two elective classes in such subjects as a foreign language, computer science, religion and philosophy.

A source said Pittman's resume lacked one of the two required math classes.

Sources said that UK was "highly suspicious" of Pittman's academic credentials and of the recruit's dramatically improved ACT score.

A source said Pittman scored a 4 the first time he took the ACT. His score improved to 11, then 12 and finally the passing 17 on June 13.

Pat Farrant, a spokesman for the ACT, said such an improvement would raise a red flag to monitors. An improvement of 13 points is "not typical," Farrant said.

Sutton called for a meeting with the *Herald-Leader*'s sports editor at the time, Mike Johnson. As Johnson recalled, Sutton did not like my reporting on Pittman's eligibility. Specifically, he did not like quoting people at Terry High School. Sutton said that quoting people about a recruit's academic record was against NCAA rules.

To which Johnson said he pointed out that NCAA rules prohibited college coaches and officials from commenting on a recruit's academic record. But high school officials could do so.

"And he said, I hate to do this, if you're going to keep publishing (such stories), I'm going to start tipping stories to the *Courier-Journal*," Johnson recalled Sutton saying. "And I just said, you're going to have to do what you have to do.

"But if we find out information that we think is important to our readers, we're going to publish it."

The *Louisville Courier-Journal* was considered the *Herald-Leader*'s chief newspaper competitor.

A follow-up meeting was arranged in which Billy Reed, then a columnist with the *Herald-Leader*, and Johnson met with Sutton.

At this meeting, Sutton said he did not like the *Herald-Leader* writing such stories, but he accepted it. And he added that he would not be tipping off the *Courier-Journal* about upcoming stories.

"Probably the biggest mistake Coach Sutton made at UK was not understanding what UK was," Barnes said several years later. "You're under a microscope for everything that happens."

Barnes said he remembered Associate Coach Leonard Hamilton repeatedly reminding Sutton of this unblinking scrutiny.

"Looking back, I think not understanding the scrutiny you get was probably his big downfall," Barnes said.

After sitting out the 1989-90 season in the wake of being fired by Kentucky, Sutton's alma mater, Oklahoma State, hired him as coach.

Sutton revived his career. In 16 seasons as the Cowboys' coach, he led the team to 13 NCAA tournaments. That included two Final Four appearances. The program had been to only four Final Fours previously.

In 2005, Oklahoma State christened its playing floor Eddie Sutton court.

"I think Eddie Sutton was probably the best bench coach we've ever had here," Kentucky alum Jim Host said in 2023. "He was a brilliant X-and-O guy, and would make adjustments during the course of the game."

Doug Barnes agreed.

"When it came to coaching the game of basketball, he was almost genius-like," the former UK assistant coach said.

Barnes attributed this to Sutton beginning his career as a high school coach and then beginning the program at Southern Idaho Junior College.

"I feel that's where you really learn to teach the game," Barnes said of this humble beginning to Sutton's coaching career. "There are people in certain professions that kind of have a sixth sense about it. . . . They make a decision and you go, wow, where did that come from? Coach (Sutton) was kind of that way."

Long after he left Kentucky, Casey said Sutton "will go down as one of the great college coaches in the history of the game. . . . I don't know how you put an adjective on 'it,' but he had 'it.'

"We're imperfect people, but he was a perfect coach."

I found Sutton distinctive in how he did not draw attention to himself during a game. He usually sat in his seat during games. If it was still competitive inside the final few minutes, he arose and tried to dictate what happened.

Barnes attributed this to Sutton assigning scouting duties and in-game observation duties to four assistant coaches. Each assistant had a distinct part of the game to watch.

"He had four other sets of eyes (watching the game)," Barnes said. "That allowed him to have more information to make good decisions.

"Basketball is such a fast game. There's so much going on. No matter how fast you are, it's too much for one person.

"Coach (Sutton) said, if you guys get a head job, you sit your tail end on the bench."

Chapman credited Sutton as a reason for his 13-year NBA career.

"He could really coach," Chapman said. "And if I had not had my two years of defense taught by Eddie Sutton, I'm not sure I could have played very long in the NBA."

In his college coaching career, Sutton won 806 games. That ranked as the 25th most by a Division I coach going into the 2023-24 season. Current Kentucky Coach John Calipari was 29th on the list with 790 victories.

Yet, Sutton never could win over the Kentucky fans. Even winning the Southeastern Conference regular-season championship with a 17-1 record in his first season brought complaints. That's because Sutton suggested that championship rings be made and presented to the players. Critics said that Kentucky was supposed to win the SEC as evidenced by having had the best overall record and/or division record in 54 of the league's 91 seasons (or through the 2022-23 season).

When asked about the criticism, Kenny Walker said of Sutton's idea of rings, "he had them made up anyway. And I still have mine. So he did honor that team. He was a man of his word."

"I Never Put Money in a Package"

As Kentucky fans of a certain age remember well, Eddie Sutton's firing as coach began seeming inevitable with the news that the *Los Angeles Daily News* was reporting that a package sent to the father of Kentucky recruit Chris Mills had come open during delivery. An employee in Los Angeles at the mailing service, Emery Air Freight, reportedly said the package coming open revealed $1,000.

Assistant coach Dwane Casey's name was on the return address.

I remember sitting in my apartment when the phone rang. My heart sank as *Herald-Leader* sports editor Mike Johnson told me about the upcoming *Los Angeles Daily News* story. I immediately could anticipate an NCAA investigation, the firing of Sutton and his staff, then a search and hiring process for the new coach. Each step along this seemingly obvious immediate future meant a lot of work and anxiety.

Sutton went to University of Kentucky president David Roselle and offered to fire Casey and administrative assistant Marta McMackin "as a sacrifice to keep his job," McMackin recalled in 2023.

When asked in 2023 about this offer, Casey added an amendment by saying he was offered a new non-basketball job.

"Well, Roselle wanted me to work in the minority affairs office," Casey said.

Casey refused the offer. "Because I hadn't done anything wrong," he recalled. "I wasn't going to quit or be reassigned and look like I was (guilty)."

Roselle decided to conduct a real investigation into how closely the program followed NCAA rules. He appointed a former Fayette County circuit court judge, James Park, to lead the investigation.

This decision put the proverbial black hat on the then UK president.

"I heard from a number of cowards in the state," Roselle told me in 2005. "They'd call and tell me what all was going to happen to me. I never took (the threats) all that seriously."

But, Roselle added, he did report each threat to the police.

At this volatile time, Todd Jones was a reporter with the University of Kentucky student newspaper, *The Kentucky Kernel*. He told me that he was among a group of reporters waiting outside the basketball office one day just in case news broke.

As Jones recalled, Sutton emerged at one point and asked the reporters, "Any of you guys have a dictionary? I need to look up the word 'absolve.'"

Ultimately, Kentucky dismissed Sutton as coach. The NCAA imposed penalties that included Kentucky being ineligible for postseason play for two years.

Looking back on those four seasons, I marvel at how available and accommodating Sutton was with reporters as his program collapsed.

"It was a mess," said Doug Barnes, who had been on the staff in Sutton's first two seasons as UK coach. "I do know this: Dwane Casey did not put that money in the envelope. I do know that for a fact. He was actually in Pittsburgh."

When I spoke to Casey in 2023, he said he was in Pittsburgh on a recruiting trip to watch the Dapper Dan Roundball Classic Tournament when the infamous package was mailed from the UK basketball office to Claud Mills.

Casey, who was represented by Bowling Green, Ky., attorney Joe Bill Campbell, ultimately filed a $6.9 million defamation lawsuit against Emery Air Freight. Evidence from the court case showed that Casey was in Pittsburgh and that the Emery Air Freight employee who claimed to have found money in the package was not a reliable witness, Casey said.

Casey scoffed at the presumption that he – or anyone from the Kentucky basketball office – put $1,000 in the package as an inducement to play for Kentucky.

Mills' father, Claud, wanted his son to play for UNLV or UCLA. "Anywhere but Kentucky," Casey said. The inference was that $1,000 was no bargaining chip.

I asked Casey in 2023 why Claud Mills did not want his son playing for Kentucky.

"He thought Kentucky was country, to be honest with you, a racist school," Casey said.

This was because of something former Kentucky Gov. A.B. "Happy" Chandler said at a UK Board of Trustees meeting in the spring of 1988.

According to a story written by Jamie Lucke, the *Herald-Leader*'s education reporter at the time, Chandler opposed the school making investments in Zimbabwe. "You know Zimbabwe is all nigger now," Chandler reportedly said at the Trustees' Investment Committee during a discussion of UK's 1985 decision to dispose of its investments in South Africa. "There aren't any Whites."

In her story, Lucke quoted Jonathan Wutawunashe, the chargé d'affaires at the Zimbabwean embassy, as saying the country's population of 8.6 million included 120,000 white people. Whites made up 15 of 140 members of the country's Parliament, Wutawunashe added.

In reaction to Chandler's comment, UK football players said they might boycott the team's annual Blue-White Game.

Chandler had a harsh reaction.

"If they'd spend more time learning how to play football, they'd be a damn sight better off," he said. Chandler later apologized.

Of the football players' criticism, Chandler said, "It hurt me because I didn't know they were that stupid."

Chandler had been Major League Baseball's commissioner when Jackie Robinson broke the color barrier. Ironically, Casey recalled that Chandler was "one of the first persons to come to my defense" when the story broke about the Emery package.

The case was settled in 1990 for a seven-figure amount. But Casey continues to see it as an example of the truism in a comment made by Martin Luther King, Jr., in his famous letter from a Birmingham jail: Justice too long delayed is justice denied.

More than 30 years later, Casey still feels like he is considered all but synonymous with money in a package sent to the father of a recruit.

"I never put money in a package," he said in 2023. "That's the only thing that hurts me or I think about with the University of Kentucky. Perception for people is reality. That hurts me more than anything. I go to a career in the NBA: coach of the year and a NBA title.

"To me, that's the hardest part of my coaching career to have to look over – what's the word I want to use? – to get over. I didn't put money in a package. So, I always have that in the back of my mind. There's nothing I can do about it. That's the only pinch I have about Kentucky. Unfortunately, that's what people are going to remember me by: for something I didn't do."

In a 2004 story published by *The New York Times*, Casey said he had accepted that others on the Kentucky staff that year did not carry that stigma. For instance, Eddie Sutton led Oklahoma State to the Final Four that season. Coincidentally, Oklahoma State beat John Calipari-coached Memphis 70-53 in the second round that year.

"I smile because of the fact they're getting second chances," Casey said in the New York Times story. "Whenever my name comes up, it goes right back to the NCAA thing. I look and I wonder why. . . .

"The one thing I didn't do (is) I didn't go out and try to blast anybody or put the blame on anybody. I took it in stride."

When I spoke to Casey in 2023, he spoke highly of Sutton.

"Coach Sutton was a great coach," he said. "He wasn't into the fanfare. Today, he'd probably struggle with the Instagrams and Twitter and all that stuff. That's just who he was. . . .

"From my experience, put him down as one of the better coaches who've coached at Kentucky."

Casey said he meant that in terms of x-and-o strategy, preparing a team and then making the adjustments a game dictated.

But Sutton did not fit the celebrity personality that Kentucky mandates for its coaches. Every move and every statement can be examined.

"There's no shame to that," Casey said. "Not at all. Kentucky is not for everybody."

For example, Casey said that Sutton did not warm to the media. This was not readily apparent. I recall practices were always open to the media. I remember Kentucky practicing three times one Thanksgiving. I was not married at the time. I had no family in Lexington. So, I attended all three practices.

"He always had a healthy disdain for the media as most coaches do after you lose," Casey said of Sutton. "But it was never personal. I never heard him say, 'I hate Jerry Tipton.'"

I remember McMackin had a drawing on her desk at the time. She was depicted at her desk by a closed door that had "Wildcats" on it. There are three shark fins swimming toward the door as the drawing of McMackin says on the phone, "Coach Sutton, Mr. Tipton is here."

In 2023, I asked McMackin about the drawing.

"I don't know where I got it," she said. "I had it on my little bulletin board."

When I asked if the drawing reflected the sentiment I evoked with Sutton, she said, "it did, yeah."

I don't remember any outright hostility. I had no personal animosity toward the coaches. I remember learning about Sutton having coached at Creighton. I innocently asked if Paul Silas had been one of his players. Sutton playfully pointed out that he wasn't *that* old. Silas' final season for Creighton was 1963-64. Sutton's first season as coach was 1969-70.

"And as much as you and I had our issues, and mainly with the $1,000 and the NCAA, it was never anything to do personally," Casey said in 2023. "It was you doing your job. I think Coach Sutton was able to compartmentalize the media and the fans. And as a coach, I think you have to. It can't be personal. I've always taken it as, hey, you have a job to do. I have a job to do. I think that's the way he looked at it. He never made a big deal out of it."

Although the settlement in the lawsuit removed any legal issue from the situation, Casey noted how an NCAA investigation is different.

"You don't need that proof," he said of an NCAA investigation. "It's not a court of law. It's one investigator saying we have one guy. He's saying $1,000. So, they act on that.

"That's the unfortunate thing about fighting the NCAA or even being investigated by the NCAA. They don't have to have the same proof that you have to have in a court of law. They just have to have that one guy's word saying it. He doesn't have to be under oath. He doesn't have to have an attorney there with him to do that."

Casey cited an example. In its investigation of Sutton's basketball program, the NCAA cited Casey for having committed an "illegal transportation." This involved giving Kentucky player LeRon Ellis a ride to his first day on a summer job.

"It sounds like you gave him a first class ticket to Switzerland," Casey said. "I said I did it. That was one of the allegations. . . . They were looking for any little thing just to throw the book at the school."

Another charge involved freshman Eric Manuel's entrance exam. The NCAA charged Kentucky with being involved in cheating on the exam.

"Probably the most serious of all the other allegations," Casey said. "I had nothing to do with that. I thought the NCAA was ruthless with that kid. They wouldn't allow him to go to any other NCAA school because of that. And of all the players, he was probably more of a pro player than Chris (Mills) was."

Casey acknowledged that the media did not differentiate between the legal system and the way the NCAA operated. Regardless of the different standards, a reporter had to report on the possible NCAA findings and punishments.

"I got so tired of talking about it," Casey told me in 2023. "I was so mad at you at the time because I couldn't convince you as a reporter. But that's water under the bridge for me. I'll never be able to get rid of that image whatever people had at that time."

I believed that players receiving money was part of recruiting. Whether the NCAA should single out an individual coach, Casey in this instance, seemed like making him a handy scapegoat.

Casey turned to professional basketball. He coached in Japan for five seasons. He returned to Japan in 1998 and guided the Japanese National Team to its best finish in the World Games since the 1960s.

Casey was an assistant coach for the Seattle SuperSonics, and Dallas Mavericks. He was on the staff when Dallas won the 2011 NBA championship. He was head coach for the Minnesota Timberwolves (2005-07), Toronto Raptors (2011-2018) and Detroit Pistons (2018-2023). He moved to a front office job with the Pistons after the 2022-23 season.

For the NBA, the package to Claud Mills was a non-issue.

"You know you'll never get that off your resume'," Casey said. "Now, in the NBA, not one owner even asked me about it."

Of course, recruiting is also a non-issue in the NBA.

"I don't miss that part of college basketball," Casey told *Sports Illustrated*. "In the NBA, it's wins and losses. You don't have to deal with some of the hypocrisy of college athletics."

The *Sports Illustrated* story noted that when news of the package emerged, Casey was interviewing for his first head coaching job. This was with the University of New Orleans in 1989. He did not get the job.

Later, Casey interviewed for the head coaching job at Western Kentucky. He told *Sports Illustrated* that the WKU president told him that the package was old news.

Then he sat in front of the Western Kentucky search committee. The *Sports Illustrated* story got right to the point by noting: "First question: 'What happened at Kentucky?'"

Casey told the *New York Times* in 2018 that he had met LeBron James's then 13-year-old son, Bronny. He said he gave a recruiting pitch for Kentucky.

"I'll probably get in trouble for that," Casey quipped, much to James's amusement, the *Times* reported.

Casey told me in 2023 that he was encouraged to sue Kentucky. He did not.

"I wasn't going to do that because now you're really doing something that was against what I wanted to do," he said.

Casey also said it was "asinine" to think a recruitment could be sealed with a payment of (only?) $1,000.

"I've seen Chris since then," he said. "We laugh about it.

"It wasn't funny at the time. But for him to think he was only getting $1,000 to go to Kentucky was even asinine."

However ridiculous, the supposed $1,000 in a package with Casey's name on the return address did lasting damage.

"It was even to this day I'll take with me the rest of my life," Casey said. "It will hurt to have that perception of who I was at that time, I felt I built a lot of goodwill throughout the state of Kentucky. I've been in every county in that state speaking, doing clinics and stuff like that. For something like that to happen, you know, you'll never get that off your resume' at Kentucky."

Kentucky Shame to Kentucky Acclaim

At the time and in retrospect, surreal could describe Rick Pitino's eight seasons as Kentucky coach. He inherited a team going on NCAA probation: two seasons banned from postseason play and any games being televised. That scandal about what the NCAA said was money sent to a recruit's father and another recruit's questionable entrance exam score inspired the famous *Sports Illustrated* cover that showed a player with his head bowed and the headline "Kentucky's Shame." A 14-14 record in his first season would normally be shameful by Kentucky standards, but it stands out as the most fun-filled season in the 41 that I covered the basketball program. The first season back in good graces of the NCAA saw a run to the 1992 East Region final, where the famous Christian Laettner shot punctuated arguably the greatest college basketball game ever played.

Four more advancements to the Elite Eight and three Final Four appearances followed in the next five years.

It seems fitting that disbelief marked the early stages of the process in which Kentucky hired Pitino as its next coach.

In the spring of 1989, Pitino was in his second season as coach of the New York Knicks. Jim O'Brien, one of his assistants with the Knicks and later at Kentucky, recalled how he learned of Pitino's possible move to Lexington. One day Pitino asked O'Brien and another assistant, Stu Jackson, to give him a ride to Madison Square Garden. Jackson drove. Pitino sat in the passenger seat and O'Brien in the back seat.

"I want you guys to know, Kentucky (and) C.M. Newton called me," O'Brien recalled Pitino saying during the ride. Newton was Kentucky's Director of Athletics. "I'm never going to go to Kentucky," Pitino said.

More than 30 years later, O'Brien remembered Jackson's reaction.

"Stu turned over his right shoulder and said, 'He's out of here, Jim,'" O'Brien recalled in 2023.

Pitino corrected Jackson.

"They're really in bad shape," Pitino said. "And, so I'd be crazy to take the job."

Once more, Jackson turned his head to O'Brien and said Pitino would take the Kentucky job.

"The more this conversation went on, the more pissed off Rick became," O'Brien said. "Stu wouldn't let up. He'd say it in different ways. He's gone. He's history."

Of course, Kentucky hired Pitino as coach that spring. But that doubt that Pitino expressed on the car ride extended into the hiring process.

Seton Hall Coach P.J. Carlesimo was the first coach brought in to interview for the job by Newton. I remember seeing Carlesimo in the school's athletic office area and jokingly asking him if he had eaten at one of Lexington's notable Italian restaurants, Lexitalia Ristorante. He laughed. But he did not take the job.

Newton's son, Martin, recalled his father's next move.

"He set his sights on Rick, and he got turned down several times," Martin said in 2023. "He offered Pitino the job, and Rick said, no. He just kind of stayed on him. He went back to New York and met with him and Joanne. He got turned down, I know, at least once and if I'm not mistaken, he got turned down a couple times."

Martin Newton, now the Director of Athletics at Samford, said Joanne questioned whether southern hospitality was real. "It seems to be a too-good-to-be-true type of thing," Martin said of Pitino's wife's perception of the south.

Another factor was C.M. Newton's honest assessment of the Kentucky program.

"He painted a very bleak picture," Martin said of his father's pitch to Pitino. "He did not want to over promise and under deliver. He wanted him to know it was in real trouble and it was going to take a while to rebuild this thing. . . . I don't know that he did a great sales job on the front end."

So, why did Pitino eventually take the job? His Knicks had just won the NBA's Atlantic Division with a 52-30 record in the 1988-89 season.

There was much talk that Pitino had a contentious relationship with the Knicks' general manager, Al Bianchi.

But O'Brien suggested another reason.

"It had the chance to be the culmination of his career if he could do what he kind of knew he could do," O'Brien said of Pitino's acceptance of the Kentucky job. "He never lacked confidence.

"It was just a funny, funny ride that day, and he was out of there."

Of course, it wasn't as simple as that. One of my stories played a part in complicating the hiring process.

I had learned that as an assistant coach at the University of Hawaii at the beginning of his coaching career, Pitino had been charged by the NCAA with rules violations. Given Kentucky basketball's recent history (the *Herald-Leader*'s Pulitzer Prize winning series about payments to players, then the implosion of Eddie Sutton's program and probation), a coaching candidate with any NCAA violations in his past was a story. I asked Hawaii to send me documentation. When I read it, it seemed significant.

In a report dated March 18, 1977, the NCAA's Committee on Infractions judged that Pitino had broken eight NCAA rules while on the Hawaii staff in the 1974-75 and 1975-76 seasons. Among the violations the committee said Pitino committed were arranging free airline transportation for Hawaii players to the mainland, using basketball season tickets to buy cars for players and helping players receive free meals at McDonald's.

The NCAA also judged that Pitino, head coach Bruce O'Neil and another assistant, Rodney Aldridge, made a false statement to Hawaii officials about their knowledge or involvement in any violations.

The NCAA Infractions Committee recommended that Pitino and O'Neil be disassociated from Hawaii athletics.

I put the information Hawaii provided in my desk drawer and quietly hoped it would stay there. I decided to write a story only if Pitino became a candidate for Kentucky's head coaching position. That decision could be second guessed. But when we learned that he would be coming to Lexington to interview for the job, it was time to write the story.

I learned that during the visit/job interview, Newton would be taking Pitino to dinner at a Lexington restaurant called The Coach House. I decided not to go into the seating area so as not to draw attention to however the interview process would go. I waited in the lobby next to the maître d's stand.

When Pitino and Newton arrived, I asked them about the violations while on the basketball staff at Hawaii.

"That was 15 years ago," Pitino said. "I've never broken an NCAA rule in my life . . . at least not knowingly."

Newton said he was aware of Hawaii being put on probation and banned from live television appearances (for two years in each case) because of the violations. He declined further comment. I wondered if Newton was being truthful.

In a telephone interview for the story, O'Neil said UK officials had not contacted him about the NCAA investigation and penalties.

"I took all the blame for everything that went on there," O'Neil said, "and I continue to do that. I don't want to bring Rick into it at all."

O'Neil described Pitino as a "young, aggressive, energetic coach" at Hawaii. Pitino began his time on the Hawaii staff at age 23.

"Young, aggressive coaches do certain things in life that they are sorry for later," O'Neil said.

Honolulu's daily newspaper, *The Sunday Star-Bulletin & Advertiser*, printed a story in May of 1977 that cited Pitino as saying he was guilty only of handing out coupons for free meals at McDonald's.

Twelve years later, O'Neil told me he had instructed Pitino to hand out the coupons.

O'Neil, who was fired as Hawaii coach because of the NCAA investigation, said Kentucky probably could not find an untainted candidate.

"You'd be hard-pressed to find a coach in America who hasn't bent a rule in his career," he said. "Anything that was done was a minor bend on Rick's part."

The intent of the story was not to kill Pitino's chances of becoming Kentucky coach. The intent was to more fully inform readers – and perhaps UK officials – of a candidate's background. Wouldn't it be better to know in advance and deal with questions related to a candidate's background rather than have it become public after the hire?

Marta McMackin, the administrative assistant in the UK basketball office, recalled that Newton considered the Hawaii story a deal breaker.

Newton told Pitino, "Rick, we're under high scrutiny here," McMackin recalled in 2023. "We can't afford any irregularity about anything or anyone. So, I think it's best that you go home."

Pitino and his wife, Joanne, packed their bags and were ready to return to New York, said McMackin, who added that Newton told her that he would be Kentucky's interim coach for a season while the hiring process continued.

Then UK president David Roselle interceded. He called Pitino and asked to meet with him. With the meeting going well, Roselle hired Pitino. "Smartest thing he did," McMackin said of Roselle.

When Kentucky hired Pitino, it was time to move on.

In a 2017 telephone interview, Roselle said he came away from the meeting convinced that Pitino was "squeaky clean" and too smart to jeopardize a promising future.

Roselle came to feel vindicated.

"I thought he did a masterful job," he said of Pitino's time as Kentucky coach. "And I thought he played it straight."

The *Columbia Journalism Review* gave the *Herald-Leader* a laurel for following up on its 1986 Pulitzer Prize-winning series on money given to basketball players that resulted in bomb threats and 400 canceled subscriptions with what it called "an in-depth report on Pitino's record of NCAA violations earlier in his career."

Said the *Columbia Journalism Review*, "history notwithstanding, Pitino got the job, and history repeating, the paper got 50 cancellations from gung-ho fans."

Mike Johnson, the *Herald-Leader* sports editor at the time, remembered a woman calling to complain about the Pulitzer Prize winning series.

"She said, my husband dropped the newspaper because of that (series)," Johnson said in 2023. "And now he sends me down to the Speedway every morning to get him one.

"I said, I appreciate you being a loyal customer."

A reader might ask why the *Herald-Leader* did not do a story on John Calipari's history with the NCAA Committee on Infractions before he was hired to be Kentucky's coach 20 years later. Two factors came to mind: (1) the infractions the NCAA cited involving Calipari's players (Memphis guard Derrick Rose's invalid SAT score and UMass big man Marcus Camby improperly accepting cash and services) were much more well known, and (2) Kentucky was not beginning to serve a NCAA punishment for rules violations as it searched for a new coach.

In his 2012 book titled *The Last Great Game: Duke vs. Kentucky and the 2.1 Seconds That Changed Basketball*, author Gene Wojciechowski wrote that Roselle's trust in Newton and Pitino led to the hire.

"If Pitino had made some mistakes as a low-level assistant more than 10 years earlier, Roselle could live with that," Wojciechowski wrote. "He was certain Pitino was the coach Kentucky needed."

It didn't take long to prove Roselle correct.

With the NCAA banning Kentucky from playing in the 1990 and 1991 postseasons, the two leading scorers from the 1988-89 team transferred: LeRon Ellis (16.0 ppg) to Syracuse and Chris Mills (14.3 ppg) to Arizona. The leader in assists, Sean Sutton (146 assists), transferred to Oklahoma State.

Six returnees averaged a combined 32.7 points the previous season. A nondescript freshman class would average a combined 18.3 points in the upcoming season.

Expectations were most un-Kentucky-like.

Cawood Ledford, an iconic radio play-by-play announcer for Kentucky basketball since 1953, predicted that the team would win, maybe, eight games in the 1989-90 season.

"I think that was one of the most optimistic views," Richie Farmer, one of four Kentucky-born players on the team, recalled in 2023. "I think people around the country thought that we may not win five or six games, seven at the most.

"We were just decimated, and nobody knew what to expect."

Surely, no one expected what I consider *the* exceptional season among the 41 I covered. The usual expectations of winning a national championship or if that didn't happen finding someone to blame were nonexistent. So was the fans' unquenchable need for the program to be exalted as peerless.

By stark contrast, basketball in Pitino's first season as coach was . . . fun. And that completely satisfied the hard-to-completely-please Kentucky fan base. Never mind a 14-14 record meant only one more victory than the previous season and only the fifth time since 1928-29 that Kentucky had failed to win at least 15 games.

Future Kentucky player Scott Padgett, then an eighth grader in Louisville, still marveled at the exceptionalism of that UK team more than 30 years later.

"They knew they couldn't go to the (NCAA) tournament, so winning a national championship was out," Padgett said in 2023. "I think you could go and just enjoy the moment and not have any stress."

That stress came in the form of annual expectations that Padgett described as "'We've got to win the championship. We've got to be the best."

In the 1989-90 season, "the fans just went and enjoyed it," he added. "I was one of them. If you had ever told me I would have cheered for a 14-14 Kentucky team, but I loved that team."

He was not alone. Style of play was a significant part of the thrill Kentucky fans enjoyed in Pitino's first season.

Fans had grumbled about Sutton having a seven-pass rule. Barring fast-break opportunities, players were encouraged to pass the ball at least seven times before shooting. Sutton had great success coaching his way. But . . .

The contrast with Pitino's frenetic style was easy to see. Full-court pressing and trapping, plus an abundance of quick trigger three-point shots made for constant action and fan emotion be it euphoria or momentary disappointment.

In the 1989-90 season, Kentucky averaged 28.9 three-point shots per game. That more than tripled the average of 9.4 the previous season. UK players took

810 three-point shots. There were 571 three-point shots the previous two seasons combined.

On defense, Kentucky averaged 11.0 steals. The average was 7.1 the previous season. Opponents averaged 21.2 turnovers as compared to 14.2 in Sutton's last season.

The style change contributed to a scoring average of 88.8 points, which was the highest for Kentucky since 92.2 points in 1974-75. The average was 69.4 points the previous season.

O'Brien, who had become Dayton coach that season, watched from afar and appreciated what he saw.

"People understand heart," he said. "They understand his teams play harder than everybody else. They really do. . . . You could see what great conditioning and great heart looked like. And people responded to that.

"Once the players bought into it, it became contagious and a thing of pride."

Competitive heart and this buy-in came at a price. John Pelphrey, one of the four holdovers from the season before who were native Kentuckians, described the 1989-90 season as "just complete survival."

There was no 20-hour weekly limit on athletic activities at that point, Pelphrey said. Of the preseason conditioning program, he said, "I thought I was on the track and cross country team all fall."

Pelphrey came to doubt his ability to meet Pitino's standard for fitness. "I'm not coming out for Midnight Madness," he recalled thinking in reference to the annual preseason unveiling of the team. "That ain't happening."

Pelphrey said he came to understand that failure to make a conditioning goal was not defeat. But meeting the standard in the long term could build confidence.

"Well, if I can do that, what else can I do?" Pelphrey said. "So, all of a sudden, you stop worrying about who's next. Whether it's Indiana and Bob Knight or Dean Smith and North Carolina or Dale Brown and LSU. . . .

"It wasn't even about them anymore. It's about let's see what we can do tonight."

O'Brien, who joined the Kentucky staff for the 1994-95 season, had seen the benefits of Pitino's emphasis on conditioning while a member of the New York Knicks' coaching staff.

"The place you start really with any team is conditioning," O'Brien said. "That's the No. 1 thing that is an absolute in coaching."

O'Brien recalled that as Knicks' coach Pitino created the franchise's first strength and conditioning program. Its immediate priority was to get Patrick Ewing to lose weight and gain fitness, O'Brien said.

There were obstacles to overcome for Pitino's first Kentucky players.

Farmer recalled a conditioning drill in a swimming pool.

"We had a gallon jug of water in each hand," he said. "We're having to tread water (he laughed). There were people going under. They had brainwashed us so much. Instead of turning loose of the jug, we were about to drown."

No one drowned. And Farmer came to see a benefit.

"When you play that style, the first thing they do is break you down to build you back up to make you what they want you to be . . . ," he said. "A lot of it is to make you mentally tough."

Another obstacle involved an off-the-court clash of backgrounds between mostly players from the South and a coach from the Northeast.

"Even though he was a Final Four coach, even though he was the Knicks coach, even though he was from New York and you couldn't understand a thing he was saying half the time and you really weren't sure if he was saying it in a way that was complimentary," Pelphrey said of Pitino, "We were on the same page in terms of basketball and the seriousness that we would take it. That's what really bound us.

"And he wasn't going to quit. He had a threshold for work that was endless, and I think he appreciates good basketball. These were things that myself, Deron (Feldhaus), Richie (Farmer) and Sean (Woods) could grab onto and do."

A sobering moment came in the season's fifth game when Kansas beat Kentucky 150-95.

Kentucky maintained its pressing, trapping style throughout the game. Kansas, which was ranked No. 2 and vastly superior, beat the press so often the game looked like a layup line.

Among the records set were most points scored in Allen Fieldhouse, most points UK had ever given up, most points Kansas had scored in a half (80 in the first half), most baskets by Kansas (52 of 85) and most assists by Kansas in a game (36).

"Worst defeat I ever had," Farmer said. "Unbelievable to score 95 points and get beat by 55. But that's exactly what happened (laughs)."

Pitino and the second-year Kansas coach Roy Williams reportedly exchanged harsh words during the game. Kansas waited in vain for Kentucky to stop pressing. Kentucky believed Williams left his starters in too long. KU starters played between 28 and 23 minutes.

"To this day, I still have hard feelings," Farmer said in 2023. "I have never liked Roy Williams because of that."

The highlight of the season came the day after Valentine's Day. Somehow, Kentucky beat a LSU team that featured Shaquille O'Neal, Stanley Roberts and Chris Jackson. All three made all-Southeastern Conference teams. Jackson led the league in scoring, while O'Neal led in rebounding.

Yet, Kentucky won 100-95. While O'Neal (14 points, 21 rebounds) and Roberts (13 points and 13 rebounds) posted double-doubles, it helped that LSU had 24 turnovers.

In 2023, Farmer said that game remained vivid in his memory. For one thing, he recalled before the game seeing O'Neal standing casually "with his hand on the backboard and his feet crossed like he was leaning against the wall."

And Farmer completed eight-for-eight perfection at the foul line to clinch an upset victory over a team ranked No. 9.

For O'Brien, this game was part of decades of evidence to prove that Pitino was and is an exceptional coach.

"Whatever mixture Rick brought to the court, it was special . . . ," said O'Brien, who added that he was eager to see how Pitino's time as St. John's coach would go beginning with the 2023-24 season. "I said to someone, within five years, Rick will have St. John's in the Final Four. Do you want to bet? I'm not a betting man . . . , that's just kind of the way he rolls."

This game was just one example of a season with memorable ups and downs.

At that time Pitino became coach, Kentucky played host to an annual Christmas holiday tournament, the UK Invitational. When the Wildcats lost in overtime to Louisiana Lafayette 116-113 in the championship game, a *Herald-Leader* photographer began taking shots of the dejection on the home team's bench. The photographer later told me that a UK official scolded him by saying the school did not want those kinds of photos.

Two weeks later, Kentucky lost 92-85 at Vanderbilt despite having five more field goals, which included three more three-point shots. But the referees called 30 fouls on Kentucky. Vandy made 31 of 38 free throws. During his postgame radio interview, Pitino said he did not realize you needed to wear pantyhose to play basketball in the Southeastern Conference.

But those were exceptions in a season that delighted Kentucky fans and fueled optimism.

As a sign that the first season was a success, Pitino opened a restaurant in Lexington before his second season. Bravo Pitino, which got its name from a favorite restaurant in Manhattan (Bravo Gianni), opened in Victorian Square, which was near Rupp Arena.

In 1990-91, Kentucky had the best SEC record (14-4), but was ineligible for the regular-season championship.

Much credit went to freshman Jamal Mashburn. It was immediately clear that he was not just another freshman. I covered a high school all-star game played in Louisville prior to Mashburn's arrival on campus. He looked like a power forward (his size listed as 6-foot-9 and 244 pounds) who played like a heady guard.

Pitino did not shy from putting the spotlight on Mashburn. In those days, Kentucky played preseason scrimmages around the state. These were always well attended and were basketball celebrations for communities.

After the first scrimmage in the fall of 1990, Pitino said Mashburn would be considered one of the best to ever play for Kentucky. Given Kentucky's history, this seemed like a startling statement.

But Mashburn lived up to this lofty standard. In three seasons, he became UK's sixth leading scorer of all time (1,843 points). He led the team in field goal percentage one season, in three-pointers made once, in rebounding twice, in steals once and was in the top 10 for career double-doubles when he turned pro after his junior season.

"I think he was the main cog that made those teams go," Farmer recalled in 2023.

Pelphrey echoed that sentiment.

"Jamal changed everything," he said. "He took us to places we couldn't go by ourselves. And that's kind of the same thing Coach Pitino did in his leadership position. . . . Jamal Mashburn was an absurd talent, right? Just unbelievably gifted. But he doesn't become who he is if he's not incredibly bright, a curious learner and a perfect fit for us."

Pelphrey suggested that the four players who did not transfer after the 1988-89 season – Deron Feldhaus, Richie Farmer, Sean Woods and Pelphrey – had only one chance to play in the NCAA Tournament. That would be in 1992. So, this one chance inspired Mashburn.

"We had a lot invested in this," Pelphrey said. "I always felt we respected Jamal for recognizing how important this was to the four of us. . . .This wasn't just a casual stroll. Others may have another year. Nah-nah. If things aren't going right on a certain day, we're going to say something."

That one chance ended in memorable fashion. Kentucky advanced to the 1992 East Regional where Christian Laettner's famous buzzer-beating shot ended a remarkable, if not unprecedented, revival of a college basketball program.

But the journey to that painful heartbreak was, as Pelphrey said, not a casual stroll. Neither were the five seasons that followed with Pitino as coach.

The 1991-92 season began with a thud. Kentucky lost at home to Pittsburgh 85-67 in the second game of the season. Future UK assistant coach Orlando Antigua scored nine points, grabbed eight rebounds and blocked four shots for Pittsburgh in the game.

The loss denied an advancement to the Preseason NIT semifinals and for Pitino a triumphant return to New York. Tickets for a Broadway play had been bought. He was not pleased.

Farmer recalled three practices a day during the following week.

"If there's ever been a hell week, that was it . . . ," he said. "He thought we were going to win, and we did, too. And we didn't. Oh man, I'm telling you (it was) hell week."

The 1991-92 season also marked Arkansas and South Carolina joining the Southeastern Conference.

Arkansas had been the dominant basketball team in the Southwest Conference. I heard the perception in SEC circles that the Razorbacks were entering a much better league now. The days of domination would be over.

Nolan Richardson, then the Arkansas coach, recalled how this perception inspired his team, which in any game played in a full-court pressure style dubbed "40 minutes of hell."

"To me and our guys, they had something to prove . . . ," he said in 2023. "We tried to prepare for everybody basically the same. We're going to get after you. That was going to be the bottom line.

"But they seemed to put that extra effort in against Kentucky because they knew and we knew Kentucky was basketball in the Southeastern Conference. If you beat them, the rest of them you're probably going to win. That became a measuring stick.

"I thought our guys looked forward to playing Kentucky because that gave them big-time bragging rights for how good they are."

In each of their first three college seasons, Arkansas seniors Lee Mayberry, Todd Day and Oliver Miller had been part of teams that won Southwest Conference championships.

This made for an electric atmosphere when Arkansas played at Kentucky on Jan. 25.

Both teams featured pressing styles. Richardson said that he and Pitino played golf together on occasion. During these rounds of golf, the UK coach sought his advice on full-court pressing, Richardson said.

Richardson said Arkansas pressed anywhere on the floor, hence the nickname "40 minutes of hell." Meanwhile, Kentucky played a "safety press" that was not anywhere on the court at all times, Richardson said.

"Rick had approached me on several occasions asking, what is it that you do," Richardson recalled.

For Richardson, the game had historic significance. He had played at Texas Western in the early 1960s. When he was a senior in 1962-63, several players who beat Kentucky in the famous 1966 national championship game were freshmen and sophomores.

"To me it was an honor to be able to play a Kentucky basketball team that had dominated in our era and everybody else's era," Richardson said.

But this feeling of respect did not translate to deference.

It seemed to me that most visiting teams doubted victory before the game started at Kentucky.

Richardson's team exuded confidence throughout the game en route to a 105-88 victory. Mayberry, Day and Miller combined for 60 points. The Razorbacks won it at the foul line, making 41 of 49 free throws. Kentucky made 10 of 18.

"They had no clue of being afraid of Kentucky," Richardson said in 2023. "None. Zero."

I liked my lead on the game story: Arkan came, Arkansas, Arkan conquered.

Kentucky made history with a comeback victory at LSU in the 1993-94 season. UK trailed by 31 points with less than 16 minutes remaining before rallying to win 99-95. The game was played at the peak of Mardi Gras (Feb. 15) that year, which led to the game being known as the Mardi Gras Miracle.

Kentucky went into the game with an 18-3 record. By then, the reporters covering the team had developed a playful habit. When feeling the outcome had been decided, a reporter would place his hand palm down on the press row table. This was to signify that you should close the book on this game, it's over.

Every other reporter had put his or her hand down at LSU by the time Kentucky trailed by 31 points. I was tempted, but continued to hold out because the power of the three-point shot made an unlikely comeback at least plausible.

Tony Delk, who made two of seven three-point shots in the game, credited Pitino's halftime speech – or is that threat? – as a key.

Kentucky trailed 48-32 at halftime.

"At halftime, coach gave the greatest speech we ever heard," Delk said. "We MFs are going to pay tomorrow. That's all we thought about. It was going to be the worst practice of our lives if we lost that game."

Kentucky had lost its last two games: 90-82 at home against Arkansas and 93-85 at Syracuse. There had not been three straight losses since Pitino's first season as coach.

"He said to all of us, you might want to transfer the next day," Delk recalled. "If there was a way we could hop on the portal and transfer, if we had lost that game, I'm pretty sure he would have had a roster of probably four or five guys left."

Pitino sat quietly on the bench as the second half began. I wondered if he was contemplating how he wanted the players to process a three-game losing streak punctuated by a blowout. Point guard Travis Ford was animated in player huddles on the court and seemed to rally the team.

Kentucky made 12 of 23 three-point shots in the second half. Behind by 31 points, UK outscored LSU 24-4 to get back in the game.

In the final minutes, Delk and Walter McCarty made back-to-back three-pointers to win the game. Those shots capped the biggest road comeback in Division I history and equaled the largest second-half comeback. Duke rallied from 31 points down to beat visiting Tulane on Dec. 30, 1950.

"We had a team that never quit," Delk recalled. "To come back from a 31-point deficit, you know you still have a chance as long as there's enough time on the clock. The threes gave us a chance in every game."

The next season saw Kentucky ranked No. 2 going into the NCAA Tournament. No.1 seed UK won three games before losing to No. 2 seed North Carolina 74-61 in the Southeast Regional championship game in Birmingham, Ala.

After the game, I sought out Pitino. I found him by himself in a room, but he immediately and emphatically ordered me to leave.

The season had been a joyride for O'Brien, who joined the coaching staff the previous fall.

"It was really nice to never take the court without expecting to win," he said.

The loss to North Carolina was difficult to accept.

"I thought it was to win the national championship or we failed," O'Brien said of the team's objective. "When we lost that game, Rick threw a switch and basically said, it was all right. Let's get ready for next year.

"The next morning at the hotel, he started meeting with guys individually. They were coming back and it kind of put in perspective what we needed to do better. . . . So he had already moved on to next year."

Almost seamless dominance marked the following season of 1995-96. Kentucky's 34-2 record including 30 victories by 10 or more points and 24 by 17 or more points.

I liked drama that would add spice to a game story. There was little of that. Most games seemed decided by halftime, thus making the final 20 minutes a ho-hum conclusion.

"It was how we approached every game knowing we were the best team not only on the court every night," Delk said. "We were the best team in the country."

Kentucky sought – and almost always achieved – dominating victories.

"We wanted the game to be over at halftime," Delk said. "Our goal was to send fans on the road home in the second half with 10 minutes on the clock. We wanted your home court arena empty before the (final) buzzer sounded. We competed. We always had our foot on the gas. If we could beat you by 50 or 60, we were going to beat you by 50 or 60."

It took individual brilliance – a reliable component for upsets in the NCAA Tournament – to beat Kentucky that season. UMass beat UK in the season's second game when Marcus Camby scored 32 points, grabbed nine rebounds and blocked five shots.

Mississippi State beat Kentucky 84-73 in the SEC Tournament finals. Donate' Jones made 12 of 18 shots (three of five on three-point attempts) and scored 28 points for State in a performance that I thought personified how any game could be decided by one player's hot shooting.

Delk credited Pitino's challenging practices as the key to Kentucky's dominance.

"As hard as we practice, you get to take it out on somebody: the team we had to face," he said. "Practices were, I would say, 10 times harder than games. We considered game day to be a day off."

Delk also cited depth as a factor. That season saw several future regulars mostly coming off the bench such as Ron Mercer (12 starts), Wayne Turner (eight starts), Mark Pope (five starts) and Jeff Sheppard (one start).

Kentucky nearly won back-to-back national championships. In the 1997 championship game, UK lost to Arizona 84-79 in overtime. Reserve big man Nazr Mohammed missed all six of his free throws in that game.

After the season, Pitino announced he was leaving Kentucky to become coach and team president of the Boston Celtics.

With Kentucky again a dynasty, why make this career change?

"Because it was the Boston Celtics," O'Brien said. "And they were in need."

The Celtics had not had a winning record in the previous four seasons, and had not advanced beyond the second round of the playoffs in the five years prior to that.

O'Brien recalled reminding Pitino of the good thing he had going at Kentucky.

"We had many, many conversations about this . . . in depth conversations," O'Brien said. "I thought and commented to Rick that we could produce at Kentucky a dynasty that would rival UCLA (during John Wooden's time as coach). His ability to recruit was there. The national championship pedigree was there. The fan base was there. And we thought we could just continue to do it again.

"But that being said, I was ecstatic he decided to go to the Celtics because I wanted to be in the NBA. That was very selfish. But I was willing to stay (at Kentucky) with him. The O'Briens were very happy there."

With a dreaded coaching search upon us, O'Brien did what a reporter would consider the ultimate favor. He pulled me aside and said that Kentucky would hire Tubby Smith as the new coach.

Christian Laettner: the Shot, the Heartbreak, the T-Shirt

Memories of Kentucky's loss to Duke in the 1992 East Regional finals – aka "the Christian Laettner game" – live on more than 30 years later. Television replays of Laettner's game-winning shot in the final second of overtime almost seem like they're on a continuous loop.

It's a game I'd like to forget. Not because Kentucky lost. Because I was overwhelmed by the magnificence I had just witnessed. I felt inadequate to the task of finding words to capture the majestic game-long drama punctuated by not one but two clutch shots.

Ever since that night in Philadelphia, I've second-guessed my decision to attend the postgame news conferences rather than go to the Kentucky locker room.

As I read the stories in the *Philadelphia Inquirer* at the airport the next morning before beginning the trip home to Lexington, my heart sank. I berated myself for not making the cruel ending of Kentucky's three-year rebuilding effort a bigger part of the story. In this case, my impulse to never overreact in writing a story was dead wrong.

In retrospect, overreaction seemed required. So, I have never read my game story since sending it to the office that night.

I assume no one needs a reminder that point guard Sean Woods put Kentucky ahead 103-102 by banking in a shot over Laettner from just inside the foul line with 2.1 seconds left. Then Laettner caught a famously unguarded inbounds pass and won the game with a turnaround jumper from the foul line as time expired.

In 2023, I asked Marta McMackin, the administrative assistant in the Kentucky basketball office, about Rick Pitino's reaction to the loss. She did not need time to reflect.

"Absolutely awful," she said. "He blamed himself for not putting a player on the inbounds (passer). He took it hard. I felt so bad for him. Even the next morning, (he was) still totally upset. We all just left him alone."

Kentucky next played Duke in the 1998 NCAA Tournament South Regional finals. For me, the occasion served as a second chance to capture the game in words.

Here was my lead to a story reflecting on that game: Duke and Kentucky. Christian Laettner and Sean Woods. To borrow a phrase from Charles Dickens: the best of times, the worst of times.

I asked Kentucky players how they remembered the Laettner game.

"We were like a little kid who's been good for a long time," Woods said. "You've been promised you'll get candy. Then somehow, it falls out of your hand and breaks into little pieces on a dirty floor."

Richie Farmer described it as a total reversal of fortune. "Like going from the highest point in your life to the lowest point in your life in two seconds," he said.

Six years later, Farmer said he still had recurring dreams about Laettner's shot. "The first three or four months, I thought about it constantly," he said. "I'd wake up in the middle of the night. Ugh, he made it."

The dreams began the second night after the game.

"I dream about what if we did this or that," Farmer said

"He makes it every time," Farmer added with a smile. "And we thought he could never make that shot again. I've seen it in my mind a million times."

First thing first, Woods remembered his shot as a product of design. John Pelphrey, whose back pick knocked the defender on Woods (Bobby Hurley) to the floor, recalled it as improvisation.

"In basketball, you can draw up a play," Pelphrey said. "But you have to play ball and react."

The evidence – a leaning, pull-up shot from just inside the foul line over a player seven inches taller (Laettner) that banks in? – suggests Pelphrey was right.

With some prodding, Woods said, "I was trying to let it hit the (front of the) rim. But when your momentum gets flowing, you can shoot it too hard. Fortunately enough for me, the backboard was there."

Pitino was hardly the only person who second guessed what happened next: not having a defender in front of Grant Hill to contest his baseball throw of an inbounds pass. From my press row seat, which was at about the top of the key on the end of the floor where Hill would inbound the ball, I noticed that there was no defender in front of Hill. But I did not think this was wise nor a mistake.

Six years later when I spoke to UK's assistant coaches at the time, they were not haunted by that decision.

"Six of one, half dozen of another," Herb Sendek said. "You could draw a line down the middle of a tablet and make logical, sound arguments on either side. It comes down to execution.

"I remember Coach (Bob) Knight told Coach Pitino at the Final Four that year that he would not have put a guy on Hill."

Billy Donovan, who was Florida coach by then, also suggested that was not an inherent right or wrong.

"We felt like if we put a guy on the ball and they threw it long and they sealed us with their size in the lane, we would have no (chance)," Donovan said. "We would be overpowered because (Jamal) Mashburn had fouled out. At least this way, if the ball was thrown in, we could double-team the ball."

Pitino's final instruction was uncharacteristically passive. He put a negative thought in the players' minds by saying, "Don't foul."

"Our guys were like, 'please miss,'" Donovan said. "It went in. I couldn't believe it. Then I looked at the stat sheet and saw Laettner was 10-for-10 from the field. And it was like, 'Wow, this guy didn't miss anything.'"

Duke was not winging it on the game's famous last sequence.

"We were very well trained in late-game situations," Laettner said of that pressure-packed 2.1-second span. After Woods put UK ahead 103-102, "we knew to call timeout right away."

The Blue Devils had practiced the game-winning maneuver, and tweaked it late in the season, he said. It wasn't a lucky shot, but he said that the Duke team had never successfully executed the play.

Laettner called getting a "good look" at the basket as key. "After that," he added, "it's up to God."

Pelphrey, who would have been guarding Hill had that been the instruction, said Kentucky's defense was well rehearsed.

"The plan we worked on many times in practice," he said in 2023. "And (in practice) the throw and the catch never got completed."

Pelphrey described himself as a free safety because his man was throwing the inbounds pass.

"Obviously, I'm back at half-court," he said. "Everybody else had a man. So, Laettner's on the baseline, and he comes flashing out to the top of the key. I'm obviously backing up because I think I'm going to catch the ball. As I stated many times . . . I saw the ball curving because of the spin of the ball. And I'm backing up, and I'm going to catch it. And at that moment in time, I literally felt I had my hands on the ball. I felt Laettner. The sensation was so real. And at that moment, I felt he had taken the ball out of my hand."

Pelphrey acknowledged later looking at the replay and realizing the sensations he felt appeared like an out-of-body experience. Pelphrey was not in front of Laettner while teammate Deron Feldhaus was behind Laettner to prevent the Duke star from getting closer to the basket.

"I never touched it," Pelphrey said in 2023. "But in that moment, I literally felt I touched the leather. I had it in my hand. I would love to have that play over."

Bob Harris, who had called Duke games on the radio for 23 seasons at that point, remembered his call of Laettner's shot as concise and unadorned.

"He catches, he dribbles? He shoots and scores!!!" was how Harris remembered his call. "I had a slight question in my voice when he dribbled because I didn't think he had time to dribble."

Pelphrey also thought that Laettner might not beat the final buzzer.

"After he caught it, he shook his shoulder like he always did in his post moves," Pelphrey recalled. "I'm thinking, 'where is the horn?'

"I don't think the shot was that tough. I think the throw and the catch were miraculous."

But Mashburn was staring at defeat.

"I knew it was going in," he said in 1998. "Usually, as a basketball player, when the ball is in the air and you continue to look at it that means something bad is about to happen."

When I spoke to the UK players in 1998, they did not seem angered by the loss. But their facial expressions harden when asked about Laettner intentionally tapping a foot on Aminu Timberlake's chest earlier in the second half. Replays suggested that Laettner intended to send a don't-mess-with-me message. In a rebound tussle a few possessions earlier, Feldhaus had shoved Laettner to the floor. The Duke star seemed to think Timberlake had shoved him.

"If he stepped on my chest, it'd be a different situation," Farmer said. "Anybody else would have jumped up and been ready to fight."

"I thought he should be thrown out of the game," Mashburn said. "But it's all part of it. He was Player of the Year that year. And they weren't about to throw him out."

"It didn't hurt at all," Timberlake recalled. "It looked worse than it was. It was like touching me with a feather. It didn't aggravate me at all."

"Because of my belief in the Lord Jesus Christ, that put me at ease with just about everything," Timberlake said. "Later, I found out I could use it in witnessing for Christ. It gets conversations going."

Timberlake clearly was not injured. He immediately stood up smiling and clapping in reaction to the technical foul being called on Laettner.

Years later, I happened to see Timberlake at a Kentucky away game. He seemed uncomfortable with being remembered as the player laying on the floor with Laettner tapping a foot on his chest.

In 2023, Farmer still seemed agitated that the referees only assessed a technical foul on Laettner.

"Had it been in today's game, he would have been ejected and suspended," Farmer said. "It wasn't like he drew back and stomped down on him with all his might. But it was obvious.

"Aminu was probably the only player on our team (not to confront Laettner). If it had been anybody else, he would have gotten up and a melee would have ensued and a punch thrown or something. And Laettner might have been ejected at that point."

Looking back 31 years, Pelphrey saluted Laettner's performance: 10 for 10 shooting from both the field and the foul line. "He was awesome," Pelphrey said.

The Christian Laettner game made the UK seniors college basketball's version of Moses. They pointed the way, yet only got close enough to see but not enter the Promised Land.

Woods, Farmer, Pelphrey and Feldhaus – with a sophomore, Mashburn, playing a lead role – restored Kentucky basketball's preeminence. That so quick a resurrection was unexpected made it all the sweeter.

"We didn't want to be remembered as the guys at Kentucky when Kentucky wasn't very good," Pelphrey said in 1998. "That was the driving force."

The Laettner game was special for more than one reason.

It was the 39th and final season for radio play-by-play announcer Cawood Ledford's career calling Kentucky basketball. As the game headed toward its dramatic and historic finish, the iconic announcer noticed sportswriter Bob Ryan of the *Boston Globe* trying to get his attention. Ryan held up a notepad on which he'd written, "Greatest game ever?"

"I shrugged my shoulders," Ledford recalled six years later. "I caught up with him in the press room and said, "Bob, I guess it was.'

"Both teams played well. It was not like Kentucky caught a flat Duke. You remember a lot of games. I guess I'd start with that game."

I still envy how Ledford ended his Kentucky broadcasting career with classic style. Many along the press row sat stunned after Woods and Laettner traded clutch shots inside the final three seconds. To punctuate his review of the game's dramatic finish for listeners, Ledford captured the moment by quoting 19th century poet John Greenleaf Whittier. Said Cawood:

"The saddest words of tongue or pen are these: What might have been.

"Kentucky almost pulled it off."

As he prepared to sign off, Ledford said he would borrow the words Adolph Rupp used in announcing his retirement.

"For those of you who have gone down the glory road with me, my eternal thanks," Ledford said. "From Philadelphia, this is Cawood Ledford saying goodbye."

Jim Host helped set up radio broadcasts of NCAA Tournament games for years. He was in the Spectrum that day and was impressed with how Ledford ended the broadcast.

"I thought Cawood's sign off was one of, if not the best, I had ever heard anyone do," Host wrote to me in a 2023 text message.

Marty Brennaman, the long-time Cincinnati Reds' play-by-play man, called the game for CBS radio. He compared it to the sixth game of the 1975 World Series when Carlton Fisk famously waved as a home run ball curved fair.

"It was one of the few college games I've seen that I was sorry it was over," Brennaman said. "You feel privileged to be there, to be part of it, because people will talk about it for the next half-century."

Bob Harris, the Duke play-by-play announcer, called it "the greatest college basketball game, period."

After the game, each team's radio announcer went to the Kentucky locker room. "I wanted to talk to the seniors who stayed there through all the crap," Harris said.

For Ledford, it led to a chance meeting with Pitino.

"He had just come out of the dressing room," Ledford said. "He'd been crying. I gave him a big hug. He was devastated."

In an interview with the *Atlanta Journal-Constitution* years later, Pitino flashed his healthy sense of humor when asked about Laettner's shot.

"Who?" he asked facetiously. "I don't believe that name rings a bell."

More seriously, he added, "That was one of the greatest games ever played at the college level. Sometimes in the NCAA Tournament, people play it close to the vest. In that game, I think both coaches sat back because they had the players. . . . Wrong ending, great game."

Kentucky players needed time to fully appreciate being part of such a game.

"That was no consolation to any of us," Pelphrey said. "We'd have loved for it to be a terrible game and be going to the Final Four."

But in time, the players took pride in the historic significance of the game.

Mashburn called it "the highlight of my career."

Of Laettner's shot, Woods said, "it was an ill feeling, like an absolute feeling. You felt just numb. I was hoping I'd open my eyes and it wouldn't be there. . . .

"You get asked about the game once or twice a day. As time goes by, it gets easier and easier. It's a conversation starter."

"It was a positive experience for me being part of one of the greatest games ever played," said Travis Ford, then a sophomore. "For the guys coming back, it made us want to get back even worse. It gave us a taste of what it took."

Laettner's embrace of the villain role proved to be no act. In October, 2011, he came to Rupp Arena to be part of a charity game.

In a story previewing the game, I wrote:

"If boos rain down on him in Rupp Arena later this month, former Duke All-American Christian Laettner will not ask for an umbrella. He's more likely to look upward, stretch out his arms and welcome the drenching."

"I miss that," Laettner said of his role as villain in the upcoming charity game. "I'm 42. I'm getting that less and less. When you retire from the NBA, you don't get the yelling and booing as much."

Laettner figured to get all the sporting hostility he'd want when he acted as coach of a team billed as "The Villains" in a charity game. The bad guys played a group of former Kentucky players called the Big Blue All-Stars in a game that benefitted The V Foundation for Cancer Research.

The game figured to revive Kentucky fans' memories of the "stomp" on Timberlake's chest.

The Free Online dictionary defines the word "stomp" as "To tread or trample heavily or violently on."

When asked if he considered "the stomp" the reason he's no favorite of Kentucky fans, Laettner said, no. "If I hit the last shot, I'd still be the No. 1 villain. Anyone who hit the last-second shot in '92 is going to be considered a villain, no matter what."

Laettner claimed to have been a "huge" Kentucky fan while growing up. Watching Rex Chapman play for Kentucky in the mid-1980s enthralled him.

"He was just an amazing player," Laettner said, "someone I looked up to and wanted to be like."

Laettner said Chapman was "a huge role model."

Laettner credited Pitino with helping him become a better basketball player. As a counselor at the famed Five-Star Camp, Pitino gave Laettner, then a high school player, valuable advice.

"I tell Pitino every time I see him, I learned some of my offensive game from Rick Pitino," he said. "He never seems to like it when I say that to him."

Laettner was philosophical about being a villain. "I realize it for what it is," he said. "It's just part of the game."

Laettner also expected an engaged crowd at the charity game.

"Nothing surprises me about Kentucky basketball fans," he said before adding that he believed those fans had "utter resentment and disdain" for him.

"It's also kind of a compliment when you get booed," he said. "They've got to hate you for some reason."

The Villains won the game 152-149 in overtime. The game drew a crowd of just under 10,000 and raised $50,000 for The V Foundation.

Judging by the boo birds and a female fan heard yelling, "Laettner, you suck" in the final minutes, the game did well in the villain department.

"Even though it's been 20 years, it's still a hurt in their hearts," former UK player Chuck Hayes said of fan reaction to Laettner's famous shot. "Just like every loss here."

Judging by the charity game, Laettner continued to enjoy his villainy. He laid it on thick by going on all fours to theatrically wipe a wet spot with a towel and then he got ejected with two ceremonial technical fouls.

"That's just part of my personality," he said. "And I think it's something that made me good. . . . You have to feed off that a little bit."

In Kentucky and surely wherever there's a love of college basketball, the game still resonates.

Curry Kirkpatrick of *Sports Illustrated* was covering the Southeast Regional in Lexington. He watched the Kentucky-Duke game on television.

"During the game, I kept thinking, 'I can't believe I'm not there,'" he said for the story leading into the charity game. "As I watched it, I thought it was really something special. Something fantastic. Just for the brilliance of the last five minutes of regulation and the five minutes of overtime. The last 10 minutes were just unbelievable."

The day after Laettner's shot, CBS ranked the UK-Duke game as the second-best ever. It put the Astrodome game of 1968 between UCLA and Houston as No. 1.

Kirkpatrick did not agree. For him, Lew Alcindor's eye injury detracted from that game.

"The artistry and excellence of that game' was not even close (to UK-Duke)," he said.

Joe B. Hall likened the Kentucky-Duke game to UK's 92-90 victory over Indiana in the 1975 Mideast Regional Finals, which he called "the best game I was ever part of."

Hall cited an uncanny number of similarities. Both games were a regional final. Kentucky's opponent in each game was ranked No. 1. Each UK team had a core of four seniors surrounding a young big man: Jamal Mashburn in 1992 and Rick

Robey in 1975. Each UK team had a point guard from Indiana: Sean Woods in 1992 and Mike Flynn in 1975. To cap it off, Hall and Pitino were in their third seasons as Kentucky's coach.

How great was "the Christian Laettner game?" Speculation is seemingly endless. "A huge therapy session" is how *Sports Illustrated*'s Alexander Wolff described the urge to rehash Duke's overtime victory.

"I can't remember a game people talked about like this one," Wolff said from the 1992 Final Four site of Minneapolis.

For Kentucky's seniors, the game evoked strong emotions both positive and negative.

Farmer spoke of a mission being accomplished. The seniors were tasked with restoring Kentucky's basketball pedigree.

"To accomplish what we accomplished I think it was really special," Farmer said. "But it was more about at the end of the year, people really thought, hey, man, Kentucky basketball is back."

Pelphrey spoke in 2023 of the difference time makes.

"It kind of takes a different place now," he said. "Obviously, there was a period of time in my life when it was extremely traumatic because it ended my career. I lost one of the things I loved most that night, and it wasn't necessarily the game. It was just the fact I would never put that uniform on again. I would never have a chance to compete with those guys. That was the devastating part."

Kentucky fans like nicknames for their favorite teams. Among the nicknames are "The Fabulous Five" (1948 national champions), "The Fiddlin' Five" (1958 national champions) and "Rupp's Runts" (beloved 1966 runner-up).

After the 1991-92 season, the UK Alumni Association asked fans to send nickname ideas for the team that lost to Duke. To prime the pump, the Alumni Association suggested such nicknames as "'92 True Blues" and "Return to Glory team." More than 200 responses came the first day.

The fans' proposals included "Faithful Five," "Mission Men" and "Rick's Rockys." The *Herald-Leader* newsroom offered "Rags to Richie," "Better Now Than Laettner" and "Five of Hearts."

The seniors became known as "The Unforgettables." And in early April of 1992, Director of Athletics C.M. Newton led a ceremony in which banners were unveiled in the Rupp Arena rafters in honor of the seniors.

"I've always said I dreamed of playing at the University of Kentucky," Farmer said in 2023. "I grew up idolizing the players, the coaches. . . . You dream of hitting game winners. You know, you dream of winning national titles. You dream of all that.

"I never even dreamed that my jersey would be hanging in the rafters of Rupp Arena. . . . I could never have dreamed of that."

Farmer said some of the other seniors had an inkling of what was going to happen at the ceremony. He did not. "To me, that was one of the most surreal moments of my life," he said. "It just meant so much."

Pelphrey was also moved.

"It's still very, very humbling," he said in 2023. "(It was) borderline a little embarrassing to be a kid in the state who grew up with ridiculous admiration and respect for the (UK) players. They are why I wanted to be there, them and the fans."

As the name suggests, "The Unforgettables" have not been forgotten. Their legacy lives on. So does "The Christian Laettner game."

For Ohio State Coach Chris Holtmann and his family, it reverberated in the 2021-22 season when the Buckeyes beat Duke 71-66 in the ACC/Big Ten Challenge.

"I will always associate that program with that particular moment in college basketball history," said Holtmann, who grew up in the Lexington area. "I think I always will. I don't think that ever leaves you."

John Michael Holtmann, the younger brother of the Ohio State coach, told me that he still remembered "the exact spot" where he sat and also where his father sat in their Nicholasville, Ky, home and watched Laettner beat Kentucky.

"I think I may have shed a few tears," he said. "I was upset after that one."

Father John Holtmann suggested Laettner's shot was more than a game-winner. It punctuated a game drenched in drama and an inspiring three-year UK rebuild led by Pitino.

"I remember we thought the game was practically over when Sean Woods hit his shot," the elder Holtmann said. "Then to see that shot from Laettner, it was, like, heartbreak."

Father and younger brother attended Ohio State's victory over Duke in Columbus on Nov. 30, 2021. Ohio State outscored Duke 14-1 in the final five minutes to win.

"There was a lot of – shall we say – redemption," the elder Holtmann said.

The Ohio State coach recalled returning home past midnight and talking about the game with his brother.

"He goes, that was the single greatest athletic experience I've ever been a part of," Chris Holtmann said. "It exorcized some demons for him for sure."

That's how John Michael remembered it.

"That healed some wounds from 1992 . . . ," the younger brother said. "I told Chris he didn't need to get me anything for Christmas this year. That gift was already wrapped up."

If you're looking for a Christmas gift for a friend who is a Kentucky fan, here's an idea. A store in Lexington called Kentucky Branded sells UK memorabilia. One t-shirt is adorned with the words "I still hate Laettner."

"That still sells after, gosh, the '70s when it happened," said store manager Linda Buch, who missed the time of the game by 20 years. "People that were young at that time come in. . . . They've heard from friends, 'you need to go see the shirt.'"

The "I still hate Laettner" shirt still sells well, Buch said. "Sometimes three a month, which is a lot. . . . Everybody gets hyped up because it's tournament time. They will say, do you remember that game? I say, 'I've got the shirt.'"

Buch made it seem that the idea for the shirt – duh – was obvious.

"I think because everybody would always walk around saying, 'I hate Laettner.' 'I hate him.' And so that's where the term came up from one of our vendors. And people say, 'I still hate Laettner' to this day."

When I asked what comments people who ask for the Laettner shirt make, Buch said with a laugh, "Some I can't say.

"It's just one of those games that went down to the wire. . . . I just remember all the (UK) basketball players crying, as we all were. We were just shocked."

As for customers still buying the "I still hate Laettner" shirt, Buch said, "They'll go on to say words (another laugh). Everybody just comes in with that hurt."

Tubby Smith: the Gentleman, the Champion . . . the Lion?

In a story leading into Tubby Smith's fifth season as Kentucky coach, I wrote about how he brought a new persona to a program that seemingly never tired of being exalted. The headline for the story, which was published five days before the opening game of 2003-04, made this clear: Tubby, the face of UK coach brings a rare warmth, humanity to his job.

His two immediate predecessors described Kentucky Basketball in splendiferous terms. "The Roman Empire of college basketball," Rick Pitino pronounced. And Eddie Sutton said he led Big Brother.

I came to refer to Adolph Rupp as the founding father of Kentucky basketball. But in this story, I used a different – although fictional – reference.

I wrote:

"The inventor of Kentucky Basketball, Adolph Rupp, affected an omnipotence that recalled the Wizard of Oz: hovering above, all knowing and unapproachable. I am Oz, great and powerful! Who are you?

"Now Kentucky basketball is . . . the man behind the curtain. UK's wizard is a Tubby."

Smith, I wrote, "brings a human dimension to an operation that counts time in 'eras' and touts its magnificence as 'unparalleled.'"

To this, Smith said in 2003, "I never look at myself (as) being different from the Joe Blow who has to go to work every morning."

To this, I wrote, "people whose lives intersected with Smith's say he's different from the Joe Blowhards in the coaching profession. Thoughtful. Considerate. A benevolent king of UK's castle."

Lexingtonian Dick Hurst, a noted bumper sticker man of the time, coined the phrase "Kentubby Basketball" for one of his products.

The difference that Smith brought was most evident in his second season as coach. The setting was his postgame news conference after Kentucky won in overtime at Georgia 91-83.

Smith had been Georgia's coach for two seasons before being hired by Kentucky in the spring of 1997. Georgia promoted his associate head coach, Ron Jirsa, as

Smith's successor. Earlier in their careers, Jirsa had been on Smith's staff at Tulsa for four seasons. "One of my best friends," Smith said of Jirsa in 2023.

Although it was only Jirsa's second season as Georgia coach, fans were already questioning his promotion.

Kentucky's overtime victory at Georgia figured to only increase the proverbial heat on Jirsa's seat. Jirsa chose to change defenses going into overtime. The move backfired as Kentucky scored on multiple possessions to start overtime.

With an easy-to-detect nervousness in his voice, a reporter for Georgia's student newspaper asked Smith in the postgame news conference if he agreed that Jirsa's decision helped Kentucky win.

As I wrote in 2003, "Smith glared at the student and spit out a putdown: What team have you ever coached?"

In 2023, Smith still remembered this exchange. "I didn't like that question," he said.

After the exchange, an interesting thing happened. Smith seemed preoccupied with thought as he responded to the next question from another reporter. Once he finished his response, he turned back to the student reporter and in an apologetic voice said he had not answered his question properly and asked him to repeat it.

This time he remained protective of Jirsa, but offered a more respectful response.

"His conscience told him that wasn't the way to answer the question," Tim Hix, the publicist for Georgia basketball, said in 2003. "He's so much more human than most other guys in the profession. And he reveals his humanity."

In 2003, Smith acknowledged the impulse to lash out. "The natural thing to do is 'I can intimidate that kid,'" he said. "Then you think about it. That's not right."

Smith even went so far as to say an effort to intimidate referees would violate his sense of fair play.

"People think he's just so nice," Smith said of himself. "He can do more to influence the game, to intimidate officials or get on players or do something with the opposing coach. I don't see it that way. It's still a game."

Time has not changed Smith's resistance to the autocratic impulses displayed by many coaches. In 2023, he cited the golden rule as the reason why.

"You want to treat people the way you want to be treated," he said. "You want to do to others what you want them to do unto you."

Anyone who has been around coaches or other authority figures might think, how quaint.

Time has not dulled the admiration others had for a humanity Smith displayed through thoughtfulness and an acknowledgement that the other person mattered, too. It was not all about placating the coach. This applied even to the Kentucky basketball coach.

Mike Johnson, the *Herald-Leader* sports editor who hired me to cover Kentucky basketball, put Smith in select company. "The three nicest people I ever had to deal with in sports were Sparky Anderson, Tubby Smith and Jerry Claiborne," he told me in 2023. "They all probably had a better understanding of what the (reporter's) job was. But Tubby was the one who seemed to have a better understanding of what your job was, and appreciated that."

Jim Host, the Lexington-based businessman who enhanced college athletics' marketing potential, called Smith "the best human being I've ever been around in my life as a coach by far, far, far, far. The best human being. Most sensitive. He always asked about my wife. Always super conscious and he never called me by my first name. He always called me mister. He still calls me that."

Former UK players also gushed about Tubby Smith, the person, as well as the coach.

"One of the best people on the planet," said Scott Padgett, a forward on UK teams circa 1994-1999. "If they had one, he would have won the NCAA Humanitarian Award on a regular basis."

Marta McMackin, the long-time administrative assistant in the Kentucky basketball office, said Smith brought a distinctive quality to coaching. "He didn't have the ego," she said.

Wayne Turner, the point guard on UK's 1998 national championship team, echoed McMackin's remembrance.

"He was a very humble guy, very humble," Turner said. "Sometimes we would forget he was the coach because he was so down to earth."

Turner recalled Smith playing pickup games with players. "He still had a little hangtime left," Turner said. "I was surprised."

When asked about not having his ego on display, Smith reacted in 2023 with a laugh before saying, "I think that's been a challenge for me in that people can look at it as a weakness. That you're always forgiving. That you're always caring about people. You're not snapping at people. You're thoughtful. You're concerned. You're emphatic. You're sympathetic.

"There are people who take advantage of that."

Smith showed empathy after Pitino became coach at Louisville, which Kentucky fans saw as a betrayal. So there was an uneasy what's-going-to-happen feeling when Louisville played at Kentucky in Pitino's first season as U of L coach (2001-02).

It was the most charged atmosphere for a home game in Smith's 10 seasons as Kentucky coach. Or as I wrote of the game two years later, "That's when Pitino, the Caesar maximus during Kentucky Basketball's Roman Empire era, returned to Rupp Arena."

Smith hoped to see Pitino in the hallway under the stands before the game so they could walk together onto the court.

"I knew the climate," Smith said. "The environment was already very tense. It was something I was thinking about: If you see Rick out here, what can you do to make this better?"

By chance, Smith and Pitino did come out of their locker rooms at the same time. Pitino accepted Smith's invitation to enter the court together.

"I wanted people to know Rick and I are friends," Smith said. "I respect what he's done and I'm sure he respects what we do. We're going to be friends no matter what. I'd walk out with any coach, but especially with Rick in that situation."

The show of togetherness defused the moment of Pitino's appearance.

"Tubby's one of the most down-to-earth people I've ever worked with in my life," Pitino said in the fall of 2003 when asked about that entrance. "I know it's tough for Louisville and Kentucky fans to understand, but he's not going to get caught up in all that."

Of course, Smith was a historic hire by Kentucky. He was the program's first Black coach. UK's Director of Athletics at the time, C.M. Newton, had a history as a progressive when it came to college basketball. As a coach, he had integrated the basketball programs at Transylvania, now a Division III school in Lexington, and Alabama. So, the hiring of Smith fit a pattern.

But Newton's son, Martin Newton, cautioned against drawing that conclusion.

Of Smith becoming Kentucky coach, Martin Newton said in 2023, "I can tell you it had nothing to do with trying to integrate or being a pioneer in that regard. (His father) talked a lot about this. He felt like Tubby's skill set with the players on that team would mesh better than with anybody else he could get."

Another factor influencing the hire was that Smith had been an assistant during Rick Pitino's first two seasons as Kentucky coach. "So he understood what being in that chair meant and how different it was," Martin Newton said. This led his father to believe "Tubby was tough enough to take it."

Smith, who had also been the first Black coach for basketball programs at Georgia and Texas Tech, said in 2023 that C.M. Newton told him that race had nothing to do with the hire.

"What Coach Newton said was there's no Black or White. We see green," said Smith, the financial bottom line reference still making him laugh 26 years later.

Smith acknowledged some uneasiness about following Pitino as Kentucky coach.

"They had already been to two Final Fours," he said of the 1996 and 1997 NCAA Tournaments. "So, I was nervous about just replacing (Pitino). What do you do for an encore?"

Of course, Kentucky won the 1998 national championship. But it was not all smooth sailing despite a 35-4 record, plus winning the Southeastern Conference regular-season and postseason tournament championships.

One notable moment came when Ole Miss beat Kentucky 73-64 in Rupp Arena on of all dates, Valentine's Day. The first home loss to Ole Miss since 1927 (and still only the second in the history of the series as of 2023) did not engender love in the Big Blue Nation. One fan famously called the postgame radio show and said Kentucky was the worst team with a 22-4 record that he had ever seen.

Jeff Sheppard, the leading scorer for Kentucky that season, said the fan's derision had no impact.

"The last thing I was concerned with while remembering the '98 season was a comment from a fan after the last loss of our season," he said.

Indeed, Kentucky went 13-0 thereafter en route to a national championship.

That's not to say that losing to Ole Miss, a program Kentucky enjoyed an all-time series record of 110-14 as of 2023, did not have an impact.

Sheppard said the loss propelled Kentucky into the immediate future.

"You refocus," he said. "For us, Coach Smith rolled out 6 a.m. morning workouts. And we were practicing at 6 a.m. and 3 p.m. It showed we weren't as good as we thought we were. He told us we weren't as bad as we thought."

In addition to the early morning practices, the team had a players only meeting after the loss to Ole Miss.

As Turner recalled, Sheppard played a lead role in the meeting.

"Jeff kind of brought up that we needed to start buying in things that coach is doing even though we don't feel like it's something we're comfortable with," Turner said. "We just have to try to get better at it."

During his Kentucky days, Sheppard played for Pitino and Smith. He recalled both excelling at motivating players.

"I've said before that I'd run through a wall for either of them," Sheppard said in 2023. "One of them out of fear. And one of them out of love."

Resilience marked Kentucky's 1998 championship. In the South Region finals, the Wildcats trailed Duke by 18 points in the first half before rallying to an 86-84 victory.

In the national semifinals, Kentucky trailed Stanford by five at halftime before winning 86-85 in overtime.

Then in the championship game, Kentucky trailed Utah by 10 at halftime, then went on to win 78-69.

"I think it was just a product of we had played a lot of games together," Sheppard said in 2023. "We had played a lot of NCAA games. . . . We were loaded down with juniors and seniors."

After you've experienced the Mardi Gras Miracle (down 31 by less than 16 minutes remaining), a deficit is nothing, Sheppard said. "So, we were OK with being down. We didn't plan it, but it's where we were. And we just had the maturity and the trust in each other to just keep playing and just stick to the plan."

Nazr Mohammed got credit for the team's nickname being "The Undeniables." But Smith playfully suggested the knack for falling behind suggested another nickname.

"That was heartache," he said in 2023. "They should have been called The Heartache Kids."

The comebacks also served to validate something I heard Smith say before and after the 1998 NCAA Tournament.

In 2023, he put it this way: "We were just a slow starting team. My whole philosophy was, fellas, we're not going to win the game in that first half.

"The most insignificant thing in sports is the halftime score."

Playing and defeating Duke in the 1998 tournament was the polar opposite of insignificant.

Memories of the loss to Duke in the 1992 NCAA Tournament (aka The Christian Laettner Game) were still fresh.

Before the 1998 game, former Kentucky players who lost the Laettner game downplayed the notion of exacting revenge. They said they respected the Blue

Devils' program, its soundness and its tradition of success. Believe it or not, Chris Harrison said he wouldn't mind being called a Duke fan.

"I used to like the way Duke played," he said in a story leading up to the 1998 game. "I always loved Johnny Dawkins. I still like the way they play."

Added John Pelphrey: "I'll be rooting for the Cats. But whether they win or lose, it won't be vindication for us. These guys probably really don't care. That game won't do anything for my sake."

Richie Farmer echoed that sentiment. "There's nothing I can do to get back at them," he said. "My career is over."

That Kentucky beat Duke in 1998 was seen as a personal triumph for Smith, whom pundits credited with wisely hoarding his timeouts in order to further sap Mike Krzyzewski's tiring team.

Jim Host, whose company owned the radio broadcast rights for NCAA Tournament games, had a courtside seat near the Kentucky bench.

"I take my headset off and I can hear what he's saying," Host said of Smith's instructions during timeouts. "He said, 'We're going to win this game and I'm going to tell you why. Wojo (Duke guard Steve Wojciechowski) can't guard you, Wayne (Turner). So, I want you guys to clear the floor and I want (Heshimu) Evans and Padgett and Sheppard to all take the shots. Wojo can't guard you, so, Wayne, you drive on him.'"

Turner finished with 16 points and had an assist-to-turnover ratio of eight-to-one. Wojciechowski had 10 points, four assists, two turnovers and four fouls.

Kentucky fans are seldom if ever satisfied, so it was not a complete surprise that some downplayed the championship. On several occasions, I heard it said that, yes, Kentucky won the national championship, but Smith won it with Pitino players.

I suspected racism played a part in this comment. When I asked former Arkansas coach Nolan Richardson in 2023 if a White coach winning the championship in his first season after replacing a Black coach would be similarly downgraded, his laughter was a guffaw.

Padgett and Sheppard both said that leading players trained by Pitino to a championship did not diminish the championship. It *enhanced* the accomplishment.

"They won doing it a certain way," Padgett said of Kentucky's 1996 championship and runner-up status in 1997. "And he won a championship by doing it his way. We were recruited by and tailor-made for Coach Pitino's system. And he could have walked in there and he could have just stayed the same. And I don't know if that team wins it."

Padgett questioned whether the players left over from 1996 and 1997 had the ability to win a championship playing Pitino's style.

Plus, Smith had to convince players who equated Pitino's style with success to change.

"For Tubby to get us to eventually buy in, to do things his way, he doesn't get enough credit for that," Padgett said.

Padgett cited defense and rebounding as significant differences in coaching philosophy. Pitino had a risk-and-reward style based on full-court pressing. Smith had more of a ball-line defense based on getting back on defense and limiting offensive rebounds.

None of Smith's teams were outrebounded by opponents in any of his 10 seasons as Kentucky coach. UK enjoyed an average rebound advantage of 8.2 in the 1997-98 season. In four of Pitino's eight seasons as coach, the opponents outrebounded Kentucky.

Pitino's system called for plays run for specific players, while Smith ran more of a motion offense.

"He doesn't get enough credit," Padgett said of Smith's coaching ability. "I hear it so many times I want to strangle somebody every time I hear it: Oh, he just won it with Pitino players."

Sheppard saluted Smith's ability to get players to accept a new coach and a different playing style.

"It's all your perspective," Sheppard said. "You think Tom Izzo could just come in and win a national championship at another school? You can look at it on the other side. You can say, wow! Tubby Smith won it with somebody else's players?!"

When I asked Smith in 2023 about the qualifier some fans put on the 1998 championship, he seemed to try to put that thought in perspective.

"Wherever you go, there's going to be players that you inherit," he said. "Did Rick win with Eddie Sutton's players? There's always going to be overlap. Whenever people say that, I say, so what? You have to coach them."

I found Smith to be approachable and considerate. I even got him on the phone as he was leaving Lexington to become coach at Minnesota. He said he was going where he was wanted. When UK honored Smith prior to a game against his alma mater, High Point, on Dec. 31, 2021, I decided not to rain on the parade by reminding readers that he had said Kentucky no longer wanted him as coach in 2007. A jersey bearing his name was put in the Rupp Arena rafters.

"You treasure the moments that you have," Smith said before adding that a full appreciation can take time.

"When you're in the midst of it, when you're here, you're working so hard . . . What I tell folks, it's 24/7/365 days of the year. And the season never really ends. But this is a special place. This city, Lexington, this state, Rupp Arena. . . . This is the longest I've served anywhere."

In 2023, Smith amended his farewell comment about going where he was wanted.

"Not so much (not wanted)," he said before adding he saw Minnesota as a coaching job "where you're celebrated, not where you're tolerated."

But despite the cooperative spirit in our relationship, Smith and I were not immune to the friction that results from a reporter covering a beat objectively. For us the story involved Kelenna Azubuike. Before his freshman season, I received calls from more than one person claiming that the player's father, Kenneth Azubuike, had defrauded them in Oklahoma.

There was a discussion with editors about whether to do a story. One factor was that Azubuike's parents had moved to Lexington, where the player's mother, Chinyelu, was working as a physician for the University of Kentucky.

If the accusations were true, how would it look if the *Herald-Leader* did not do a story and a person or persons in Kentucky were cheated. It was ultimately decided to do a story.

"It certainly looks bad if you take money from friends and declare bankruptcy," the elder Azubuike told me. "That looks terrible. But that's not what happened.

"My reaction is obvious. I deny the key point: that I went out with intent to defraud the people who are concerned. I absolutely deny that I tried to defraud anybody ever. I never ever defrauded anybody."

The UK player's father added that he would fly to Tulsa to answer the charges.

Gene Abell, the *Herald-Leader*'s sports editor at the time, said that UK Director of Athletics Mitch Barnhart confronted him at a Kentucky home game and voiced his objection to the coverage.

Abell said he told Barnhart that the newspaper had an obligation to alert readers to be wary. He said Barnhart thought the coverage was unfair to Kelenna.

In February of 2005, Kenneth Azubuike was found guilty on 41 counts and sentenced to four years in prison. He was told to pay $340,000 in restitution to investors.

Years later, I spoke to Kelenna Azubuike about his entry into the broadcasting business. He became a color commentator for the Golden State Warriors. We had a pleasant conversation.

When I asked why he wanted to become a broadcaster, he said, "Because I love sports and I love basketball. And I love talking about it with my friends. It just kind of seemed like a natural fit."

In 2023, I asked Smith about his reaction to the coverage of Azubuike's father.

"You know, when you see that, you go, oh no! How it's going to affect others," he said.

Smith questioned whether the story was written to protect people in Kentucky or whether it was a story that could sell newspapers. I said it was written with Kentuckians in mind, plus it was also a good story.

Smith said a desire to "protect your flock," in this case Kelenna Azubuike, fueled his concern.

He noted that former Georgetown Coach John Thompson used intimidation as a tool in protecting his players.

"I'm not sure I was intimidating enough," Smith said.

Coincidentally, Smith and I attended the same Methodist church in Lexington: St. Luke.

In 2023, I spoke to Gene Strange, who was the minister at St. Luke at the time. He gushed about how Smith and his wife, Donna, contributed to a growing church.

"Tubby was just Tubby," Strange said. "What people didn't understand was there was no pretense.

"And Donna was the mother. She had a very motherly attitude about her."

During our conversation, I told Gene of Smith's exchange with the Georgia student newspaper reporter. I added that Smith might be the only coach to publicly express regret for scolding a reporter.

Strange agreed, adding that other coaches "might have told you where to go. And it wouldn't have been to the good place."

I remember one Sunday service when Smith and I happened to be kneeling side by side while taking communion.

This led someone – I don't remember who – saying this replicated the Bible reference to the lion and lamb laying together.

"I would never put it that way," Strange said. "I never saw (Smith) as the lion. He would be a person I would describe as velvet steel."

Nor did Strange see me as a lion.

"I always thought you were fair," he said. "And I read your columns. I'm sure there were times you had to say things you wish you didn't have to say. But you had to say them or write them."

When I told Smith I had spoken to Strange about the lion and the lamb reference, he smiled and asked, "Who was the lion?"

Smith playfully said he thought Strange would see me as the lion "because you were writing stuff and going after this poor lamb in Tubby Smith."

Smith then laughed. Then he added of himself, "He's such an innocent guy. Why is Jerry Tipton beating up on him?"

Then Smith again laughed.

Billy G's Time was Brief, but Eventful

Looking back on his 10 seasons as Kentucky coach, Tubby Smith was philosophical about his need to move to another basketball program.

"You can wear out your welcome if you're not careful wherever you go unless you just win, win, win all the time," he said in 2023. "Unless you're Mike Krzyzewski or Roy Williams.

"Even at that point, there's going to come a time where it's going to come to an end."

Smith's end-time came after the 2006-07 season. Back-to-back seasons with the number of losses reaching double digits inspired fans with an apparent appreciation for alliteration to dub him "10-loss Tubby." Overall, he had 10 or more losses in five of his 10 seasons as coach.

By then, I thought that fans think of coaches as toys. After a certain amount of time, fans want a new toy to play with.

Mitch Barnhart, who became UK's Director of Athletics in 2002, knew that Smith's endearing humanity made the already challenging job of hiring a new coach even more difficult.

"He represented this place with incredible class," Barnhart said of Smith in 2023. "So, it's tough to replace someone like that."

Speculation centered on Billy Donovan. He had begun his coaching career on Rick Pitino's Kentucky staff. Near the end of the 1993-94 season, I was asked to go to the coaches' locker room after practice. This was an unusual request, and I wondered what prompted it.

I found out that Donovan was considering an offer to become Marshall's head coach. Knowing that was my alma mater, he wanted to know if I could provide insight into the Marshall basketball program.

I figured he wanted to know how important basketball was to Marshall officials and fans. I said it was considered *the* sport. To emphasize that point, I said that if Donovan took the job and was successful, Marshall officials would erect a statue of him on campus. That drew a laugh, but I wasn't trying to be funny.

Later that spring, Donovan became Marshall coach. His won-loss record was 35-20 in two seasons before he became coach at Florida.

When Kentucky was looking for Smith's replacement, Donovan had led Florida to nine straight NCAA Tournament appearances. The streak included a Final Four appearance in 2000 and back-to-back national championships in 2006 and 2007.

A few days before the 2007 Final Four, the *Atlanta Journal-Constitution* asked me if Kentucky might be interested in Donovan.

"I believe Kentucky will make a sincere all-out effort to land Billy," I told the *AJC* for a story that was published the Wednesday prior to the Final Four. "I wish I knew how Billy would react. Barnhart wants to hit a home run with this hire. Billy would be a Mark McGwire moon shot into the upper deck."

From the perspective of 2023, Barnhart said that hiring a new coach can be more difficult than fans imagine.

"I think everybody has this notion when you go to hire a coach that the pool is as large as you want it to be. . . . There's 400 candidates for every job. You just pick the plum. And it's really not that way at all."

Kentucky is no exception, Barnhart said. The program's history makes for unblinking scrutiny and something close to national-championship-or-bust expectations. The prize that is a victory over Kentucky inspires opponents.

"When you put all of that together, the pool (of potential candidates) gets a little tighter," Barnhart said. "You might call it a puddle. And out of the puddle, some of those folks are just unavailable. They are already at places they like."

Four days after Florida beat Ohio State 84-75 in the national championship game, my story updating Kentucky's search for a head coach ran on the *Herald-Leader*'s front page. The headline did not mince words: "From Billy D. to Billy G?"

Donovan had said he was not interested in moving to Lexington. At a news conference, he saluted Barnhart as "a terrific athletic director," but added, "I felt at this time in my life, the best place for me was the University of Florida."

Then Texas Coach Rick Barnes discouraged speculation that he might move to UK, the story said.

The first coaching candidate Kentucky seriously considered for the job was P.J. Carlesimo.

Then UK president David Roselle recalled his conversation with Carlesimo.

"He sat at my breakfast table and he said, 'Dr. Roselle, if you hire a basketball coach and he cheats, would you fire him?'" Roselle recalled. "And I said, 'No, I'd shoot him.'

"He just said, 'you talk plain.'"

Kentucky scratched Carlesimo, Donovan and Barnes.

"That left Texas A&M Coach Billy Gillispie, college basketball's hottest commodity not named Donovan," I wrote. Gillispie had a reputation as "the total coaching package." He had led a revival of The University of Texas at El Paso program (six victories the season before he became coach and 24 in his first season). At A&M, he inherited a team that had had an 0-16 record in the Big 12 Conference. His first A&M team won 21 games and played in the National Invitation Tournament. The 24 victories at UTEP led Gillispie to be a finalist for a National Coach of the

Year award for the 2003-04 season. At Texas A&M, he was twice named Big 12 Conference Coach of the Year (2004-05 and 2006-07).

The day before the story appeared Barnhart had asked A&M's athletic director for permission to speak to Gillispie about the job.

This came a week after Gillispie-coached Texas A&M beat Kentucky's archrival Louisville 72-69 in a second-round NCAA Tournament game played in Lexington.

Barnhart smiled in 2023 when asked how beating Louisville affected Gillispie's stature as a candidate for Kentucky's job.

"Everyone likes to point to that," Barnhart said. "But I think he had done a lot of really good things leading up to that. That was not the end-all-be-all. For our fans, that might have been a little icing on the cake."

But, Barnhart added that watching in person how A&M defended and played with zeal in Rupp Arena made a positive impression.

Less than two weeks later, Gillispie agreed to a new contract with Texas A&M that called for a pay raise of about $500,000 that would take his annual salary to $1.75 million, a three-year extension and a retention bonus of $750,000 if he remained Aggie coach through 2015.

Yet, a short time later, Kentucky hired Gillispie.

When Kentucky announced Gillispie as the new coach, optimism overflowed. There was a pep rally in Memorial Coliseum (the on-campus arena that was formerly UK's homecourt) after his introductory news conference that drew a big and enthusiastic crowd.

"It was great," Barnhart said of the rally.

In its preseason yearbook, *Athlon Sports*' cover headline hailed "A New Hope" at Kentucky. It included Gillispie welcoming the unblinking interest and pressure to succeed that is Kentucky basketball.

"The harder it is, the better I like it . . . ," he told Barnhart during the job interview, according to the story. "You can't put any more pressure on me than I put on myself. I'm a 24-hour-a-day guy."

The September, 2007 edition of *Basketball Times* had Gillispie on the cover with the headline reading "Big Blue Billy Clyde." The headline on the three-page story said of Lexington: "This is Billy G's Town." The story's second paragraph referred to "the new king of Kentucky's Big Blue Nation."

Of course, the reign of this king lasted only two fitful years.

An early warning sign came before Gillispie's first season as Kentucky coach when he refused to speak to the Lexington Rotary Club. UK coaches had given the Rotarians a preseason preview of the team dating back to Adolph Rupp.

In 2023, Lexington Rotary Club officials impressed upon me how anticipated the coach's annual appearance was.

"We'd have more requests for that program than any other event during the year," former Club president Kevin Weaver said. At a time before social media, "you weren't getting stuff every day. So it was very exciting for people to come and hear about the new players."

Another past president, Martha Riddell, said this was especially true "with him being a new coach that year."

Weaver did not remember an exact reason given for Gillispie declining to speak to the Rotary Club. The feeling was "something like he was here to coach and not to glad hand and do that part of the job," Weaver said.

Upon learning that Gillispie would not continue this tradition, it was easy to see a news story there. I spoke to Rotary Club Executive Director Nell Main, who was in charge of lining up speakers. When we spoke, I could hear concern, if not panic in her voice. What could the Rotary Club do for a speaker for a meeting only a week or so in the future? I then heard myself volunteer to speak to the Rotarians. Main immediately agreed, which caused me to wonder what I had just done.

I was uneasy about public speaking. But the Rotarians' gratitude made filling the void a pleasant luncheon experience.

Main introduced me to the audience as "the pride and joy" of the *Herald-Leader*. Hopefully, I kept a straight face. I spoke optimistically about Gillispie "creating a buzz" about Kentucky basketball and, according to the Rotary newsletter, said that it was "too easy to forget that the players are young guys with feelings."

In the next Sunday's newspaper, I wrote a note about my speaking to the Rotary Club.

As I told the Rotarians, my appearance was like thinking you might be dating Angelina Jolie and instead you get Olive Oyl.

Gillispie spoke to The Rotary Club before his second and final season as Kentucky coach. He lightened the mood by saying, "I've had a lot of fun since I was here last . . . uh, I wasn't here last year."

Gillispie's first season brought more departures from the Kentucky basketball norm.

Kentucky lost its second game: 84-68 at home against Gardner-Webb.

December began with four straight losses: against North Carolina, at Indiana, against UAB and at Houston. UK had not lost four straight since Rick Pitino's first season: 1989-90.

The nadir of the first season came in a 93-52 loss at Vanderbilt on Feb. 12. That continues to be Kentucky's most lopsided loss in Southeastern Conference play. Ever.

My story eight days later for the *Herald-Leader* began with an anecdote.

Shortly after Kentucky's chartered flight from Nashville touched down at 2 a.m. last Wednesday, Billy Gillispie sought out freshman walk-on Dusty Mills.

"He looked at me, confronted me and said, 'you're done,'" Mills recalled on Tuesday. "I said, 'yes, sir,' because, you know, I had no idea what he meant."

Returning home from a historic 41-point loss at Vanderbilt on Feb. 12 didn't strike Mills as a good time to ask for an explanation.

He waited until Thursday afternoon. During the "one-sided discussion," Mills said, "Gillispie used a lot of profanity in telling Mills he had been kicked off the team. Mills said he never got a chance to give his side of the story."

By then, Gillispie had gotten a reputation for being disagreeable. I felt I needed to talk to him with a story about kicking a player off the team. I did the story, in part, because I thought Mills would pull the curtain back on just how tyrannical Gillispie was. Thinking I needed to talk to Gillispie related to regret about the story in the Huntington *Herald-Dispatch* in which I did not speak to the owners of the bowling house in reference to a story about lanes being improperly oiled.

During the telephone conversation, Gillispie was cordial in explaining his side of the action in a matter-of-fact manner. He said he gave Mills a chance to explain.

"They all get chances," the UK coach said in the *Herald-Leader* story. "He (Mills) was a real good member of the team for a little bit." Gillispie denied using profanity in meeting with Mills.

Mills said he believed Gillispie dismissed him because a television camera showed the walk-on laughing with teammate Morakinyo Williams on the bench as Ramel Bradley lay on the floor, suffering a concussion during the game at Georgia. While acknowledging that Gillispie could mete out any punishment he saw fit, Mills was left frustrated because he said he never got a chance to tell the UK coach what led to the ill-timed laughter. Nor did Gillispie bring up the subject until the flight from Vandy landed even though, Mills said, he explained to assistant coaches what led to the laughter.

"The whole thing is his decision, which I respect 100 percent," Mills said. "I understand he said there's a zero-tolerance walk-on policy. But the way it went, the way I was not able to explain myself, the way he really treated me was difficult to accept."

Why the laughter?

Mills, an end-of-the-bench fan favorite from Noblesville, Ind., said he and Williams laughed because of what happened after a Dave Bliss foul flattened Bradley. Perhaps recalling Gillispie's irritation that no one helped a UK player confronted by Houston players earlier in the season, a teammate left the bench to head toward Bradley at the other end of the court. Thinking of a possible technical foul, Mills said he played peacemaker by grabbing the teammate and steering him back to the bench. Mills and Williams laughed at the thought of a 5-foot-8 freshman taking charge of a much larger teammate. Adding to the comical effect, the teammate stumbled on the return to the bench.

But Mills, who subsequently apologized to Bradley, did not get the chance to tell Gillispie what happened. Instead, "he bashed on me pretty much," Mills said.

Rather than meet in Gillispie's office privately, the coach took him to an assistant coach's office and left the door open so anyone nearby could hear, Mills said.

"It was like he had a total power trip on me," Mills said. "Instead of explaining things, he decided to use intimidation. 'You're below me. This is how things are going to be.'"

Mills' hopes of explaining what happened or at least persuading Gillispie to allow him to finish out the season gave way to a hard reality. Mills, who again expressed his gratitude for the chance to play for Kentucky, realized he was off the team.

"Eventually, at one point, I was moved to tears," Mills said.

Regaining his composure, Mills tried to explain to Gillispie why he laughed at Georgia as Bradley laid on the court.

"He cut me off and just went berserk," Mills said. "He cussed me out. Just basically said he didn't care what I had to say. Said he was sick of me. That was a quote. He actually said he was sick of me.

"At one point, he said something along the lines of, why don't you transfer to, and named some small school, and said, complain to somebody there because I don't want to hear it."

Gillispie invited him to tell reporters of the meeting, Mills said.

Dave McCollough, who coached Mills at Noblesville High School, said that Mills was a good kid who could be "squirrely" like a lot of kids. When asked to explain what he meant by squirrely, the coach said, "You know, nudging a guy next to him or talking when they shouldn't be talking or joking around or rolling his eyes when you're not supposed to be rolling your eyes."

Mills and his mother, Cathie, said there had been no problems before the Georgia game. Mills, who was nicknamed "Ollie" after the player-manager in the movie Hoosiers, said several teammates voiced support.

Bradley offered to lead a team effort to have Mills reinstated. But the walk-on declined the offer, which Bradley said could have been successful.

"I think we could have (persuaded Gillispie)," Bradley said. "He was our teammate. I think if we came as a team, (Gillispie) would have accepted him."

Mills said he did not want to be a distraction.

A few days later, I wrote a follow up story that tried to put into perspective Gillispie's coaching style and how Mills became the third player to leave that Kentucky team either voluntarily (Alex Legion and walk-on Kerry Benson) or by edict (Mills).

The headline, which I wish I had written, read: "The End Justifies the Mean."

Mills told me he had hoped to develop a relationship with Gillispie like the open-door access he enjoyed with his high school coach.

"But immediately, off the bat, I realized he was really unapproachable," Mills said. "He has more basketball knowledge than any person I've ever met in my life. But I just feel like he has – I don't know if it's no people skills or bad socially or however the heck you want to word it – but he doesn't seem to be very good with people."

Gillispie said that the long-range benefits of his demanding style outweighed any hurt feelings. He cited long-lasting relationships with former players as evidence of the merits of his coaching style.

Josh Johnston, a walk-on for Gillispie at UTEP, followed him to Texas A&M and was a walk-on for the Aggies.

"I just felt he was sincere and genuine," Johnston told me. By then, he was an assistant coach at the College of Eastern Utah. ". . . Nobody cares more about kids on a Billy Gillispie team than Billy Gillispie."

Although he had been a star as a senior for A&M, Acie Law IV said he thought about transferring more than once. His parents would not let him quit.

"Once I matured a little bit and got used to it, I look at coach as a father figure," he said of Gillispie. "I love him to death."

When Kentucky played Florida International in late December of 2007-08, FIU Coach Sergio Rouco defended Gillispie. Rouco said he considered Gillispie a friend as well as his former boss.

Rouco said Kentucky players had to adjust from "a mild-mannered man" (Tubby Smith) to a "Baby Saddam."

That drew laughter from reporters at the postgame news conference.

Gillispie said he was just trying to motivate players. He likened himself to the character played by Sean Connery in the movie *The Untouchables.* When Eliot Ness (Kevin Costner) tries to add the tough Chicago cop to fight organized crime, Connery has a question: What are you prepared to do?

"I really believe that's relevant to what we do as basketball players," Gillispie said. "What are you prepared to do? Everybody wants to be an NBA player. But what are you prepared to do to make yourself become one of those guys?

"That's just my whole philosophy."

Mills likened Gillispie to another no-nonsense, this-will-be-good-for-you coach who drew admirers and detractors: Bob Knight.

"I think we're teaching life through basketball," Gillispie said. "Life isn't always easy either. The people most prepared to be successful are the people who've probably gone through some trials and tribulations."

In a special section previewing Gillispie's second – and last – season as Kentucky coach, I asked players what actor should play him in a movie.

Patrick Patterson said Robert DeNiro. A.J. Stewart asked, who is the meanest actor? Jack Nicholson? Josh Harrellson said Samuel L. Jackson "because he yells a lot in all of his movies."

In 2012, I revisited Gillispie's time as Kentucky coach when there were reports of him conducting marathon practice sessions and mistreating players as Texas Tech coach.

Call it Déjà Blue, I wrote before adding, "or is that Déjà Black and Blue?

"I was not surprised by one thing I read," Mills said of the stories coming out of Texas Tech. "Nothing was outrageous to me."

Mills called Gillispie "the smartest X-and-O guy I've ever met in my life." He likened Billy G to then Ohio State football coach Urban Meyer.

"He'd draw up a play and it'd work every single time," Mills said of Gillispie. "But he couldn't really relate to players. I'm not sure (about) the reasons behind that. But it makes it difficult to play for someone you're not happy to be there with."

When asked about the rumors that such players as Jodie Meeks, Derrick Jasper and Patrick Patterson practiced despite injuries, Mills said, "I can't really confirm Gillispie technically made them practice. That's not fair for me to say.

"But it was clear they practiced and were not happy about it. Physically, they were playing in pain, and it was hard to watch at times."

Texas Tech players went to the athletic director to protest how they were treated. In Mills' aborted season at Kentucky, the players endured. "It bonded us and united us as a team," he said.

Mills said he held no grudge against Gillispie. He said he had reached out to his former coach, but had not gotten a response.

"He gave me an opportunity no other human being on earth would have given me," Mills said. "I'll be forever grateful for the opportunity he gave me, and I'll always praise the Lord that he gave me that chance.

"I think he does really care for his players. I think he does. He just has a very odd way of showing it. Obviously, something is going on there and I'm not sure what it is."

Mills could serve as an example of how wildly a relationship with Gillispie could fluctuate. His teammates teased him about being a favorite of Gillispie's, Mills said. Before UK played Tennessee Tech early in the 2007-08 season, assistant coaches rushed him video tape to study because they suspected the walk-on might start, Mills said.

In 2012, Mills aspired to coach on the college level. His backup plan was to use a master's degree in accounting to find a job. His coach at Ball State, Billy Taylor, was an accountant before getting into coaching.

Mills had coached on the high school and AAU levels. He said he tried to be encouraging.

"If a kid messes up or does something wrong, I talk to them about it (and) try to figure out what they were thinking . . . ," he said. "Rather than yelling at them or demeaning them."

Tornado Time

As if Billy Gillispie's first season as Kentucky coach hadn't been chaotic enough, the next-to-last game involved chaos on a historical and potentially horrific level. It came at the 2008 Southeastern Conference Tournament.

Surely no one wants to relive that frightening night of March 14, 2008. But the return of the Southeastern Conference Men's Basketball Tournament to Atlanta in 2011 evoked an unstoppable flood of memories that included a tornado hitting the Georgia Dome, an all-night scramble to keep the tournament going, a move to nearby Georgia Tech and an unforgettable Cinderella championship run by Tech's archrival, Georgia, which finished last in the SEC's Eastern Division that regular season (4-12).

As Alabama and Mississippi State played in the third quarter-final game of that Friday, a rhythmic thump-thump-thump sound suddenly took attention away from the court.

"I thought a lot of people in the upper part of the arena were stomping their feet," recalled Damon Evans, then the University of Georgia athletics director.

But the thumping sound kept getting louder and louder.

Public address announcer John George wondered about air traffic into Atlanta's Hartsfield International Airport. "Good night," he thought. "Maybe an airplane is coming real close."

Referee Tony Greene heard what he thought sounded like the rumbling of a freight train locomotive. A resident of Atlanta, he knew there were railroad tracks near the Georgia Dome.

"So I look across the court, and here I see all the people in stands standing up and looking over my shoulder," he remembered. "What in the world is going on? People are standing up, and there's nothing exciting happening on the court."

Tim Brando, the lead announcer for the telecast of this Southeastern Conference Tournament game, knew what was going on.

"I knew this was a tornado," he said. "Just the sound, a freight train kind of sound."

For Brando, that unnerving sound was perversely familiar.

"Shreveport, La., is on the back end of Tornado Alley," he said of his hometown. "It's not like Oklahoma or Kansas, but we have our fair share. We've had tornadoes come over us since I was a kid."

From my courtside media seat, I heard the thump-thump-thump sound. I, too, thought the fans were creating this rhythmic sound. But when I looked across the court to the seats, the fans were looking up at the ceiling rather than down at the court.

At the moment the 2008 SEC Tournament started becoming a surreal experience, Robin Keller Hix, a member of the University of Kentucky statistics crew that worked the event each year, pointed toward the Georgia Dome ceiling. One portion of the fabric roof had been blown out of its attachment to the beam structure. She told her fellow stat counters to put their shoes on and get under the scorer's table. She sent a text message – "Take cover" – to her fiancé, Georgia basketball publicist Tim Hix, who sat with reporters across the court.

Everything hanging from the roof or beam structure was swaying.

"I look up and see the scoreboard swinging," George, the public address announcer, recalled. "You think that's got to weigh a couple tons, and it shouldn't be swinging."

Kentucky Director of Athletics Mitch Barnhart stood with his son, Scott, at the end of one of the media rows. "A really good-sized bolt" fell a few feet from Scott, Barnhart said.

"We decided at that moment it was time to go," added Barnhart, the memory flushing his face with emotion three years after the fact.

Greene had the same I'm-outta-here idea. He went to the scorer's table to say he'd be in the referees' dressing room. "I do remember laying there on a table and sort of taking a nap," he said.

When asked how he could relax enough to sleep at such a moment, Greene said, "It wasn't a deep sleep."

SEC Associate Commissioner Charles Bloom was in the locker room area under one section of stands. He heard a boom and came to the court. "I could see the scoreboard swaying," he said. "Not going from 3 to 9 o'clock, but 5 to 7 o'clock."

It was 9:40 p.m. There was 2:28 left in overtime and the Alabama and Mississippi State teams were leaving the court.

Before retreating with the players to their locker room, Alabama Coach Mark Gottfried got his wife and children out of the stands to join the team in relative safety.

Mississippi State Coach Rick Stansbury, understandably frazzled, went into the stands looking for his family.

"I forgot my two boys had been sitting on our bench," he said. "They were already headed back through the tunnel with the players."

I also wondered about my family. My wife and two sons had made attending the SEC Tournament an annual spring trip. Earlier in the day, I had gone up to their seats near the top of the lower deck. Now, I hoped being under the upper deck would protect them from anything that fell from the ceiling.

Fortunately, they got back to their hotel room after the all-clear signal was given.

Recalling that night, my wife said in 2023 that she and our sons saw cars overturned and other damage on the walk back to the hotel.

Communication was limited to cell phones. My wife said her mother and a neighbor texted her to make sure she and the boys were OK.

When my wife got in line the next morning to get her car and make the six-hour drive back to Lexington, she noticed that several cars had windows blown out. Her car had a crack across the windshield, but it was drivable, she said.

More threatening weather came the next day as my wife and sons returned to Lexington.

Meanwhile, on that long Friday night-Saturday morning, players for Kentucky and Georgia, who were scheduled to play in the next game, waited in their locker rooms. Rumors swirled.

"I was thinking it could have possibly been a terrorist attack or something," UK guard Ramel Bradley wrote in a 2011 text message from Israel where he had been playing professionally.

Mike Griesinger, a meteorologist with the National Weather Service, was sleeping in his Atlanta-area home. Threatening weather was expected the next day. As for that Friday night, there were "two little cells" in northeast Alabama late that afternoon. "Outside of that, there was nothing else out there," he said.

When Griesinger reported to work at 5 a.m. Saturday, one of his co-workers told him he'd just seen the video of the storm hitting the Georgia Dome.

Tornado strength is rated on the Enhanced Fujita Scale, from an EF0 (the mildest winds) to EF5 (the most destructive winds). The tornado that hit the Georgia Dome was an EF2. Its winds were in the 111 to 135 mph range.

It touched down just west of the Georgia Dome at 9:38 p.m., thus becoming the first tornado to hit Atlanta since records began being kept in the 1880s. It lifted off the ground at the Fulton-DeKalb County line at 9:50. In those 12 minutes, which is a typical length of time for a tornado to be on the ground, this 200-yard-wide twister cut a six-mile long scar. Damages were estimated at $150 million.

About 100 such storms hit the United States each year.

"If it had not gone where it went, we would have forgotten about it," Griesinger said. "It went through downtown Atlanta. Because of that, it's a memorable tornado."

George, who had just completed his 30th season doing the public address announcing for University of Arkansas basketball, was working his second SEC Tournament. At the time of the Gulf War in the early 1990s, he had trained with federal agents and bomb squad experts on how a public address announcer can help crowd control.

"I had to remain calm," he said, "and every two or three minutes, max, I needed to say something to what I just said. But not the same thing so the crowd would realize it's not a recording. A crowd of 15,000 to 20,000 can only be fooled for a few minutes. Once they realize the people telling them what to do are not there, they begin to panic again."

Varying word choice and cadence, George confirmed a "weather event" had occurred and advised fans to stay inside the dome. He worked without a script.

"It's really surreal," he said. "I'm sitting there. After 10 or 15 minutes, I look down both sides of stat row. I was the only one sitting there."

The announced crowd of 20,025 – the largest SEC Tournament crowd in three years – waited.

Any conversation about the 2008 SEC Tournament must mention Alabama guard Mykal Riley as an unwitting hero. He hit a three-point shot at the buzzer to send the Tide's quarter-final game with Mississippi State into overtime. If Riley had missed the shot, the game would have been over and fans would have been streaming out of the Georgia Dome when the tornado touched down.

"I really believe that three-pointer saved lives," Gottfried said. "I really do."

Georgia guard Sundiata Gaines was named the tournament's Most Outstanding player. "But the real MVP was Alabama's Riley, who rattled in a three-pointer to send the game into overtime," Ron Higgins wrote for the *The Times-Picayune* (New Orleans). "If he didn't hit that shot, a sizable portion of the crowd of almost 15,000 would have headed out the door about the time the tornado struck."

Higgins then quoted Riley as saying the next day, "I believe it was God. I keep thinking about how the ball just rolled in. It was supposed to happen so that no one would be hurt. I believe God had His hand in that to protect the people who were in the dome."

Higgins wrote about the moment the tornado hit.

"I remember being at courtside looking at State guard Ben Hansborough guarding Mykal Riley and facing the direction of where the tornado hit," Higgins wrote. "I saw Hansborough mouth the words (which I later confirmed) to Riley, 'I think that's a tornado!' Riley quickly agreed."

Higgins wrote about the light supports and a large replay screen beginning to shake.

"Further down from me at courtside on press row, a giant bolt the size of Shaquille O'Neal's fist that had been ripped from the roof rocketed to a landing between two writers without miraculously touching a soul," Higgins wrote.

Within 10 minutes, Higgins ran to the media entrance. He wrote that he saw "debris everywhere."

Mississippi State forward Charles Rhodes told him, "the last time I was that scared, a bat was in our gym."

One of Riley's teammates, Alonzo Gee, had been fouled just before the tornado hit. The teams waited for more than an hour before resuming the game with Gee shooting free throws. Talk about icing a shooter. "He missed," Gottfried said.

When asked in 2011 about being iced, Gee said, "It was crazy. But I wasn't even thinking of the free throws. I was really concerned about my family because my family was there."

Bob Holt, longtime reporter covering Arkansas basketball, was – for once – thankful that he was "a pretty slow writer." He recalled in 2023 that he had finished his game story on Arkansas' victory earlier in the day and was about 10 minutes from leaving the Georgia Dome with colleague Tom Murphy when he heard a booming sound.

"My first thought was that a plane had crashed into the Dome," he wrote in a 2023 email. "Not a terrorist attack, but just a small plane that had lost power or something . . .

"I remember being very relieved we hadn't been outside. If I had filed (the story) a few minutes faster, who knows what might have happened?"

After Mississippi State beat Alabama 69-67, SEC officials met with Georgia Dome staffers long into the wee hours of the morning. I was among a crowd of reporters who waited – and waited – for decisions. Should the tournament continue? Was the dome safe? Carl Adkins, the general manager of the dome, told the SEC that engineers and designers needed to do a thorough inspection. Coincidentally, those people were on hand to supervise an ongoing renovation. But it was decided that the dome could not be opened to the public that weekend.

Eventually, damage to the Georgia Dome was estimated at $2.2 million, a pittance compared with the $55 million damage done to the Georgia World Congress Center next door. The dome reopened in little more than a week for an Easter sunrise service held by one of the Atlanta area's megachurches.

Unlike the other teams winning in that Friday's quarter-final round, Georgia had no other way of getting an NCAA Tournament bid except by winning the SEC Tournament. So when the SEC wondered about canceling its tournament, "we really spoke out," Georgia's athletic director at the time said.

But where to play? The tornado did not damage Phillips Arena, the home of the Atlanta Hawks. But it was booked for that Saturday.

The SEC's commissioner at the time, Mike Slive, was in Indianapolis serving on the NCAA selection committee. Associate executive commissioner Mark Womack led the discussion about how and where to play the rest of the SEC Tournament.

"Since this is the 75th anniversary of our league, we figured we'd come over to Georgia Tech and invite one of our original members back in the league," Womack said of the change of venue.

Khalil Johnson, the CEO of the dome's governing body, called Paul Griffin, a senior associate athletic director at Georgia Tech. Tech and the Georgia Dome had collaborated on Atlantic Coast Conference and NCAA tournaments.

Griffin, who was at the ACC Tournament in Charlotte, N.C., saw the news of the Atlanta tornado on a television in the media workroom.

"If that's serious damage, we need to be prepared to see if we can help," he said to a Tech colleague. "By the time the sun comes up, let's be ready to do everything to help them."

Tech was closed for spring break. So its Alexander Memorial Coliseum (capacity 9,191) was available.

The SEC limited attendance at Georgia Tech to family, friends, media and anybody who had a tournament credential. Each of the remaining schools were allotted 400 admissions.

The league established a refund policy for fans who weren't allowed to attend the rest of the tournament. This resulted in a loss of almost $1.5 million in ticket revenue.

"I felt like I was at a high school tournament . . . ," Higgins wrote. "It was the second and last time Georgia won the league tourney, and basically no one was there to see it."

Once the decision was made to move to Georgia Tech, a frenzy of activity included the UK stats crew and television staffers returning to the dome to dismantle equipment, pack it and install it in Tech's arena.

Locker rooms, training rooms, media work rooms and interview space had to be cleaned and/or erected.

Griffin left Charlotte at about 4 a.m. and arrived at Alexander Memorial Coliseum at 9. He couldn't believe his eyes.

"All the people in blue jackets and blue sweaters and blue coats walking around our facility," he said. These were Kentucky fans.

Georgia Tech did not charge the SEC rent. "That's not how you treat family and neighbors in time of need," Griffin said.

At noon, Kentucky played Georgia to complete the quarter-final round.

Kentucky had already overcome a lot this season. But a tornado, a short night's sleep, scrambled reformation of the SEC Tournament format, lack of the usual Cat-mosphere, Bradley's poor shooting, an inspired opponent, a gutsy freshman's clutch shot and Gillispie's coaching gaffe proved too much to overcome.

Barely.

Georgia outlasted Kentucky 60-56 in overtime on Saturday.

Freshman Zac Swansey hit a three-pointer with 1.2 seconds left to give Georgia a 57-56 lead. He hit the shot over Ramon Harris, UK's best perimeter defender. Harris made Swansey eat up precious seconds changing direction three times as the freshman dribbled up court. But on the final change, Harris anticipated Swansey handing the ball off to junior Billy Humphrey.

Instead, Swansey pivoted and fired from the right side to put Georgia ahead. It had to be the biggest shot in a young college career for a player who had made 19 percent of his three-point attempts against SEC teams this season.

When asked how many spinning three-pointers he'd ever made, Swansey laughed and said, "Not many. I think the only time you do that is in a gym shooting by yourself. You work on stuff like that. Not really a typical game shot."

Georgia, which improved to 15-16 and kept its flickering NCAA Tournament hopes alive, sealed the victory in bizarre fashion. After Michael Porter inbounded a pass over Bradley and out of bounds, Kentucky fouled walk-on Corey Butler before Georgia could put the ball in play. Butler, an 82.8-percent free thrower, hit the first free throw with 1.2 seconds left.

Then something happened that made a tornado seem like a ho-hum regular occurrence.

Shockingly, Perry Stevenson goal-tended the second free throw attempt. That was a technical foul. Butler was awarded the free throw. Then Humphrey made one of two technical free throws to set the final score.

"It was a plan," Stevenson said of his goal-tend. The Cats did not want Georgia to purposefully miss the second free throw, thus giving Kentucky only a second or so to rebound and get off a shot. UK wanted to give Georgia the point, but have a chance to set up an inbounds play for a tying three-point basket.

When asked what he expected to achieve, Stevenson said, "Not a technical."

Gillispie took the blame. "I didn't know the rule," the UK coach said. "I didn't know it was an automatic technical. So that's my fault on that."

Only once that season (the 41-point blowout loss at Vanderbilt) did Kentucky shoot poorer than the 35.3-percent accuracy against Georgia. Bradley, UK's all-conference guard, made only four of 17 shots (one of six from three-point range).

"Let's give Georgia credit," Gillispie said after noting that Bradley made two straight down the stretch of regulation. "They played great defense. It was a very physical game on both ends, and it was hard to catch the ball. It was hard to do anything with the ball."

That the game was played marked a victory for the SEC.

The announced crowd of 1,458 – the fewest to attend a Kentucky game in many years, if not ever? – watched an unsparing, if hardly pretty, competition. The teams combined for 16 assists and 30 turnovers.

Georgia had to play overtime without its team leader, point guard Sundiata Gaines. He fouled out with 1:33 left in regulation. A surprise was Terrance Washburn, who led Georgia with 17 points after making only nine of 31 shots against UK in two regular-season games.

Bradley put UK ahead 56-54 with a foul-line jumper.

Then Swansey, who replaced Gaines, hit the big three-pointer to show Georgia the way to a second straight overtime victory in this SEC Tournament.

The shot inspired a postgame news conference question about magic.

"Well, I think it's a lot more grit and toughness and sweat than anything about magic," Georgia Coach Dennis Felton said.

Bradley remained unconvinced. "We would have won that game if it wasn't for that damn storm," he wrote in an email message.

For Georgia, it was a second straight overtime victory produced by a last-second shot.

Later that day, Georgia beat Mississippi State in the semifinals. Then in Sunday's championship game, Georgia beat Arkansas. A team that won only four SEC games in the regular season won four in four days, the final three in barely more than 24 hours.

"It was kind of fitting with everything going on around us," Evans said of Georgia's unlikely championship. "I knew anything could happen in a tournament. In that particular year, anything did happen."

Incidentally, Atlanta's forecast for the week of the SEC Tournament's return in 2011: Thursday: chance of showers, high 49, winds 22 mph gusting to 30; Friday: sunny, high 56; Saturday-Sunday: highs in the upper 60s, mostly sunny.

In 2020, I wrote another look back at the 2008 SEC Tournament.

Lexington's own Tom Hammond worked that tournament as a play-by-play announcer on Jefferson Pilot's telecasts.

"It was just an eerie feeling," he recalled. "There was just no enthusiasm whatsoever. But it was understandable because the story was about (the tornado). Nobody cared much about the basketball game."

Higgins wrote that he thought of that night every time he walked by the Georgia Dome, which was torn down in 2017.

"The first time I walked into the new Mercedes-Benz Stadium built next to where the Georgia Dome once stood, the first thing I noticed was one end of the stadium had a huge glass window with a view of downtown Atlanta," Higgins wrote. "My first thought: 'Nice view. At least they can see the tornado coming this time.'"

Coach Cal

During the 2009 SEC Tournament, I happened to intercept Billy Gillispie in the locker room area. I casually noted that being Kentucky's basketball coach was like being a celebrity. Gillispie objected to this description.

Kentucky fired Gillispie as coach a few weeks later after the team lost an NIT game.

In 2023, I asked Director of Athletics Mitch Barnhart if Gillispie's refusal to accept the star power and notoriety that goes with being UK's basketball coach played a part in the decision to change coaches.

"I don't think you really truly know till you get here and feel it," Barnhart said of this celebrity status. "There are some who will grasp it. Cal, he got it before he ever got here. He knew exactly what it was."

Barnhart was referring to John Calipari, who replaced Gillispie as Kentucky coach beginning with the 2009-10 season.

Calipari was no stranger to Kentucky fans. His UMass teams played Kentucky six times. He made an immediate impression in the first game. It came on Dec. 4, 1991, which was just two days after the Minutemen won the Great Alaska Shoot-out. So, the travel plans meant the long trip from Anchorage to Lexington, then playing Kentucky the next night.

Despite the travel, UMass was competitive. UK led 46-41 at halftime. Perhaps fatigue set in as Kentucky went on to win 90-69.

Former Kentucky player Mike Pratt, who was providing color commentary on radio broadcasts of games, was helping UK in the hiring process.

"I wanted Mike around just to listen to the basketball side of it," Barnhart said. "Mike had a really good feel and touch for this place. You know the game. You've coached it. You've played it. Tell me what you hear."

I happened to have a casual conversation with Pratt at this time. With a slight bit of concern in his voice, he mentioned that Kentucky did not have a candidate in mind to replace Gillispie.

I said that I would hire John Calipari. To which, Pratt asked about the NCAA violations that occurred during Calipari's time as UMass and then Memphis coach. I shrugged it off as old news.

Pratt never mentioned this conversation, Barnhart recalled in 2023. Meanwhile, Calipari made an immediate and positive impression when interviewing for the job.

"Oh, he commanded the room," Barnhart said. "He knew everything you needed to know about the place. He knew what it meant to lead a program of this stature. You could tell in his heart, it was something he really, really wanted. And I think any program wants to know someone wants their job. . . .

"To start a conversation with a candidate, and the first thing they said is, 'well, I'm not sure.' OK, next! The first thing I want to hear is 'I'm so excited to think of the possibility of being a Wildcat.' Perfect!"

Calipari made Kentucky synonymous with the so-called one-and-done player. To some fans' annoyance, the UK program could be seen as a waystation en route to the NBA rather than a destination.

When asked in 2023 about one-and-done players being the foundation of his Kentucky program, Calipari said, "it wasn't by design."

Calipari said his reliance on one-and-done players started with Dajuan Wagner at Memphis in the late 1990s. In checking with the NBA people, Calipari learned that Wagner would be picked in the top 10 of the 2002 NBA Draft.

"I tore up his scholarship and said you can't come back," Calipari recalled in 2023. "That's it. You've got to go."

Wagner became the sixth pick in the 2002 NBA Draft. He averaged 13.4 points as a rookie with the Cleveland Cavaliers. Although injuries cut short his career, Wagner "made a lot of money," Calipari said before adding another longer term benefit. "Because I did right by him, I got to coach his son."

That would be Dajuan Wagner, Jr., a highly-regarded prospect who would be a freshman for Kentucky in the 2023-24 season.

It would seem that one-and-done is selling something most recruits – and their families – would want. Not necessarily, Calipari said. "Some of them want more than just he'll make it (to the NBA)."

Some families want assurances that their son will be the brightest star among Kentucky stars. "Shoot all the balls," Calipari said.

John Wall set the one-and-done precedent at Kentucky. Calipari said he challenged Wall to not simply work to be taken in the next NBA Draft, but to try to help teammates follow that same here-today-gone-tomorrow route.

Calipari credited Wall with helping four teammates get drafted in 2010.

As for the UK program, advancement to the Final Four in 2011 and a national championship in 2012 showed that reliance on one-and-done players did not prevent the kind of ultra-success Kentucky fans view as routine.

"It proved that it doesn't matter," Calipari said of reliance on freshmen being a hindrance. "It just showed you could be about the guys. If they wanted to come back, just explain to me. 'Patrick, why?'"

This Patrick was Patrick Patterson, who scored 1,020 points in the two seasons before Calipari arrived in Lexington. Yet, Patterson wanted to return for a third season.

Why?

Jerry Tipton, age 10

Jerry in Hamtramck, Mich., age 10, November 1961.

Jerry takes a shot during pick-up basketball games involving Huntington *Herald-Dispatch* staffers, Feb. 17, 1978. Photo by reporter Don Ruane.

Co-workers from Huntington *Herald-Dispatch* along with players in pickup basketball games. Jerry is on the far left.

Drawing of Jerry inspired by pickup basketball in Huntington, W.Va. "HUPCO" stands for Huntington Publishing Company.

Jerry at Glacier National Park in Montana, ca. 1980s. Photos by Chris Thompson, friend from the *Huntington Herald-Dispatch*.

Caricature of Jerry for *Herald-Leader* promotions. Drawing by Camille Weber.

After covering UK sports for more than four years, Jerry Tipton has Big Blue eyes. His keen game observations, drawn from more than 12 years as a sportswriter, put his personal stamp on your *Herald-Leader's* reports of each Big Blue contest.

Before each UK game, Jerry analyzes opponents' key players, team strengths and weaknesses, and game tactics, as well as the game plan Sutton's 'Cats will employ. After the game, Jerry takes you behind the scenes for candid comments from coaches and players.

When you want to know what's happening in Big Blue sports, Jerry Tipton is there for you.

he's there for you...

LEXINGTON HERALD-LEADER

For Home Delivery, Call 253-1314 or toll free 1-800-432-9548.

Advertisement by the *Herald-Leader* to promote Jerry's coverage of UK basketball.

Jerry pitching for the *Herald-Leader* (slow pitch) softball team.

UK head football coach Jerry Claiborne speaks to the media in 1982. Jerry is pictured in the striped shirt and tie over Claiborne's right shoulder. Photo by *H-L* photographer E. Martin Jesse.

Jerry (far right in sweater vest) with Cliff Hagan, then UK athletic director. Hagan played for UK and is in the Naismith Memorial Basketball Hall of Fame. Photo by Chuck Perry.

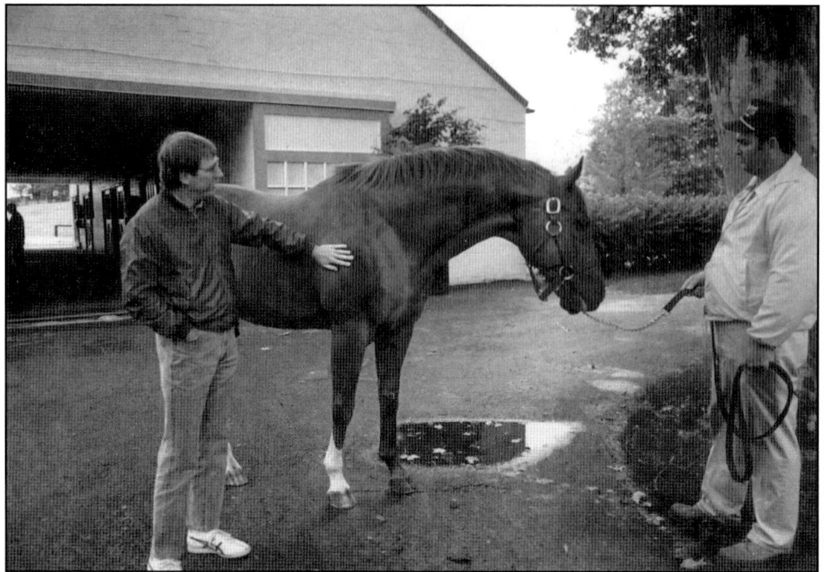

Jerry with horse-racing legend Secretariat at Claiborne Farm in Paris, Ky.

Drawing posted on the desk of Coach Eddie Sutton's administrative assistant, Marta McMackin, in which Jerry is compared to sharks circling in the water.

Jerry with Coach Rick Pitino.

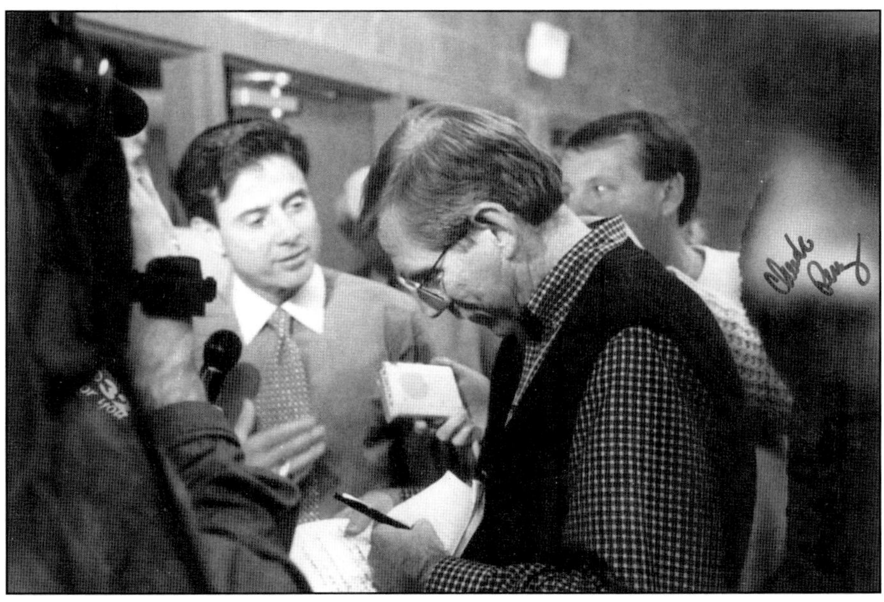

Coach Rick Pitino answers a question while Jerry (sweater vest) takes notes. Photo by Chuck Perry.

Pictured l-r: Paula Anderson, Jerry Tipton, John Clay, and Cindy Clay in 1998.

Jerry (white shirt with tape recorder) at "Billy Gillispie Day" early in his time as UK head basketball coach.

Jerry enjoys beautiful Maui, Hawaii, during the Maui Invitational basketball tournament in 2002 or 2006. Photos by Chris Thompson.

Coach John Calipari answers questions during a new conference. Jerry is seated in the third row in front of the center column.

David Byrd (left) with Jerry at Marshall's football stadium in 2003. Byrd was a friend of Jerry's and a manager on the football team during the 1970 season in which the team's plane crashed. There were no survivors. Byrd was not on the plane.

Jerry poses for a photo for a story about men and their cleaning habits and supplies at the *Herald-Leader* studio in Lexington, March 26, 2008. Photo by David Stephenson.

Jerry with UK basketball player Travis Ford. Photo by Chuck Perry.

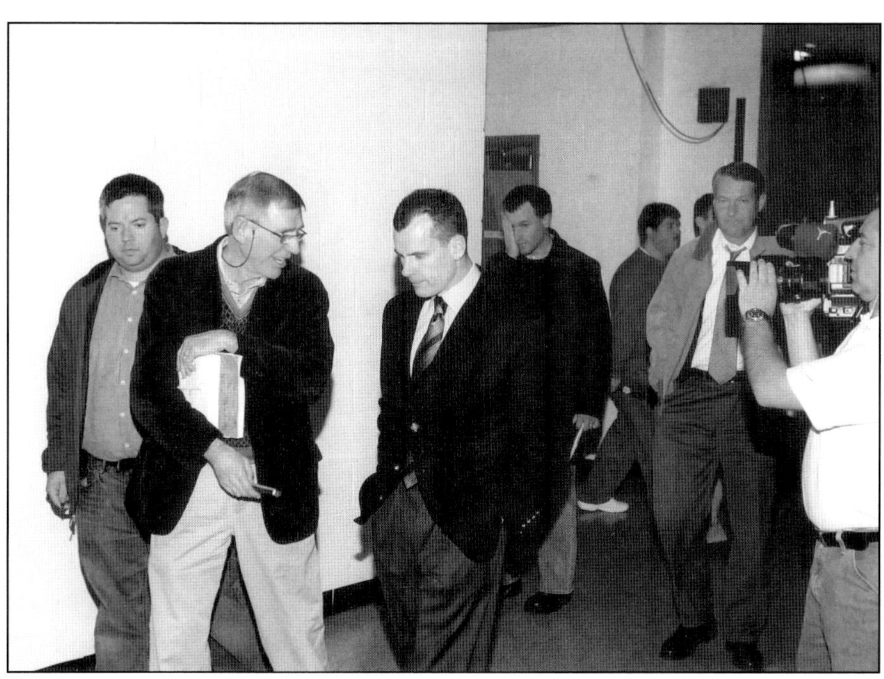

Jerry interviews then Florida Coach Billy Donovan at the SEC Media Day.

Jerry watches a UK men's basketball team practice at the Superdome in New Orleans on March 30, 2012. The practice was in preparation for a game against the University of Louisville in the NCAA Final Four. Photo by *Herald-Leader* photographer Charles Bertram.

Jerry watches a UK practice at the Superdome in New Orleans on March 30, 2012. The practice was in preparation for a Final Four game against Louisville in 2012.

Jerry and American basketball sportscaster Dick Vitale. Photo by Chuck Perry.

Jerry speaks with UK player Sam Malone during the University of Kentucky's basketball media day held on the practice floor in the Joe Craft Center on Oct. 11, 2012. Photo by *Herald-Leader* photographer Charles Bertram.

Jerry works on a story during a reunion of the University of Kentucky's 1978 championship men's basketball team held in Rupp Arena. Photo by *Herald-Leader* photographer Charles Bertram.

Jerry takes notes during a UK press conference. Photo by Chuck Perry.

Cartoon that ran protesting Jerry's coverage of UK basketball.

Jerry talks with Immanuel Quickley. Univeristy of Kentucky photo.

Jerry with his two sons, Stephen on the left and Jackson at right, at The Arboretum State Botanical Garden of Kentucky in Lexington, November 13, 2014. Photo by Charles Bertram.

Jerry after making a hole in one at a media golf outing held annually at the University of Louisville Cardinal Club, August 12, 2013. Photo by Mike Fields.

Jerry talks with Willie Cauley-Stein. University of Kentucky photo.

Kevin Grevey, Jerry, and Kenny Walker. University of Kentucky photo.

Jerry and David Byrd on the Marshall University campus in front of the memorial in remembrance of those who died in the football team's plane crash on November 14, 1970.

Jerry asks a question during a UK press conference. Photo by Chuck Perry.

Jerry during a John Calipari press conference after a Yahoo Sports report linked past (and current) UK basketball players to an FBI investigation into college basketball, February 2018. Photo by *Herald-Leader* photographer Charles Bertram.

13
KEN

Jerry and Dick Vitale before a UK basketball game.

Jerry and Rick Bozich before a UK basketball game. Rick is a former columnist with the *Louisville Courier-Journal* who now works for Louisville radio station WDRB.

Jerry was inducted into the Marshall Journalism Hall of Fame in 2018.

Headshots through the years for the *Herald-Leader*.
Photos by *Herald-Leader* photographer Charles Bertram.

Jerry in 2022 for his *Herald-Leader* retirement story. Photo by Mark Cornelison.

He told Calipari he wanted to get his degree, play at long last in the NCAA Tournament and get to show his versatility as a player.

"'I played under the basket, and you're going to let me play out on the floor,'" Calipari said, speaking in Patterson's voice.

Patterson took only four three-point shots in his first two Kentucky seasons. He missed all four. In his one season with Calipari, he made 24 of 69 (34.8 percent) and was a lottery pick (No. 14) in the 2010 NBA Draft.

During my time covering Kentucky in what could be called the one-and-done era, the national championship season of 2011-12 was the obvious pinnacle period. As a 38-2 record suggests, Kentucky was dominant. The national championship run included two always celebration-worthy victories over Louisville, the second in the Final Four semifinals.

But the SEC Tournament in Calipari's first season was memorable.

On Feb. 16, Kentucky won 81-75 in overtime at Mississippi State. I referred to it as the "plastic bottle game." State led by seven with four minutes left. From that point through overtime, 10 calls went against State and none against Kentucky. After UK won, State fans protested by throwing plastic bottles onto the court.

In the postgame news conference, I asked State Coach Rick Stansbury about that disparity. He replied by asking me if I would contribute money to help pay the fine he would get from league officials.

The 2010 SEC Tournament finals a month later gave that response new life. Referees did not detect Kentucky guard John Wall breaking into the lane early from the top of the key to try to rebound an intentionally missed free throw in the final seconds of the second half. Instead of play being stopped because of the violation Kentucky got the rebound. DeMarcus Cousins made a layup at the buzzer to send the game into overtime. UK won 75-74.

Afterward, Stansbury's frustration boiled over when he said the SEC had an ongoing invested interest in Kentucky's success. Commissioner Mike Slive fined him $30,000, which would have been tip money if Stansbury had gotten his contractual bonuses for State winning the SEC Tournament, getting the automatic NCAA Tournament bid and winning an NCAA Tournament game.

Stansbury, a Kentuckian who grew up in Meade County, had a reverence for Kentucky basketball.

"I took pride in putting our programs together at Mississippi State," he said years later. "And there was always one team in mind. And it was Kentucky. . . . That was my measuring stick all through those years."

Fast forwarding to the 2012 national championship season, Anthony Davis was dominant. He led the team in scoring (14.2 ppg), rebounding (10.4 rpg), steals (54) and blocks (186). The blocks are a UK record for a single season, and 80 more than the two players tied for second: Willie Cauley-Stein and Nerlens Noel.

I remember early in the season, Davis had not been dominating. A reporter – thankfully not me – asked Calipari about his concern about Davis' play. The expression on Calipari's face took on a are-you-kidding-me quality. It soon became evident why.

Kentucky won its first eight games, which included victories over Kansas at Madison Square Garden and North Carolina. Davis saved the latter 73-72 victory by blocking a shot in the final seconds.

Then came a memorable game at Indiana. Christian Watford made a shot at the buzzer to give Indiana a 73-72 victory.

But the action was hardly over. Fans started rushing the court at IU's Assembly Hall. The media seating was in front of a student section. As the students began rushing the court, there was no exit to take. I hovered over my computer and hoped the computer and me wouldn't be crushed by the onslaught. We got nudged, but fortunately we stayed in place.

The Indiana fans made no mystery of their disdain for Kentucky. As of 2023, that remains the last game Kentucky has played at Indiana.

Kentucky's 71-64 loss to Vanderbilt in the Southeastern Conference Tournament finals made a lasting impression. That's because of Rick Bonnell, who covered the NBA for the *The Charlotte Observer.*

I could count on Rick to help me with insights whenever the story might involve a Kentucky player and the NBA, which was frequently the case.

Rick attended the 2012 SEC Tournament in New Orleans. Before the championship game, he came to my media seat behind a sideline and asked how I thought the game would go.

I said I thought it would be competitive and Vanderbilt might win. Rick reacted with a skeptical look.

Vandy had played competitively in the two regular-season games against Kentucky, losing by six and nine points. Plus, Vandy had a center in Festus Ezeli who could compete with Davis. In two regular-season games, Ezeli had scored 28 points, grabbed 12 rebounds and blocked five shots.

Wouldn't you know it? Vandy beat Kentucky 71-64 in the SEC Tournament championship game.

When it became obvious Vandy would win, Bonnell returned to my seat and playfully bowed in recognition of my speaking of the possibility of an upset.

A much bigger surprise came in the days leading up to the Final Four, which was again in New Orleans.

Greg Bishop of *The New York Times* approached me and asked if he could do a story on me covering Kentucky. Me? I was blown away. Of course, I agreed.

Bishop was looking for off-beat stories on each of the Final Four teams: Kentucky, Kansas, Louisville and Ohio State.

True confession: It was a thrill, but also somewhat educational being the subject of a story. Afterward, I could relate better with those I interviewed.

It was odd sitting at the news conferences on Friday previewing the national semifinals and hearing Bishop ask then Louisville Coach Rick Pitino about me.

"He didn't always write good things about me, but I wasn't bothered by it," Pitino said. "He's a good guy."

Whew. I was relieved when we got to the next question.

The next season began with surprising gladness, but ended on a sad note.

Kentucky opened the 2012-13 season by beating Maryland 72-69 in Brooklyn's Barclays Center. The unlikely hero was freshman walk-on Jarrod Polson. His hometown of Nicholasville, Ky., practically borders Lexington.

In the postgame news conference, I asked Maryland Coach Mark Turgeon how much Polson figured in his team's pregame planning.

"Absolutely zero . . . ," Turgeon said. "When he subbed into the game, I said, 'Who's that?'"

Kentucky led by 15 points early in the second half. Then Maryland rallied to tie the score with more than 11 minutes remaining.

Polson, who scored six of his then career-high 10 points in the final 5:10, made two free throws with 7.7 seconds left to ease Kentucky to victory.

When asked about stepping to the foul line with the outcome of the game to be determined, Polson did not fake false bravado.

"Nah, I was nervous," he said. "I was pretty nervous (because of) not expecting to play that much."

In a follow-up story, Polson said he did not mind high-pressure situations.

"I just like that feeling of being nervous," he said. ". . . I've always liked that feeling even though it is a little scary. I feel I play better when I'm in those situations."

Polson played because starting point guard Ryan Harrow was ill.

Polson told reporters that he received more than 100 phone calls or texts in reaction to his play against Maryland. A text from former UK walk-on Cameron Mills hit home.

"Pretty cool because I looked up to him a lot," Polson said.

Polson's mother, Chrisi, planned to attend the Maryland game. But the weather forecast for New York called for Hurricane Sandy followed by a northeaster. She decided to cancel the drive from Nicholasville to Brooklyn. His parents watched the game telecast.

"All of a sudden, it was all about him," George Polson said of his son. "I turned to my wife and said, 'Can you believe we're sitting here listening to Dick Vitale and Digger Phelps talk about our son, and he's the difference in the game?'

"It is surreal. Sort of like high school all over again, but on steroids."

Technically, that season ended on March 19. But it really ended on Feb. 12.

That's when Nerlens Noel tore an anterior cruciate ligament during a 69-52 loss at Florida.

Two weeks earlier, Noel made me think of Bill Russell. No other player did that before or since. In a 87-74 victory at Ole Miss, he scored only two points, but grabbed seven rebounds and blocked a UK record 12 shots.

I didn't fully appreciate what his absence would mean. That became clear four nights later in a 88-58 loss at Tennessee. It was Tennessee's biggest margin of victory in a border state series that spans more than 200 games. My game story hit the theme of a preview of what Kentucky's remaining schedule would look like without Noel.

Kentucky was 17-6 with a healthy Noel. But only 4-6 without him.

The season concluded with a 59-57 loss at Robert Morris in the NIT first round. My vivid memory of that game was in the final minute seeing myself alone on press row as Robert Morris fans gathered to rush the court in celebration. My colleagues anticipated the rush and retreated to the media workroom. Fortunately, no damage was done.

I remember asking Calipari in the postgame news conference if he was glad to get a season without Noel finished. He said that wasn't the case.

Kentucky made amends the following season with a run to the 2014 Final Four capped by a 60-54 loss to Connecticut in the championship game. Florida had beaten Kentucky three times that season, but UConn rallied to beat the Gators in the semifinals.

Kentucky made history in the 2014-15 season by winning the first 38 games.

"While you're going through it, you knew how unprecedented everything was," recalled Joel Justus, the Director of Analytics that season and later an assistant coach. "I had been part of basketball for 30-some years at that point. Winning one game is really hard, much less winning 38 in a row."

Kentucky was good, but not as invincible as the won-loss record suggested. UK needed overtime to win a home game against Ole Miss. It helped when Ole Miss's leading scorer that night, guard Stefan Moody, cramped late in the second half and had to go to the bench rather than shoot clutch free throws. Kentucky got to pick who shot – and missed – the free throws.

Four nights later, Kentucky needed double overtime to win at Texas A&M.

Of all things, how Kentucky substituted also marked the 2014-15 season as distinctive.

Because twins Aaron and Andrew Harrison surprised everyone by returning for their sophomore seasons, Kentucky had an over-abundance of players.

Calipari decided to use a platoon system of substitution. He used six exhibition games in the Bahamas during the summer of 2014 as a time to experiment. Mass substitutions occurred about every four minutes.

As Tyler Ulis recalled in 2023, the players needed time to adjust.

"At the beginning, we're McDonald's All-Americans," he said of several incoming freshmen that season. "We didn't know the twins were coming back. . . . Obviously, we wanted to start and play 30-plus minutes.

"I don't think me and 'Book' (fellow freshman Devin Booker) ever had a time where we were, like, thinking about not coming (to practice or games). It was tough, you know. You want to play. You're playing four minutes at a time. But once you start winning, what can you say? 38-0. Yeah! Everybody's got to be happy at some point. So, it was fun."

In 2023, Justus credited Calipari with having the willingness to depart from the norm.

"For Cal to have that kind of foresight, I thought was genius," Justus said. "And how he managed it day by day was genius. That was such a unique year when you get that many good players on the same team. But I don't think that's something that's very sustainable."

That thought was the subject of much debate in a loss to Wisconsin in the 2015 Final Four.

But a key game I thought got overlooked was a tense 68-66 victory over Notre Dame in the Elite 8. The Irish led much of the first 30 minutes. But led by Karl-Anthony Towns' low-post dominance (25 points), Kentucky rallied to gain what seemed an improbable victory. I recall the UK players leaving the court with a stunned, but relieved look on their faces.

"I feel like that was the game we definitely should have lost," Ulis recalled, "and not Wisconsin."

Interestingly, Towns came to Kentucky with a reputation for being a face-the-basket shooter. Justus noted how Towns trusted Calipari and assistant coach Kenny Payne with developing a low-post game.

The loss to Wisconsin stirred fan emotion because Ulis and Booker were on the bench while the Harrison twins played down the stretch. Kentucky was called for two shot clock violations which helped the Badgers win 71-64.

Justus said he did not know precisely why the twins played and the freshmen sat. But he added that a case could be made for that decision.

The twins had won a lot of games for Kentucky. Each scored double-figure points against Wisconsin. Andrew, the point guard, had a 4-to-1 assist-to-turnover ratio. Ulis and Booker each scored six points.

When asked in 2023 about sitting on the bench, Ulis said, "it was tough. But, honestly, if people kind of go back to the game, you feel Andrew was having the best game. 'Book' got a few fouls.

"But I'd definitely like to be in at the end. But, hey, that's tough. That's still tough to this day."

Kentucky returned to the Bahamas for more exhibition games in the summer of 2018. I wrote a story referencing a similar trip in 2014 during which Calipari experimented with a platoon system of substitution for a team with abundant depth.

I began the 2018 story by writing: If you feel the urge to singe tender ears in Kentucky's basketball program, there's a word much worse than an F-bomb.

Whatever you do, don't associate Kentucky with the platoon system of substitution.

"No," associate coach Kenny Payne said in a scolding voice. "Don't say that word. We are not platooning. Coach (Calipari) says we don't want to go through that ever again."

A roster bursting with talent accepted mass substitutions at regular intervals as a fact of basketball life in the 2014-15 season. Winning the first 38 games made platoons a much-ballyhooed part of Kentucky basketball that season.

But the P-word became a derogatory term when rival recruiters used platoons as an argument against UK. Don't go to Kentucky, they said, if you want to play more than 20 minutes a game.

When asked in 2018 if the P-word was verboten in the UK program, Payne said, "Yeah. Yeah. We don't want to go through that again."

My final three seasons covering Kentucky served as further proof that you have to expect something memorable will happen regularly.

The opening game of the 2018-19 season was a stunner. Led by Zion Williamson, Duke beat Kentucky 118-84. The Blue Devils won each half by an identical score of 59-42.

The first television timeout of the second brought something I thought I'd never see. Kentucky fans began walking up aisles and heading for the exit. Besides UK getting routed, another factor had to be the 10 p.m. start to the game.

Of course, the coronavirus canceled the SEC and NCAA tournaments in 2020. Calipari spoke of Kentucky having a real chance to win both.

My last season (2021-22) saw Kentucky post a 28-8 record. But the season was hardly seamless.

Kentucky got off to a roaring start. In mid-December, Kentucky routed North Carolina 98-69 in Las Vegas.

Then in late January, Kentucky rolled to an 80-62 victory at Kansas.

Kellan Grady credited early-season losses to Duke and at Notre Dame as key.

"A lot of people were questioning how good we were," he said. "I think that was kind of a catalyst for our season.

"By the end of January, middle of February, I thought we were arguably the best team in the country. I thought a lot of people also believed that, especially after we went into Phog Allen Fieldhouse and were up 51-31 at halftime.

"So, it was really cool and fulfilling and rewarding, frankly, to see how everybody really became stars in their roles."

Fans will not easily forget how the season ended.

Kansas beat North Carolina in the championship game of the 2022 NCAA Tournament.

Meanwhile, Kentucky lost to 15-seed Saint Peter's in the first round.

Injuries to guards Sahvir Wheeler and TyTy Washington were factors, Grady said.

"That rhythm that we had then I think was disrupted a little bit," he said. "And once we put the pieces back together, I just don't think we had the same jazz to our team."

Fortunately, I recalled before the Saint Peter's game that former UK player Scott Padgett was on the staff at Manhattan. Saint Peter's was in the same league.

So, I called Padgett and asked for his assessment of Saint Peter's. He was more than willing to help and practically gave me a scouting report.

He noted Saint Peter's competitive toughness, defense first mindset and quality guards. I came away thinking it would be a competitive game, but Kentucky would take control at some point, probably in the second half.

But as the game remained close heading into the final minutes of the second half, I knew either team would win.

Helped by Kentucky missing free throws, Saint Peter's won 85-79 in overtime.

Grady scoffed at my suggestion that the game showed how there was greater parity in college basketball.

"If we played them nine more times, I think we would have won all nine," he said. "I firmly believe that. It was their night that night. We didn't show up to play at a high enough level."

The sting of that loss had not subsided more than a year later.

"Every time I talk about it, it feels too soon," Grady said.

Nor did Grady get much relief from Saint Peter's subsequent advancement to the Elite 8.

"To a degree it makes it look not quite as bad," he said. "But at the end of the day, we were a 2-seed, and we deserved that 2-seed. . . . But, no, it still sucks. There's no doubt. And it always will."

In a sense, Kentucky's loss to Saint Peter's was a fitting punctuation to my time covering the program.

It was never boring, especially when Calipari was coach.

His sometimes uneasy relationship with referees hit a peak in the 2015-16 season.

The coach-referee dynamic had been a continuing theme that Kentucky basketball season.

Doug Sirmons' ejection of Calipari at South Carolina inside the game's first four minutes and Pat Adams' technical foul on Isaac Humphries at Texas A&M put referees front and center. Sort of like a punching bag in front of a boxer.

Author Bob Katz tried to humanize referees in a book titled *The Whistleblower: Rooting for the Ref in the High-Stakes World of College Basketball.*

Katz laughed when I asked if defending referees made him something of a modern-day Don Quixote.

"It's less defending than illuminating what they do," he said. "It is my belief that what they do requires something like athletic skills and managerial shrewdness. How do we make the games fair in the midst of confusion and not an inconsiderable amount of deliberate deception?"

J.D. Collins, the NCAA coordinator of men's basketball officiating, summed it up in a quote from *The Whistleblower.* He said, "Our job is to absorb the chaos, create calm and provide hope that the outcome will be fair."

Of course, players and coaches are not keenly interested in fairness. They want advantage, and are willing to go to great lengths to achieve it: Flopping, pointing to indicate the decision about possession should go their way, flailing arms, screaming in pseudo pain, sideline tirades, flinging off sports coats.

Katz said referees and coaches inevitably clash. They have different missions.

"Coaches understand working the refs is part of their strategy," he said. "They want to get favorable treatment down the stretch (of games). They don't want the refs to forget they're there. The refs, of course, want to ignore them.

"They're on a collision course."

After the South Carolina game, Sirmons did not work another Kentucky game for some time. This raised the question of whether a referee involved in a particularly contentious situation should be quietly removed from assignments involving that team in the immediate future. Katz thought so.

"My guess is there's no need to set up that collision for a while," he said. "So, let's avoid it for a while."

Katz said that referees are not happy when one of their brethren ejects a coach. "Provoking coaches is too easy," he said the refs believe. "It shouldn't be done."

During his radio call-in show, Calipari lamented how opponents had shot more free throws in the 2015-16 season. Opponents hadn't shot more free throws than Kentucky in a season since 2007-08.

As formerly UK's Director of Analytics, Justus said a key was shooting more free throws than opponents.

Calipari downplayed the notion that a lack of a low-post game that season reduced Kentucky's chances of getting to the foul line.

"Some (opponents) may jam it in the post," he said. "Well, we're driving it into the post. It's the same deal."

Calipari said it might appear at times that Kentucky is playing "against eight," which Katz called "a complete mischaracterization of the function of the refs. And he knows that."

Calipari's speech to fans attending the Big Blue Madness in 2013 sparked a story lead I liked.

It read: Today we ponder John Calipari: the man, the Mist.

Former Georgia Coach Hugh Durham laughed uncontrollably when told how Calipari mentioned the Blue Mist in his state-of-the-program speech at Madness.

Said Calipari: "The Big Blue Nation extends far beyond the hallowed halls of college basketball's greatest arena. It's a nation that stretches across 120 counties in Kentucky, all 50 states and to every country in the world.

"We are borderless. We are everywhere. No corner is left untouched by the Blue Mist."

Durham, who coined the term Blue Mist more than 20 years earlier, reacted by flashing his signature sense of humor.

"There's a lot of people who think Calipari is full of (pause) a lot of stuff," he said. "Now we know it's just Blue Mist."

Rather than oozing into and out of every nook and cranny, Durham said that the Blue Mist is concentrated in Rupp Arena.

"Let's be honest about it," he said. "Kentucky is Kentucky. All 50 states? Give me a break."

For example, Indiana and Kansas have their own forms of mist, Durham said.

As for Kentucky, he said, "You don't hear anybody talk about the Blue Mist in football season. It must be an indoor disease."

Durham, who grew up in the Louisville area as a fan of Kentucky's Fabulous Five, first mentioned there being a Blue Mist in Rupp Arena during a postgame news conference. It was a way for him to discreetly comment on the officiating.

"It starts at the top (of Rupp Arena) and starts to come down," he recalled. "Pretty soon it changes the color of the officials' shirts from black and white to blue and white."

Durham cited two calls within a few minutes of each other, one favoring Georgia and one Kentucky. Both were correct calls, he said, but the referees made the calls in strikingly different ways. On the call favoring Georgia, the referee was subdued. "Almost apologetic," Durham said.

On the call favoring Kentucky, the referee's body language spoke of enthusiastic approval.

The Blue Mist could also affect reporters, said Durham, who added, "They look through mist-colored glasses."

Dependence on one-and-done players and having a keen sense of marketing possibilities seemed to make Calipari something of a polarizing figure.

That contributed to an under appreciation for sacrifices made by UK players in the platoon system of substitution, ESPN commentator Jay Bilas said in 2015.

"Some of it is John Calipari, frankly," Bilas said. "People have views of John, and they're entitled to like or dislike him. I have zero problem with that. That's a matter of taste. I happen to like John very much, and I don't like people . . . questioning why I like him."

Kentucky Fans are "Passionate" and "Spoiled"

While the media should adopt an objective distance, Kentucky fans are the polar opposite. They are – duh – zealous.

My favorite story about Kentucky fans dates back to the 1980s. Because I had started doing a Sunday notes column, the search for material to fill up the space was almost non-stop. This was especially true during – quaint reference alert – the off-season.

At the time, I thought *Street & Smith* was *the* preseason magazine for the upcoming college basketball season. I don't remember the year, but when I saw that Kentucky was ranked No. 2 in its preseason top 25 poll, a call to the editor, Jim O'Brien, seemed like a good idea. The obvious question: Why did Street & Smith rate Kentucky so highly?

O'Brien said Kentucky would have good guard play and its big men made for a better front line than most teams figured to possess.

I immediately thought I needed something else to enhance the note. After a moment's thought, I asked how Kentucky fans had reacted to *Street & Smith* ranking the Wildcats No. 2. I expected a happy, upbeat reaction.

Oh, they're really mad, O'Brien said of the feedback.

This was a surprise. So, I asked why Kentucky fans were not happy with the magazine's poll.

They can't believe we ranked Kentucky so low, O'Brien said.

No. 2.

In 2023, I bounced that exchange off Dan Wann, a psychology professor at Murray State University who helped me whenever stories involved fans. In the fall of 2023, he began his 33rd year teaching sports psychology, sports fan psychology and social psychology.

When I told him about Kentucky fans being upset with a No. 2 ranking, Wann said, "Exactly. That's outstanding. How dare you put us down there with the hopeless?"

Of course, preseason rankings – and rankings during much of the season – are meaningless, Wann said before adding a qualifier. "But if you think your program is the best, then how dare someone insult you by saying you're the second best."

During my 41 seasons covering Kentucky basketball, fans many times made me wonder if I could really understand them.

I asked Wann how he would describe Kentucky basketball fans.

"I definitely think 'passionate' is a word that immediately comes to mind," he said before a moment later explaining why he thought that was accurate. "They travel so well. And it's statewide. There's more love for Kentucky basketball in Murray than there is for Murray State basketball.

"All these years I've been doing this research, I don't ask their level of fandom for Murray State as often as I ask their level of fandom for Kentucky because I get more rabid fans that way."

Wann also used another word to describe Kentucky fans.

"Right after 'passionate' (comes) 'spoiled,'" he said. "But I don't necessarily mean that in a negative connotation. . . . Fan bases would rather be spoiled than not."

In this regard, Wann likened Kentucky fans to fans of the New York Yankees, Kansas basketball and Ohio State football.

I've thought of such rabid rooting as the sportsworld's version of a legal term: crimes of passion. In each case, passion leads a person to do something he or she would otherwise not do.

"Absolutely," Wann said. "Fans don't wake up one morning and decide, hey, it's a Kentucky basketball game tonight. Here's another opportunity to embarrass myself and my family.

"But their passion wraps themselves up so much into the event."

Wann pleaded guilty of such a crime of athletic passion. He recalled a fan's reaction when an unhappy Murray State player, Vince Rainey, chased a referee.

"The fan was yelling, 'punch him, Vince, punch him,'" Wann said. "And I always follow that up by saying that wasn't my best moment. I was really embarrassed I was up there yelling that."

Wann grew up in the Kansas City area, got an undergraduate degree from Baker College before receiving a PhD in social psychology at the University of Kansas in 1991.

Why study fan psychology?

"It was a combination of a few things," Wann wrote in a text message. "First, I knew that when I got to KU for my doctoral program in social psychology, that I would need to start a research program. I wanted to pick something I was interested in and I'd always been a sports fan. So that made sense.

"Additionally, very few (like nobody, lol) were systematically studying the psychology of sports fandom. So, I thought I could carve out a niche for myself. And given that so many people are sports fans – as in BILLIONS – , I figured people might be interested in what I found in my research."

Wann seemed thoroughly entertained as I asked him about several examples of Big Blue Nation passion that I've observed.

In the summer of 2014, the Kentucky team went to the Bahamas to play six exhibition games. I went to cover the games via a travel package offered to fans.

Kentucky won the first five games, but then lost the sixth game. Early the next morning, our group boarded a bus for the trip to the Nassau airport to catch the flight home.

I sat silently after making eye contact with a fan who proceeded to express his unhappiness with Kentucky losing. He capped his criticism by saying, "Cal is running out of excuses."

My immediate thought was that Coach John Calipari had led Kentucky to a national championship only two years earlier. But I remained silent and kept my head down.

"That was a combination of passion and spoiled . . . ," Wann said. "The fans are so used to success that they just expect it at a level that's not reasonable."

In the summer of 2018, Kentucky played four exhibition games in the Bahamas. I learned that fans were being charged $100 for a game ticket. And that UK required each fan to buy four tickets. That figured out to be $800 for a couple and $1,600 for a mother, father and two children. Then Deputy Director of Athletics DeWayne Peevy said the money was used to ensure better competition by paying a portion of the other teams' travel expenses.

When I checked on how much some other blueblood programs charged their fans for similar exhibition trips, I was told the tickets were either free or much less costly.

I bounced that off some Kentucky fans in the Bahamas. One fan told me if, say, Kansas charged $100 a ticket, he'd pay $200 for UK.

"That's just a point of pride," Wann said. "You can't search for any logic in this. This is void of any logic because it doesn't make any sense. . . . It's how can you show that your fan base is the best fan base? Well, because we're willing to spend the most money."

In 1988, Kentucky played in the Great Alaska Shootout. A fan told me he drove to the game. He said driving through Canada was the best route to take. A drive from Lexington to Anchorage is about 3,935 miles.

"They should have bought an Atlas and called a travel agent because there's no way they saved money on that," Wann said. "If you say it's a three-week trip and you're retired, I get that. But if you're saying we travel (to see the games) and we don't like to fly, you better hope they're not playing in Puerto Rico."

One summer when C.M. Newton was Kentucky's Director of Athletics, the NCAA put a priority on saving money. This inspired me to write a tongue-in-cheek suggestion: Kentucky could save money on road games by staying at the second-best hotel at the site.

This led a woman to send me a note saying she would contribute to a fund to ensure that the Kentucky team stayed at the best hotels.

"How dare you?" Wann facetiously said of my suggestion of the UK team staying at the second-best hotels. "And you know what, she would have. For all we know, she did."

I remember a Kentucky player struggling to make free throws. I believe it was Andre Riddick, who made only 41.3 percent of his free throws in his college career (1991-92 through 1994-95).

During that time, a fan called into Rick Pitino's weekly radio show. The fan offered advice on how Riddick could improve his free throw accuracy. By banking in the shots, the fan said.

For me, this was a case of someone knowing just enough to be dangerous. Banking the ball off the glass is a good idea when shooting from an angle. But banking the ball when shooting a foul shot would make it more difficult, not less.

"They don't make fans take tests, right?" Wann said. "On any level of knowledge, (the school) will take your money and give you a ticket."

Tubby Smith's first season as Kentucky coach saw at least one fan flunk. Kentucky lost to Ole Miss 73-64 on Valentine's Day, 1998. It was only the second home game Kentucky had ever lost to the Rebels. The first came in 1927.

While Kentucky's record fell only to 22-4, a fan called into the post-game radio show and proclaimed the Wildcats the worst 22-4 team he had ever seen.

Tom Leach, the radio play-by-play announcer and host of the postgame radio show, later likened the comment to "dating the least attractive supermodel."

Kentucky did not lose another game. A 13-game winning streak to end the season was capped with the 1998 national championship.

"I wonder what he was saying then," Wayne Turner, the point guard on that UK team said in 2023 about the fan.

In 2007, Kentucky hired Billy Gillispie as its new coach. This led to an interesting comment by a fan. It occurred at an annual fun experience for fans. There was a campout outside the on-campus gymnasium, Memorial Coliseum, for free tickets to Big Blue Madness, which was the fans' first chance to see the upcoming season's players on a court.

I went to the campout each October to chat with fans and try to fashion a feature story.

It was already known that Gillispie was not married. I overheard a fan say it was a good thing that Gillispie was not married. A wife is a distraction, the fan said.

In 2023, I asked Marsha Poe, a retired postal worker and regular participant at the campout, if she thought the fan really meant that.

"Oh yeah, they mean it," she said of startling fan comments.

It didn't take long for a fan to question Gillispie's coaching. It came during Big Blue Madness, which is more showmanship than any kind of setting for basketball assessment. During a scrimmage, little if any defense is played. The players run and jump and dunk pretty much at will.

Yet, I heard a fan complain. The basis of the griping was the well-chronicled fan complaints about the offense played under the guidance of the previous coach, Tubby Smith.

Gillispie's first Madness scrimmage, if you want to call it that, was only a minute or two old when I heard a fan grouse, "It looks like Tubby ball."

This did not surprise Wann.

"Ok, yeah, what I think about that response is this: they do not require you to take a test to be a fan of the team," he said. "In other words, you can have some pretty unknowledgeable sports fans out there that are diehard."

The psychology professor agreed with me that a Madness celebration is not a setting to make any kind of assessment.

"It also looks like everybody else's Midnight Madness," he said of Kentucky's basketball show. "At that time, it also looked like Bill Self basketball. Roy Williams basketball. Mike Krzyzewski basketball."

When I suggested that Madness does not really look like the basketball you would see in a season, Wann said, "that's better yet. It looks like NBA All-Star Game basketball, which to your point also does not look like basketball."

As noted at the beginning of this chapter, Calipari has not been immune to fan complaints despite the 2012 national championship and three other advancements to Final Fours.

One memorable moment along these lines came in the 2014-15 season. On Feb. 10, Kentucky won 71-69 at LSU.

The coach's weekly radio call-in show aired the next night. For whatever reason, assistant coach John Robic substituted for Calipari on the show. It was their 17th season on the same coaching staff.

A caller said he had thought of ways the Kentucky team could improve. The show's host, Tom Leach, asked the caller to share how there could be improvement.

The caller had a long list. After about six or seven pieces of, uh, advice, he seemingly paused to take a breath.

Robic used the moment of silence to calmly remind the caller and the radio audience, "we're not doing that badly."

I chuckled. The victory at LSU improved Kentucky's record to 24-0. Eighteen of the victories had come by a double-digit margin.

"These stories just resonate with me because I've been studying this stuff for 35 years," Wann said. "Nothing is ever good enough. Plus, I think sports fandom is that passionate, they all think they have the answers, right?"

Wann put this in perspective.

"There are people who have gone to over 100 Grateful Dead concerts," he said. "Do they sit out there and complain about the order of the songs that were sung? I don't know. Maybe they do. But certainly fans, they all think they have the answers. And they think of the answers before any questions are asked.

"If you're 24-0, everybody in sports who knows anything would say you would never change a thing."

Wann then quoted Crash Davis, the character Kevin Costner played in the baseball movie Bull Durham: "I told him that a player on a streak has to respect the streak."

Kentucky's winning streak that season ended in the Final Four. A 71-64 loss to Wisconsin in the national semifinals included a startling inconsistency from some fans.

In the days leading up to Selection Sunday, I heard about fan complaints that the NCAA would try to thwart Kentucky by putting Big Ten champion Wisconsin in the same region.

That didn't happen. Kentucky was the No. 1 seed in the Midwest Region. Wisconsin was the No. 1 seed in the West Region.

But after Wisconsin beat Kentucky in the Final Four, fans sounded stunned that the Badgers could win the game.

Huh?

Wann cited two observations. "There's no logic there whatsoever," he said before adding, "No. 2, fans are constantly looking for ways to protect their ego if their team loses. . . . It's way easier to say we lost because the NCAA is against us than it is to say we lost because we just can't seem to find a way to a championship anymore."

More than once leading into Selection Sundays, Calipari (playfully?) hinted that the NCAA would try to stack the path so as to prevent Kentucky from advancing to the Final Four and a national championship.

Wann scoffed at that notion.

"It cracks me up . . . ," the sports psychology professor said. "The NCAA wants Kentucky playing (in the tournament). Kentucky travels. The NCAA wants stories. The Loyolas, the Saint Peter's, that's good, too. But Saint Peter's is not selling out the arenas and the hotels and the restaurants during the week of the Sweet Sixteen."

Kentucky lost to Saint Peter's in the first round of the 2022 NCAA Tournament.

Fans complained that Calipari did not call a timeout before the last possession of regulation. He said on several occasions that he does not like to call a timeout in such a situation because it gives the opponent a chance to make an adjustment/ spring a surprise.

When I later saw the Celtics not call a timeout yet win a playoff game by seemingly improvising a last-second layup, I decided to do a note. Basketball has been played for more than 100 years. If there was only one way to handle a decisive last possession, it would be settled by now that a timeout should or should not be called. Either approach can work. Either can fail.

This sparked angry emails accusing me of defending Calipari rather than pointing out the coach's supposed mistake.

"No, there isn't going to be perspective and logic," Wann told me. "Have you not learned?"

Another thought came to mind. Fans usually blame the coach and seldom, if ever, blame players.

"Never," Wann said. "Because the players are who they are living through. They're identifying with the players."

Wann added that fans do identify with some coaches. He mentioned San Antonio Spurs Coach Gregg Popovich as an example.

"But in the vast majority of scenarios, kids that are going to go try to grab an autograph at Kentucky, I'm not saying no one is running up to Calipari," Wann said. "But no kid is going to Walmart in Lexington and grabbing a Calipari jersey."

Rick Pitino had an interesting relationship with fans. If he thought a fan was ridiculous, he might say so. One example involved Richie Farmer, an iconic high school player idolized by fans.

On one of his radio shows, a caller asked Pitino to speculate on what kind of NBA career Farmer would have. Pitino ridiculed the suggestion that Farmer, a 6-foot guard, would have an NBA career.

The fans seemed to like being corrected.

"They can change the narrative later on when they were telling their friends, well, I had a good conversation with Kentucky's basketball coach," Wann said. "Make it sound like they helped out with game planning or something."

I asked if even a reprimand can be a good thing if seen as a form of acknowledgement.

"Exactly," Wann said. "Being told you're an idiot by your hero is better than never being able to talk to your hero, I suppose."

This is not to say Kentucky fans are a hindrance or a nuisance.

Joel Justus, a Kentucky basketball staffer during Calipari's time as coach for seven seasons, applauded how much the Big Blue Nation feels invested in the program.

"That's great," he said. "And that's what you want. When you're in our line of work, you want to be where people care because the opposite is way worse."

I've heard coaches welcome how the fan interest translates into ticket sales, leaving the coaches free to concentrate on basketball.

From the media standpoint, surely every reporter wants to cover a beat that intensely interests the readers. I've thought of how it seemed every reader was like a copy editor. Kentucky fans who can be judgmental about every double dribble also seem to be checking for spelling errors or mistakes in facts. Not that mistakes were eliminated, but fan zeal further motivated my effort to get the story right.

Sam Bowie credited the Kentucky fans for helping him with a stress fracture that sidelined him for the 1981-82 and 1982-83 seasons.

"During that two-year ordeal, without the support, it would have been much more difficult," Bowie said in 2023. "I was at a convenience store in Lexington. There was a kid. When you're 7-feet, you can't hide and a lot of people knew me. . . . I remember signing a cast (for) a kid seven or eight years old on the leg. The other leg there was no cast because his leg was gone. It's easy to say it puts it in perspective. So, no way I can say, why me? That sums it up. He thought he had three legs after we got done taking pictures and talking (about) Kentucky basketball. His mother and father were so thankful."

Scott Padgett, who scored 1,252 points over four seasons in the 1990s, noted that Kentucky did not have a monopoly on rabid fans. Arkansas fans stood out in his memory.

"Like going to Arkansas and they're chanting "Wooo pig sooie" at 3 in the morning outside our hotel," he recalled in 2023. "My first year in '95, . . . loudest I ever heard an arena. I was standing two feet from Coach Pitino and I couldn't hear a word he was saying. It was a good thing I wasn't playing because I didn't know what he was saying.

"Then I remember '97. We went into the tunnel to go into the arena, and they were up in the overpass throwing snowballs at us. So we threw them back as we were going in."

That T-shirts displaying the words "I Still Hate Laettner" continue to sell well at a Lexington store more than 30 years after the Duke star made the winning shot against Kentucky in the 1992 NCAA Tournament region final surely says something about the zeal of Kentucky fans.

"That's outstanding," Wann said. "It's almost like a badge of honor."

Hard Questions

Somehow I gained a reputation for asking "hard questions." That was not my intent. I wanted to ask "good questions" or "pertinent questions."

The goal was to improve the story. I might wonder what questions readers might have. Then, sometimes after taking a breath to steady myself, ask the question.

Perhaps it was a fitting conclusion to my time covering Kentucky basketball that I asked such a question during my last post-game news conference. It came after Kentucky's 85-79 overtime loss to Saint Peter's in the first round of the 2022 NCAA Tournament.

Sitting near the Kentucky bench, which was a nice change from media seats being much farther from the court in the regular season, I felt I had a better feel for how the game transpired. It seemed obvious that if Kellan Grady had made more than one of nine shots (one of seven from three-point range) Kentucky would have won.

So, in the news conference I asked him why he had been shooting poorly (two for 17 and one of 12 from three in the last two games, plus six of 29 from three in the last seven games) and what impact this had in Kentucky's season-ending defeat.

As I expected, Grady responded thoughtfully.

"If I could pinpoint it exactly, I wouldn't have shot like crap," he said. "I feel bad I couldn't help – in a better fashion – us win.

"But it is what it is."

Later that night angry emails reminded me that fans can watch news conferences on the Internet.

Ross got to the point.

"That was a pretty lame question to ask Kellan after the game," he wrote in the email. "I get you think you have to ask the 'tough' questions because you're an old decrepit jerk. But this guy was clearly in his head for the past month, and you asking that stupid question I'm sure really helps his confidence.

"I'm sure you were the happiest guy in the world when UK lost tonight. Can't wait for you to retire. Won't be long."

Ross ended the email by saying I had a small penis.

If a reader took the time to send me an email, I always tried to reply. I thanked Ross for the email and said I would ask the *Herald-Leader* sports editor and other reporters what they thought of the question I asked Grady.

"I meant no disrespect and I thought Kellan handled it well," I wrote.

Another email came from Ray. I noticed it included several F bombs including more than one F you directed at me.

Near the end, Ray wrote that he doubted I'd read his entire email. Then he ended it by writing, "I hope you lose your job and someone else reads this so it doesn't go to waste."

I read Ray's entire email twice, the second time to count the F-bombs. There were six.

I sent Ray a response that read: "Thanks for the email (I mean that). And I read it to the end. I will ask my editor and colleagues about the question. That kind of review is typical. For what it's worth, I thought Kellan handled it well."

In a response to my email, Ray apologized for his "vulgar language." He said he still disliked my question, "but should've had my emotions a little more in check."

Ray added that Grady handled the question "perfectly and like a true professional."

In 2023, I spoke to Grady and asked him about my question in the news conference.

"Honestly, that's your job," he said, "and your job is to ask, 'Hey, Kellan, . . . you shot like crap today. Do you think that had an effect on the overall team performance?' Well, of course it did."

Grady acknowledged not being in the best of moods during the news conference.

"I think that frustration came more from our result and had nothing to do with the question you asked," he said. "I was not offended by that."

When I reached out to Ray and Ross in 2023, they both apologized for the emotional emails they sent after the game.

Mike Johnson, the *Herald-Leader* sports editor who hired me, did not mind me asking pointed questions. "One of the things I knew we needed in the job was you had to ask hard questions," he said in 2023.

Gene Abell, who followed Johnson as sports editor, agreed.

"I thought you were there just asking the obvious question," he said in 2023. "Later on, you were going to wait to see if somebody else was going to ask the question. And if then if they didn't, 'OK, I'm going to have to do it.'"

In John Clay's 2022 story announcing my retirement, Abell said much the same thing.

"Jerry asked the tough questions," Abell said in the story. "He was not trying to win a popularity contest. He covered teams as a journalist, not a fan. He was targeted on gathering all the information possible and being accurate. Coaches may disagree with him but I am confident they respected and admired him. His worth ethic was unparalleled. He was tough but fair."

When speaking with Rex Chapman, I noted my reputation for asking, "hard questions." To which he injected, "which is ridiculous. Really. I mean the questions that you ask are legitimate questions."

Well after Chapman had moved on to the NBA, he happened to be at a practice the Kentucky high school all-star team was conducting for its annual games against Indiana high school stars.

After the practice ended, I stood on the court. Chapman approached me and made a memorable comment. He said when he played for UK, he did not understand why I asked certain questions. But upon playing in the NBA and being around the NBA reporters, he now understood my questions.

In 2023, Chapman elaborated. He noted how dealing with uncomfortable situations was part of his Kentucky experience: an NCAA investigation, speculation about Eddie Sutton having a drinking problem.

"It's a huge advantage Kentucky players have going through it even for guys who come and play for a year and transfer," Chapman said of the interview process and media scrutiny that comes with being a Wildcat. "They understand and will definitely have a better appreciation for the media and the media's role."

Scott Padgett, who played for Kentucky about a decade after Chapman, also spoke of his UK experience with the media being a long-term benefit.

"I felt it prepared me for life after Kentucky . . . ," he said in 2023. "It got me ready for maybe some hard-hitting questions. Maybe today I don't answer your question the way you want. That happened a lot in the NBA. They didn't get the answer they wanted, but I gave them an answer."

I told Padgett that I only wanted to improve the story by asking a question.

"I think that came from you being a person who reported on Kentucky for a long, long time. You were in Lexington, so you're supposed to be a homer. You were supposed to ask all the fluff questions."

With that Padgett laughed.

Dwane Casey also spoke of playing for Kentucky and later serving on Sutton's staff as good preparation for life in the NBA.

"Having had scrutiny from the media for 15 years in the NBA asking all kinds of questions," he told me in 2023. "Questions about your rotations, your substitution pattern, your defensive calls, your offensive calls. . . .

"When I look back, there were hard questions at the time because so much of the media at Kentucky is, you know, promoting the program and not wanting to get on the bad side. Looking back, you did probably ask the hardest questions. They weren't tough. They were good questions."

When I said I sought to explain something to the readers, not second-guess a coaching decision, Casey said, "in the cocoon of Kentucky, that seems like a hard question, which it is not."

I gained a reputation for asking "hard questions" early on. Kenny Walker, who played for Joe B. Hall and Sutton in the 1980s, said Kentucky coaches would alert players to be careful when talking to me.

"They would always say, when you're talking to Jerry, be careful," Walker said in 2023. "He's going to ask you tough questions. I always laughed. . . . They may be tough, but they're fair questions. I guess there's a way to ask whatever question you're going to ask. Me, I never really thought your questions were that tough."

When I said I asked questions to help the story, Walker said, "I don't see anything wrong with that. And I kind of liked it. And, yeah, you did get the reputation from my teammates and coaches as a guy that was going to write the tough story. I appreciate that. I think in a lot of ways it made us better.

"I often thought it was constructive criticism, not anything personal toward a coach or player."

Sam Bowie recalled my name coming up in preparing players for interviews.

"A guy like Jerry Tipton, be careful," he said. "Almost like trying to warn someone who's a little wet behind the ears that there can be poison pens out there. I'm not saying anyone said Jerry Tipton had a poison pen. But we were warned to answer the question and really don't elaborate."

Any questions from all reporters could be hard for Wayne Turner. As a point guard, he could have in depth knowledge of what happened in a game.

When asked if he did not want to divulge team strategy, Turner said, "exactly, and get killed by Coach Pitino the next day because (coaches) watched the interviews."

Part of the team's tutorial program involved preparing players for interviews.

"It helped me relax my nerves and answer questions without feeling so much anxiety or like I'm going to mess up," Turner said. "It may not seem like it, but I'm a perfectionist."

Joel Justus, who had several jobs during seven seasons on John Calipari's staff, said assistant coaches also felt their interview sessions would be scrutinized. Later in Calipari's time as coach, an assistant would do the day-before news conference previewing the next game.

"You knew you had to have your chin strap buckled when you walked down those steps in the Kraft Center you never knew what you were going to ask," Justus said. "You just hoped you answered the question correctly because you had to walk back upstairs to see John. So, you just hoped you answered it correctly."

Most times any friction in a reporter's interaction with a player or coach did not go public. That was especially true before the Internet made news conferences available to the public.

I never forgot a Marshall journalism professor telling students that it was never good if a reporter was the story. So, I tried to accept any criticism and keep it out of the story.

One exceptional exception involved Calipari and me in the fall of 2017.

The setup for our notable exchange came two years earlier. Kentucky had a player whose eligibility was in question. I believe it was Skal Labissiere. So, I asked Calipari if this case should be likened to John Wall, who gained his eligibility after sitting out an exhibition game and that season's opening game, or Enes Kanter, who the NCAA ruled permanently ineligible.

Perhaps not liking me bringing up the multiple times his program had added players with eligibility issues, Calipari scolded me and said I had no right to ask the question.

I did not respond, but I thought the person being interviewed should not have the power to forbid certain questions.

This played on my mind for several days. The thought that stuck with me was that this scolding came on Media Day, the first formal interview sessions each preseason.

Fast forward to Kentucky's Media Day in 2017. A big story at the time was an FBI investigation into corruption in college basketball recruiting. The focus of the investigation was programs involved with Adidas.

With talk of the investigation expanding to schools affiliated with Nike, I asked Calipari how concerned, if at all, should Kentucky fans be.

Again, Calipari told me I could not ask that question.

I responded by saying I had a right to ask the question. Fortunately, I did not insist on an answer. I simply said he could refuse to respond, but I could ask the question.

After all, I concluded, it was *Media* Day, not coach's day.

I became identified with that statement.

Justus said the coaching staff was amused.

"There was always the banter that we would always laugh about," he told me in 2023. "Kind of with Cal about his dry sense of humor and your dry sense of humor. Kind of a battle of wits in press conferences."

John Clay's story for the *Herald-Leader* about my retirement included a quote from John Calipari that suggested there was nothing personal involved.

"Jerry Tipton has been synonymous with Kentucky basketball for 40 years and that should be applauded," Calipari said. "He's never been afraid to ask tough questions, even when I might not have liked it! But his dedication to the Lexington community and unwavering work ethic has resulted in a Hall of Fame career. I wish him nothing but the best in his retirement."

Here, in more or less chronological order, are some of the hard questions I asked during my time covering UK basketball.

Joe B. Hall announced his retirement on the post-game radio show after Kentucky lost to St. John's in the 1985 NCAA West Region semifinals. Reporters huddled by the table and took notes as Cawood Ledford interviewed Hall.

Reporters were told that Hall would be available for a news conference in his hotel room the next morning.

Before the news conference began, Hall's wife, Katharine, scolded reporters for never helping readers/viewers/listeners appreciate "the real Joe B."

I asked her to talk about "the real" Joe B. She declined, saying we had had our chance and struck out.

Much to the UK fans' delight, Rick Pitino brought in a new, exciting style of play. Johnny McGill, then the *Herald-Leader* sports columnist, memorably dubbed the players "Pitino's Bombinos."

When Kentucky played Indiana, there was a stark contrast in playing styles. So, in the day-before-the-game news conference, I asked Indiana's irascible coach, Bob Knight, what he thought of the Pitino style?

"Why ask me?" Knight responded.

Because I consider you knowledgeable about the game to the extent of being a historian, I replied.

Knight agreed that he was exceedingly knowledgeable about basketball. But he declined to comment on the Pitino style.

When Arkansas joined the SEC for the 1991-92 season, the league added a fan base that rivaled the Big Blue Nation in terms of fervor. This was clear before Kentucky's first league game at Arkansas began. The date was Feb. 10, 1993.

By habit or theatrical appreciation, Pitino liked to make a dramatic late entrance. Cozy Barnhill Arena, still my favorite arena, was buzzing when he entered the court.

At this time, the Arkansas pep band played the theme to The Godfather.

I wondered what Pitino thought of this. Maybe Kentucky's 101-94 defeat stifled media curiosity. Maybe reporters remembered, as I did, that Pitino objected when a radio announcer referred to him as an "Italian." When no one asked during the postgame news conference, I asked about his entrance accompanied by The Godfather theme.

"To me, that's good-natured fun," Pitino said. "You laugh at that."

Kentucky Director of Athletics C.M. Newton was not amused.

"Orchestrated cheers to deride opponents is not good for college basketball, particularly the ethnic things," he said, "To me, it steps over the line. It gets into the area of being cute rather than supportive."

Pitino's refashioning of Kentucky basketball extended to, uh, fashion.

A story I did about how he had jazzed up the UK basketball look began with:

The fashion world sees Rick Pitino and says, "Armani."

The fashion world sees his Kentucky team and says, "Are you kidding?"

Pitino ordered a design change in the uniforms and voiced his approval.

"It's more uniform (clean in appearance)," he said in the story that was published on Dec. 22, 1994. Last season's design "wasn't as organized. It was a little too busy."

In making a fashion statement the previous season, Kentucky's uniform had a pajama look with an aimless zigzag design. Tony Delk disapproved, saying the uniforms "look like swimming trunks."

Pitino worked with APEX, a sports clothing manufacturer whose clients included the Dallas Cowboys. Pitino and equipment manager Bill Keightley picked the design.

"It's catchy," Pitino said. "Kids love it more than anyone else. . . . It's a young, hip thing. No question about it. That's the audience we're trying to attract."

Traditionalists recoiled. Wallace "Wah Wah" Jones, one of Kentucky's celebrated Fabulous Five, objected.

"Kentucky is like the New York Yankees of basketball," he said. "I think 95 percent of the people agree."

This inspired a pertinent question. Pitino grew up in New York and was a Yankees fan. "Very much so," he said.

So, I asked how would he feel if the Yankees bowed to a marketing impulse and slashed a rainbow across the iconic pinstripes?

"I would say the Yankees are getting into the '90s look," he said with a self-conscious smile.

During the later seasons of Tubby Smith's time, the North Carolina job became available. Some fans slyly hid their desire for a new coach by talking about Smith moving to UNC.

Newton tried to shut that down by asking, "Why would Tubby take a step down to go to North Carolina?"

I followed up as soon as I could by asking Newton why he considered North Carolina "a step down."

Newton smiled a you-got-me smile and said his "Kentucky pride" got the best of him.

Calipari almost annually belittled the Southeastern Conference Tournament. He said it got in the way of the element of March Madness that mattered, the NCAA Tournament, and served no useful purpose.

One year during his time on the NCAA Tournament Selection Committee, SEC Commissioner Mike Slive happened to be at the site where Kentucky was playing. I used the occasion to ask Slive how he felt about the coach of the league's marquee program lamenting that his team had to play in the conference tournament.

Slive smiled as I finished asking the question. He then pointed out that before he entered athletics administration, he earned law degrees from the University of Virginia and Georgetown University. He practiced law in New Hampshire and then served as a judge of the Hanover District Court from 1972 to 1977.

This background made him aware of the First Amendment's guarantee of freedom of speech. So, he said, he had no objection to Calipari exercising this right.

One time when Howard Schnellenberger was Louisville's football coach, the school had a promotion involving the Beach Boys singing group.

Schnellenberger came to a news conference wearing a Beach Boys shirt.

I could not resist asking him what his favorite Beach Boys song was. This question stumped Schnellenberger.

I've been on the other side of pointed questions.

When Pitino was Kentucky coach, I got caught by surprise while eating a pregame meal in the media dining area inside Rupp Arena. Ken Ford, aka Jersey Red, was something of a court jester for Kentucky basketball at the time. For instance, he once said he'd like to see me strapped to a rocket and have it fired off the big blue building in downtown Lexington.

Ford came and sat at my table and began asking me questions: What did I think of Pitino? How good of a coach was Pitino?

I immediately thought Ford would be relaying my responses to Pitino. I saluted the job Pitino was doing without – I thought – sacrificing my professionalism.

This did not seem to satisfy Ford. So, he turned up the heat. He asked: Did I think Pitino was a better coach than Adolph Rupp?

I mulled this over for a moment before responding: In 30 years, people will think the Kentucky coach is better than Pitino.

Ford gave up and departed.

Another time I faced a pointed question came on a flight home from a Kentucky road game. In those days, I flew regional jets to most away games. With two seats on either side of the aisle, it was a real treat to get a two-seat area to yourself. You could stretch out and relax.

So, if no one was sitting next to me, I'd watch the front of the plane closely as passengers boarded and all but celebrate if the seat next to me was unoccupied when the entry door was closed.

While I was watching the door on this flight from Atlanta to Lexington, a man got on the plane. He slowly made his way along, seemingly stopping at about every row to glad hand passengers and exchange pleasantries.

I took an instant dislike to him and hoped he'd find his seat and sit down. He finally stopped . . . at my row and pointed to the seat next to me as his seat.

I got up and let him inside to his window seat.

We introduced ourselves. After a few minutes, he asked me what I did for a living. I said I was a sportswriter with the *Lexington Herald-Leader*.

I then asked him what he did for a living. He said he was a Methodist minister on his way to Asbury University for a religious gathering.

After a few minutes of small talk, he asked a pointed question: Where was I in my faith journey? I wondered if I should be honest or simply brush the question off by saying all was good.

I decided to be honest. I told him I wished my faith was stronger.

I expected him to invite me to a church service. Instead, he pointed out that when John the Baptist was imprisoned, some of his followers came to him and asked what they should do. John told them to go to Jesus and ask if he was the one promised in Scripture.

To ask that question suggested some doubt, the minister said. So, he added, it was all right to have doubt.

I then felt thankful that the man had taken the seat next to me.

Sunday Notebook

A notes column called the Sunday Notebook became a signature part of my coverage of Kentucky basketball. This weekly collection of notes spurred me to move beyond the day-to-day routine and look for enterprise stories, albeit ultra-short stories or as the title suggested mere notes.

Two factors played a part in this idea. One involved my reading habits. For several years I had been a regular reader of notes columns that ran in *The Boston Globe* each Sunday.

Plus, the *Herald-Leader* budget in the 1980s going forward allowed me to fly to most of Kentucky's away games. The only exceptions in the Southeastern Conference were games at Tennessee and Vanderbilt.

The flights home almost always involved changing planes in Atlanta. After Saturday road games, I'd fly back Sunday and buy *The Atlanta Journal-Constitution* at the Atlanta airport. Its Sunday notes columns in the Sports section were a fun read.

The other factor was space limitations on stories. In these days before the Internet, the length of stories was limited to the space available in the newspaper. As a result, some information frequently had to be left out. This led to frustration.

I thought these missing elements of stories could be part of a notes column.

Approval to do a Sunday notes column was not automatic.

The *Herald-Leader* sports editor at the time, Mike Johnson, recalled in a 2023 text message that the initial hesitancy "had more to do with length and space in the Sunday" newspaper. Obviously, it paid off to do it because ultimately it gave readers information they might not have gotten."

Here is a chapter in the style of the Sunday Notebook.

Life as a Teenage Celebrity: 'It's Tougher Than it Looks'

During my high school years, I did not want to stand out. My self-esteem was not strong. I thought everyone else had it together. I wanted to blend in and not be noticed.

A stark contrast came to mind as I got acquainted with Kentucky basketball. All the players are celebrities. All the recruits are hyped as stars. It's impossible for such a person to blend in.

But what fascinated me most were the players who moved beyond mere stardom to basketball icons by the time they were eligible to get a driver's license.

What was it like for a teenager to be venerated?

Two Kentucky players I covered came immediately to mind.

When it came to celebrity, Rex Chapman and Richie Farmer were Beatles even before arriving to the Kentucky campus as freshmen. No doubt, being Kentucky natives helped enliven their celebrity immensely. Of course, so did their obvious basketball skill.

Chapman, who was from Owensboro, was named Mr. Basketball and The Associated Press Athlete of the Year as a high school senior. He scored 2,286 points for Apollo High School, was a three-time All-State selection and *the* must get in the recruiting circus of 1986. Adding to the must-see component of his recruitment, Kentucky or archrival Louisville was the choice he had to make.

When I spoke to Chapman in 2023, he said he had not been comfortable with unblinking notoriety as a teenager.

"I was not a confident kid," he said. "Insecure about whatever: my looks, my hair, what it was."

As the son of a basketball coach and a former UK player, Chapman found solace in his ability to play the game.

"I started to realize I might not have friends at the beginning of the day, but after P.E., I would have friends," he recalled. "I was good at all that stuff. So that gave me an identity and probably this is probably also why I struggled some because my only identity was my physical, my athletic."

Chapman said he did not like speaking to the media, especially when he got to Kentucky. He discovered that reporters who covered college sports were not so enthralled with the star players.

"In high school, everyone just loves us," he said. "College reporters are trying to write accurate stories. . . . That's our first experience, really, with criticism publicly."

I was viewed as a reporter trying to write accurate stories, Chapman said. "I didn't even know who you were. . . . And I can remember getting to Kentucky and meeting with Bret Bearup and Rob Lock and all of them. As soon as your name came up, well, (screw) Jerry Tipton. And for no reason. That was just passed on for years. I'm sure from generation to generation, for no real reason."

Farmer was arguably even more of a basketball phenomenon. He was named Kentucky's Mr. Basketball as a senior in 1988. He was also named Most Valuable Player in the 1987 and 1988 state tournaments with his Clay County team winning the state championship in 1987. Clay County was State Tournament runner-up twice in Farmer's four-year high school career.

A three-time all-state selection, Farmer broke the state tournament scoring record previously held since the 1940s by Wallace "Wah Wah" Jones, who went on to become one of the players on UK teams known as Fabulous Five. Farmer scored 317 points in 14 state tournament games. That included 51 points in the 1988 state championship game against Louisville Ballard.

Overall, Farmer scored 2,937 points as a high school player. Clay County's record in his four seasons as a starter way 141-22.

No wonder more than 1,600 people came to the Clay County High School gym to watch Farmer sign a letter-of-intent to play for Kentucky.

When asked in 2023 about being a celebrity as a teenager, Farmer said, "Obviously, people would sit back and think that it'd be great, but it's difficult, especially when you're a young person. I've said, when you're like that, then everybody judges you. They may only see you that one time and they judge you from that meeting."

Farmer had experience on the other side of that dynamic. He couldn't remember whether he was in the eighth or ninth grade, but he recalled being in line for 20 or 30 minutes waiting get to an autograph from Kentucky big man Melvin Turpin.

When his turn for an autograph finally came, Turpin said he had to leave.

"I'll never forget that feeling of how I felt," Farmer said.

How did he feel?

"Oh, I was crushed," he said before adding, "Later, after I saw how it was, he probably did have something to do and had to go. But I've always tried to never leave anybody with that feeling. It's impossible to always make everybody happy. But that's a lot more difficult to be kind of a celebrity at a younger age. It's tougher than it looks."

Another teenage celebrity joining the Kentucky team as a freshman in 2023-24 will be Reed Sheppard. He will come to the UK program having led the state in scoring as a sophomore for North Laurel High School with an average of 30.1 points. He was the Kentucky Gatorade Player of the Year as a high school junior and the state's Mr. Basketball as a senior. He finished his high school career with quadruple points (3,727), assists (1,214) and rebounds (1,050).

Adding to his celebrity are parents who starred for UK. Father Jeff Sheppard scored 1,091 points and was named the Final Four's Most Outstanding Player in leading the Wildcats to the 1998 national championship. Mother Stacey Reed Sheppard was a 1,000-point scorer for the UK women's team and finished college ranked in the program's top 10 in career steals, assists, three-point baskets and starts.

Jeff said he and his wife have given their son the same advice as Kentucky Coach John Calipari.

"It is to have fun and to just really enjoy every moment," Jeff said in 2023. "Enjoy every moment in high school. Enjoy the recruitment. Enjoy the process and the transition into college. Really enjoy it because not many people get the opportunity.

"And, second of all, just be yourself. You don't have to be anybody other than you."

Sheppard said it helps Reed that his parents serve as role models for dealing with celebrity at a young age.

"We have our background and our stories to be able to help him," Sheppard said. "He's also seen us his whole life be Kentucky ball players. So, you know, he understands the mentality of the fan and how fans love Kentucky basketball. It's not new to him."

Reed grew up a UK basketball fan. His bedroom has pictures of Devin Booker, Tyler Ulis, Anthony Davis, Karl-Anthony Towns and Rajon Rondo.

"What does that mean and look like for him?" Jeff asked. "I don't know. Stay tuned. See how it plays out."

Sports and Religion

Paul Prather, the minister at Bethesda Church in Mount Sterling, Ky., writes a Sunday column about spiritual matters that appears in the *Herald-Leader*'s editorial page. When he was a full-time reporter of church news, his desk was next to mine.

We would playfully debate about which one of us was really covering religion.

In 2023, Prather conceded.

"I was covering the formal area of religion," he said. "But if you look at how dedicated people are to something based on how they vote with their feet, I would say you were the real religion writer because people are way more devoted to UK basketball than they tend to be to their churches."

When asked why devotion to Kentucky basketball is stronger, Prather said, "I think in a lot of ways basketball is more real than God is. It's real and it's tangible and you can feel it, taste it, see it, hear it, watch it. And it's always to some extent or other a cliffhanger. The outcome is uncertain so it's exciting. . . .

"Religion is very much different from that because you can't see God and church, frankly, to a large extent, tends to be boring. There aren't a lot of cliffhangers as far as we know."

Dan Wann, the Murray State psychology professor who has a keen interest in fan thinking, noted that sports and religion have several similarities. Both have hallowed grounds, ideas that you just don't challenge, deities and music "designed to raise the fervor," he said.

Wann said he was part of a study in which fans were asked to make a list so as to identify themselves to a stranger.

"What always made me laugh, the five or six people who, like, on the third line they'd say 'I'm a Kentucky basketball fan.' The very next line below that (was) 'I'm a Baptist.'

"It's like they had their hierarchy set. Basketball and then Baptist. We giggled for years about that."

Prather noted that as a reporter he wrote a story centered on a county-by-county breakdown of religious affiliations in the United States. About 80 percent of respondents in some counties in western Kentucky were Baptists.

"So it doesn't surprise me at all that people would self-identify as UK fans and Baptists," he said.

Sports and religion crossed paths in a note I did published on Aug. 16, 1992.

The lead got to the point:

Matthew, Mark, Luke and . . . Richie?

The note detailed how further evidence that Kentucky basketball was like a religion would hit bookstores that week. It would come in the form of a 100-page autobiography by Richie Farmer.

The Lexington publisher, Antex Corp., was offering a blue-letter edition. In a biblical touch, every Farmer quote would be in blue type. It could be likened to how every statement by Jesus is printed in red in some versions of the Bible, Antex spokesman Tim Lester said.

"I never tried to equate myself with Jesus or God," Farmer said in 2023. "It really wasn't meant to be that. . . . (It was) just a gimmicky little thing that we came up with. It seemed to work. I think it sold almost 50,000 copies. We had to do a second printing."

What If?

Richie Farmer and John Pelphrey were among "The Unforgettables," players who had jerseys hung in the rafters of Rupp Arena because they did not transfer after the NCAA penalized the Kentucky program in 1989.

Tony Delk, the leading scorer on Kentucky's 1996 national championship team, ranks fifth on the program's career scoring list with 1,890 points.

It's interesting to think how close we came to none of that happening.

Farmer recalled hearing that Eddie Sutton did not want to recruit him. Perhaps because his son, Sean Sutton, was on the team, Farmer said. Both were guards.

Then LSU Coach Dale Brown made a recruiting pitch that envisioned Farmer joining Chris Jackson in the backcourt with Shaquille O'Neal and Stanley Roberts in the front court.

"He said I'm going to put you guys out there to shoot and I'm going to put them under the goal and let them rebound," Farmer recalled Brown saying.

Yes, Farmer conceded, "that was a pretty attractive offer."

But Farmer chose to commit to Kentucky. He recalled writing a paper as a first grader that said what he wanted to be when he grew up was "to be a UK Wildcat."

When Pelphrey made his recruiting visit, he was not offered a scholarship. He was told that if one of three other prospects declined UK's offer, he could have that scholarship.

"I said, fine, I'll take that deal," Pelphrey recalled.

While only one of the three prospects committed to Kentucky, Pelphrey still did not get an offer.

"So, I had to deal with the disappointment, the pain and suffering," he recalled in 2023.

Ultimately, Kentucky made a scholarship offer. Pelphrey accepted. But more mental strife lay ahead.

Pelphrey recalled being chosen only once in a whole day when the UK players played pickup games.

"Wow, I'm here," he said he thought. "That's exciting. But in the next 30 seconds, am I here? Was I being seen? Is there any value to me?

Pelphrey stuck it out and said he learned "pain and suffering is good."

Delk's crisis was coming in as a McDonald's All-American and then hardly playing. In the first 16 games of his freshman season for Kentucky, he averaged 5.6 minutes. He did not play in three of the games, and played four or fewer minutes in six of the games.

"I was thinking of transferring," Delk recalled. "Man, I could be on somebody else's roster and getting PT and doing what most of my peers who came out that year were doing."

Delk said he was considering a transfer to his "second option" of Memphis, which was relatively close to his hometown of Covington, Tenn., or Arkansas. He told the UK coaches and his parents of his intention to leave.

He credited then assistant coach Billy Donovan for working with him and getting him to ride it out.

Overreaction Is Everywhere

Jeff Sheppard said he paid no attention when a fan labeled the 1997-98 Wildcats the "worst 22-4 team" he had seen after a home loss to Ole Miss in mid-February set that won-loss record in the 1997-98 season.

"The last thing I was concerned with when remembering the '98 season was comments from fans after the last loss of our season that propelled us to an SEC championship and an NCAA championship run," Sheppard said in 2023.

He suggested a lesson could be drawn from that fan's comment.

"It just shows, in sports especially, sports media, we use words like 'best' and 'worst' way too often," Sheppard said. "And it makes the story sound better. It drives home, I guess, viewership. And we swing really, really fast to both of those words. And I understand it. And that's what's going on at the moment also. We have the perspective now of looking back and we have the whole story."

I've thought the same thing and tried to base my stories on an adage I heard many coaches say: It's not as bad as it seems and it's not as good as it seems.

Sheppard said Kentucky's 2021-22 season, which was my last covering the program, served as a good caution against overreaction.

"Two years ago, Kentucky had the best team in the country in January," Sheppard said. "We beat Carolina. We blew them out. We beat Kansas at Kansas. And we were incredibly strong. We were the best team in the country, and we lost in the first round of the tournament."

A Salute to Professors, Tutors

Among Kentucky players, Wayne Turner ranks first in career steals (238) and fourth in assists (494).

But when asked about memories from his UK playing days, Turner added perhaps overlooked contributors.

After saluting the program's tradition, the fans and his teammates, Turner added, "my professors, my tutors. People who kind of go behind the scenes that run through my mind a lot."

Given the travel involved and the time devoted to basketball, academics were a challenge for all players, Turner said before adding that he took "a lot of pride" in how he did in the classroom.

Turner recalled skipping one class in his four years as a UK student. "It wasn't so much that I didn't want to go to class," he said. "I was just tired. I wanted to sleep more because, you know, practice is coming up soon.

"But one of my main goals was to get my degree."

Turner said that one of Kentucky's recruiting advantages in his case was the Cawood Ledford Scholarship Fund, which allows former players to return to school after their eligibility expires and complete work for a degree. Turner returned and earned a degree in Community Communication and Leadership Development. He now works at Atherton High School in Louisville as a youth service coordinator and coaches the girls basketball team.

'Death by Basketball'

While collecting – and recollecting – memories of my time covering Kentucky basketball, I came upon something that would have made a wonderful lead note to a Sunday Notebook.

Frank X. Walker, a professor in the University of Kentucky English Department, wrote a poem titled "Death by Basketball."

The poem included a reference to Wayne Turner:

Before and after school
he stood
On a milk crate
Eyeballed the mirror
And only saw Wayne Turner
At tournament time

I learned that Walker was Kentucky's poet laureate in 2013 and 2014. A UK graduate, he was program coordinator of the school's King Cultural Center and founder/executive director of The Bluegrass Black Arts Consortium.

I asked him what message he hoped "Death by Basketball" would give readers.

"That poem is really about little kids who see sports as their only option to success and the individuals in the education system who support that notion," he said before adding a minute later, "for me, that intellectual underdevelopment is kind of a death."

As Bill Russell did during an appearance at Marshall University in the early 1970s, Walker saw benefit in college athletes spending more time with fellow students and not existing exclusively in an athletic cocoon.

"Particularly these uber superstars who are basketball players," Walker said. "They just separate them from the general community. I'm not sure that's good for them in the long run.

"I really think it can be done differently with a richer outcome for students and the athletes."

Walker saw long-term benefits in a lifestyle that extends beyond a sport. He suggested players can progress from teenage celebrities to millionaires living in isolation.

"There's all these social cues that they've missed," he said. "I think that particular past makes them kind of vulnerable to predators and people who would prey on their celebrity and their money."

Walker is a UK fan. He grew up in Danville in a family of Wildcat fans.

Walker was not sure when exactly he wrote the poem. "That was 13 books ago," he said with a chuckle. "It would have been after the amazing run they had in the (1998) tournament."

The obvious follow-up question was why include Turner, the point guard on that Kentucky championship team, in the poem.

"Let me just say Wayne Turner at tournament time really meant something . . . ," Walker said. "He wasn't seven feet tall. Much of what he succeeded at was because of his heart and his gut. It made him kind of a superhero without superpowers."

'It's Unfathomable'

When Kellan Grady played for Davidson, the team went on a trip to eastern Europe. One stop was at the Auschwitz-Birkenau concentration camp where Germans killed millions of people during World War II.

"It's gruesome," Grady recalled in 2023. "It's unfathomable. You're not sure how this could happen.

"When you see everything there, it's tough. You're going to have a pit in your stomach. There's going to be a sense of uncomfortability. It's really a tough thing to experience and witness. But it's a very moving experience. And I'm very fortunate that we were able to do that."

Grady made a donation while at the camp. "I thought it was the least I could do," he said.

Kudos to Bradley

Although Dusty Mills' experience as a Kentucky player was short and not sweet, one teammate made a winning impression. When Mills entered the locker room for the first time, Ramel Bradley welcomed the freshman walk-on and gave him his cell phone number.

"If you need anything, you can get me at this number," Mills remembered Bradley saying in a story I wrote for the *Herald-Leader.*

Mills became a fan as well as a teammate.

"He easily could have been a senior who saw a worthless walk-on," Mills said. "'We don't need this kid.'

"He always made me feel part of the team."

'That Happened'

A note published on March 13, 2016 marked the upcoming 50th anniversary of the landmark Kentucky-Texas Western championship game.

Louie Dampier, a guard on the UK team known as Rupp's Runts, and his wife, Judy, went to see the movie *Glory Road*, which told the story of Texas Western beating Kentucky.

"At certain points of the movie, I'd lean over and say, 'That didn't happen,'" Dampier recalled. "'That didn't happen. That never happened.'

"Then Bobby Joe Hill stole the ball from me. I said, 'That happened.'"

Empty Seats

Much to the annoyance of twitter responders, I got in the habit of tweeting pictures of empty seats at Kentucky home games. This was based on how Kentucky had led Division I in attendance in 28 seasons since Rupp Arena opened in the fall of 1976. Kentucky had been no lower than second in attendance the other 18 seasons as of the summer of 2023.

So, empty seats seemed notable.

Thanks, in part, to an enhanced home schedule created by its entry into the Atlantic Coast Conference, Syracuse in 2013-14 snapped Kentucky's eight-season streak of leading the nation in attendance.

Kentucky's popularity remained undeniable. Big crowds braved ice and snow to get to several home games that season. The same was true despite a tornado watch the night Kentucky played a home game against Eastern Michigan.

But, I had long noted that the announced attendance at UK's home games didn't match what you saw in the Rupp Arena stands.

Open records obtained by the *Herald-Leader* indicated about a 20-percent markup in attendance. I included this in a note for the Feb. 9, 2014, Sunday Notebook. Lexington Center Corp., which operates Rupp Arena and the adjoining Lexington Center, counts the ticket holders admitted into Rupp Arena.

The official average announced attendance to that point of the season was 22,662. The average number of ticket holders in Rupp Arena was 18,110.

DeWayne Peevy, then Deputy Director of Athletics, acknowledged that determining an announced attendance was "kind of an imperfect science."

Lexington Center Corp. scanned the number of people admitted into Rupp Arena to help determine how many concession workers and other employees to assign to games, said Bill Owen, then the CEO and president of LCC.

The "scan number" is given to UK officials during a game. To arrive at an announced attendance figure, Kentucky then factors the total number of tickets sold, whether or not the ticket holder is actually there. UK then added media types, pep band members, cheerleaders, dance team members, referees, security, players, coaches, ushers and practically anyone else in the building.

The NCAA keeps attendance figures as one of its statistics. But the NCAA provides no guidelines on who should and shouldn't be counted. Spokesman Cameron

Schuh said in 2014 that the NCAA depended on the schools to be "honest and accurate" in their counts.

Syracuse, which had led Division I in attendance 17 seasons as of the summer of 2023, based its count on tickets sold and/or distributed, spokesman Peter Moore said in 2014.

There was a consistency in Kentucky's announced attendance figures. Open Records obtained by the *Herald-Leader* showed a 16-percent markup in the 2012-13 season.

"Leading the nation every year in attendance is one of those things you'd like to continue to do," former Director of Athletics Larry Ivy told me in 2014. "I think Kentucky is a premier program. So, obviously, you'd want the number to be there."

We Are in Trouble

Among all-time Kentucky players, only Anthony Davis (4.7 per game) averaged more blocks than Nerlens Noel (4.4 per game).

On Jan. 29, 2013, Noel blocked a program record 12 shots in Kentucky's 87-74 victory at Ole Miss. It was the only time Bill Russell came to mind as I watched a game.

Two weeks later, Noel torn an anterior cruciate ligament in a 69-52 loss at Florida.

John Calipari recalled seeing Noel crying in his seat as the team traveled back to Lexington.

"I reached over and put my arm around him," Calipari said. "I said, you're going to be fine. This is an injury you will recover from. I said, we will not. We are in trouble."

Kentucky lost its next game by 30 points at Tennessee.

Kentucky had a 17-6 record when Noel was healthy and lost six of 10 games with him sidelined.

Calipari noted the importance of shot blocking as a factor in Kentucky's first-round loss to Saint Peter's in the 2022 NCAA Tournament.

"Anything can happen if you don't have shot blocking . . . ," he said. "If you have rim protection, it's hard for those teams to beat you."

Media Game

Early in Rick Pitino's time as Kentucky coach (I think before his first season), there was a game arranged at a Lexington high school pitting UK basketball staffers against the media. The word was that whatever reporter was guarded by strength coach Ray "Rock" Oliver was not in good standing with the program.

Oliver guarded me. I had nothing to prove. I missed the one shot I took and tried to enjoy the game.

Tubby Smith, then an assistant coach, scored something like 36 points in the UK staff's breeze to victory.

The *Herald-Leader* sports editor at the time, Gene Abell, had broken an ankle the previous year. So, he was the media team's coach.

"Boy, they were serious," Abell said in 2023 when asked about the game. "I remember early on thinking, I thought this was supposed to be fun. I can remember when it was over thinking were they trying to make a point or something? Or show dominance?"

No Offense

When freshman Terrence Jones took and missed a shot inside the final minute of a 68-66 loss at Alabama in the 2010-11 season, a TV camera caught John Calipari calling him a "selfish motherfucker." I was not initially aware of this, but it made for much social media chatter.

Jones' family took no offense. They said they understood the coach-player dynamic could be contentious.

When I next spoke to Jones (in the locker room after a home game), I used a nonchalant voice to playfully say I had heard he was a selfish motherfucker. He laughed.

Obituaries are Part of the Job

With covering Kentucky basketball for 41 seasons came the inevitable need to write obituaries. I came to feel like the grim reaper when learning that another prominent figure in the program's history was seriously ill and there was a need to gather information for the obit. It was helpful that I regularly read obits in *The New York Times*. That served as a form I tried to follow.

Among those for whom I wrote an obituary are:

Joe B. Hall

When Joe B. Hall died on Jan. 15, 2022, I had already prepared a 100-inch obituary. That was the longest story of my journalism career. It helped immensely that Hall agreed to talk to me about the obit. We met more than once a few years earlier to discuss his life and career.

I thought the lead captured Hall's place in Kentucky basketball history. It read:

"Joe B. Hall, who made his mark on Kentucky basketball by successfully following a legend and then becoming one himself, died early Saturday morning. He was 93."

The obituary detailed Hall's lifelong connection to UK basketball. It began as a child keeping score as he listened to games on the radio, continued as a reserve player on the 1948-49 national championship team, included seven seasons as an assistant coach for Adolph Rupp, then following the man I liked to refer to as the founding father of UK basketball with a 13-season run as head coach before retiring in 1985 and returning to the role of fan.

"The Big Blue circle was unbroken," I wrote.

As of 2023, Hall remained the only native-born Kentuckian to be UK basketball coach since Basil Hayden in 1926-27.

"It was not just another coaching job to him," Hall's son-in-law, Mike Summers, said. "It was *the* coaching job."

Longtime friend and Lexington attorney Terry McBrayer saluted Hall as "about as decent a person as I've ever dealt with. But he took the program so seriously, and had to defend the program at all times. He was the defender of the program."

One of the critics Hall had to fend off was Rupp, who made no secret of his desire to remain coach. With Hall having gained a reputation as a good recruiter and likely successor, Rupp felt threatened by his assistant coach.

"I just don't think he ever wanted anybody to really succeed him . . . ," Lexington businessman Jim Host said of Rupp. "Joe really connected with the followers and the fans, yet Coach Rupp was never ready to turn it over to him. He saw him as a competitor."

Kevin Grevey, who was a freshman in Rupp's last season as coach (1971-72), recalled Rupp openly criticizing Hall during practices. Rupp made no secret that he favored another assistant, the newly hired Gale Catlett, who had little chance of becoming Kentucky coach.

"Gale Catlett could do whatever he wanted to do," Grevey said. "And Coach Hall had to step aside. It was kind of weird. I got the feeling Coach Rupp was losing any kind of love he had for Coach Hall, for sure."

In a forced retirement, Rupp made the already high-pressure job of Kentucky coach even more difficult for his successor. He did not attend the news conference formally introducing Hall as the new coach. He maintained an office in Memorial Coliseum. He continued to do a weekly television show on which he second-guessed Hall.

"Coach Rupp would say things on the show and in the paper, and he'd criticize Coach Hall," Grevey said. "You know, 'I'd never have done that.' 'I don't know why he was running the 1-3-1 zone.'

"He was an armchair quarterback and not helping Coach Hall through this transition which was already difficult in itself and made it almost unbearable."

Billy Reed, a longtime columnist for the *Courier-Journal* in Louisville and later the *Herald-Leader*, recalled Rupp saying on the television show, "I can't believe it. They got beat by Georgia! Georgia!!"

Tom Hammond, then the sports anchor at Lexington's NBC affiliate, WLEX, said Hall probably internalized the hurt he was feeling.

"I think that rolled-up program he always had in his hand was pretty indicative of how he was feeling," Hammond said.

Hall refused to criticize Rupp publicly.

But in 2017, Hall conceded that Rupp made the difficulty of the job "10 times worse."

Reed called Hall "almost a tragic figure."

When John Wooden retired as UCLA Coach in 1975, Hall famously said about following an iconic coach that *The Huffington Post* included in a listing of "25 idiosyncratic sports quotes."

Hall jokingly suggested that UCLA should hire him to follow Wooden. "Why ruin two lives?" he quipped.

Hall called the 92-90 upset of unbeaten Indiana in the 1975 NCAA Tournament "a pivotal game in my career. . . . That was kind of the break over with the fans and everybody."

Besides winning games, capped by the 1978 national championship, Hall also fully integrated the Kentucky program.

After retirement, Hall worked for a bank and later co-hosted a radio show with former coaching rival Denny Crum.

Before the 2017-18 season, Jack Givens, the hero of Kentucky's 1978 championship game victory over Duke, said Hall had become "everybody's granddad."

Summers' voice softened as he responded to a question about his father-in-law becoming a beloved figure in Kentucky basketball history.

"Personally, I'm so happy," Summers said. "People now realize what we in the family have always known about him. That he is a person with impeccable character, and genuinely a great person."

Frank Ramsey

Frank Ramsey, a native Kentuckian whose basketball legacy includes helping the University of Kentucky win the 1951 national championship and then becoming the original Sixth Man of the Boston Celtics, died in July of 2018. He would have turned 87 five days later.

Ramsey teamed with Cliff Hagan on UK teams that won 86 of 91 games in the early 1950s. That run began with UK compiling a 32-2 record en route to winning the 1951 NCAA Tournament. After a 29-3 record in 1951-52, the Ramsey-Hagan era ended with the only unbeaten season in Kentucky basketball history: 25-0 in 1953-54. The Wildcats were ineligible to compete for the national championship that season.

"He was the one who came in and sparked them," former UK Coach Joe B. Hall said of Ramsey's role for Kentucky. "He played with a lot of enthusiasm and a lot of toughness. No one intimidated him."

Although only 6-foot-3, Ramsey's 1,038 rebounds rank second on UK's career list (Dan Issel had 1,078).

Ramsey ranks 27th on UK's all-time scoring list with 1,344 points.

A first-round pick of the Boston Celtics in 1953, Ramsey played on seven NBA championship teams. In 623 NBA games, he averaged 13.4 points.

Boston's coach, Red Auerbach, made Ramsey the team's Sixth Man, a role previously unrecognized. Ramsey began a tradition of famed Sixth Man players for the Celtics that was to include John Havlicek, Paul Silas, Kevin McHale and Bill Walton.

"I knew I was playing behind two all-star guards in Bob Cousy and Bill Sharman," Ramsey told me in 2009. "They were established pros when I got there. So, I didn't take it as an affront."

As a high school student I read a book in which Auerbach explained the thinking behind the Sixth Man role. At that time, teams started their best five players. Any substitution diminished the five-player contingent. But if the Sixth Man was one of the five best players, the substitution improved the five-player group, thus gaining the team an advantage.

Ramsey said Auerbach did not give him any explanation. "I was just the first substitute," he said.

Ramsey cited a reason he accepted coming off the bench. He said that at the time he and many of his teammates had served in the military, which contributed to accepting whatever role the coach assigned.

"We all knew to take orders," he said.

Ramsey came to enjoy the role. He noted that opponents had grown accustomed to a reserve entering the game as a sign of weakness. A substitute was presumed to be less of a threat, so the opposition relaxed. "So I got a whole lot of shots," Ramsey said. "To me, it was great. I was playing on a good team. We were all friends. There were no jealousies. And we were winning."

As his career wound down in the 1963-64 season, Ramsey mentored Havlicek in the Sixth Man role. The NBA began a Sixth Man of the Year Award in the 1982-83 season.

In preparing Ramsey's obit, I spoke to one of my sportswriter heroes: Bob Ryan of *The Boston Globe*.

"Frank was famous for being able to get on the floor and first touch he could make a shot," Ryan said. "He didn't need much warm-up time."

Ramsey "wrote the book on the job," Ryan noted in his history of the Celtics.

"Ramsey could handle more than one position and affect the game in numerous ways,' Ryan wrote. "Though just 6-3, he was tough enough and clever enough to play forward. Auerbach reasoned that bigger forwards would have more difficulty keeping up with Ramsey than Frank would have handling them. . . . And when Ramsey played guard, he was a real big guard for the era. He had an incredible capacity to come in cold and hit his first shot.

"It seldom took him long to get his name on the stat sheet."

Ramsey became something of a controversial figure in his final NBA season. In the Dec. 9, 1963, issue of *Sports Illustrated*, he spoke candidly of how players would try to deceive referees into making favorable calls.

In the introduction to the article written in the first person, the magazine said of Ramsey, "no one has ever been better at the art of suckering an opponent into committing fouls than this former All-American from Kentucky."

Ramsey demonstrated this ability to *S.I.* writer Frank Deford on a court at his Madisonville, Ky., home. "Drawing fouls chiefly requires the ability to provide good, heartwarming drama and to direct it to the right audience," Ramsey said. "I never forget where the referees are when I go into an act. The most reliable eye-catcher is still the pratfall. Particularly on defense. When everything else fails, I fall down."

Then NBA Commissioner J. Walter Kennedy called Ramsey to his office to express his displeasure.

"The officials let me get killed after that," Ramsey said in 2014.

Ramsey was born on July 13, 1931, in his grandfather's house in Corydon, Ky. His father, also named Frank, ran a dry goods store. His mother, Sara, was a housewife and later taught school after her only child grew up.

His father wanted him to play baseball. He was an All-Southeastern Conference baseball player for UK. But basketball was his sporting future.

The 70-year bond between Ramsey and Hagan included being roommates at UK as juniors and seniors. And as Ramsey pointed out, he and Hagan both married women named Martha Jean.

Ryan recalled how Ramsey would write the number 5,000 on the blackboard before the start of each playoff season. That was the amount of bonus money each player could receive if Boston won the championship.

"He was very conscious of the monetary aspect of the playoffs," Ryan said.

Perhaps not coincidentally, Ramsey worked in banking after retiring as a player. In 1896, his grandfather founded the bank in Dixon, Ky., that Ramsey joined in 1964 as a board member. He became president in 1972. He was still at his office when he agreed to an interview in 2014.

There was nothing on display in his office to show he had a place in basketball history. In a hallway leading to his office, I happened to see a photograph on the wall. It showed the Celtics posing with U.S. President John F. Kennedy in the Oval Office.

Ryan, who lamented how the passage of time can cause a person's legacy to fade, suggested something grander was appropriate. Ramsey was inducted into the Naismith Memorial Basketball Hall of Fame in 1982.

Ramsey was part of "one of the handful of greatest traditions in college (basketball), so he's an integral part of that," Ryan said. "And he's an integral part of . . . one of the two greatest traditions (in the NBA).

"What a legacy to be part of both of those traditions."

Reggie Warford

Reggie Warford, a transformational figure in the history of the University of Kentucky's men's basketball program, died in May of 2022. He was 67.

As UK's first Black player to have a four-season career and graduate, Warford keyed the full integration of the program. Six years before he arrived on campus in 1972 as new coach Joe B. Hall's first recruit, an all-White UK team lost in the NCAA Tournament finals to a Texas Western team that started five Black players. Two years after he graduated, UK won the national championship with a team that had six Black players among its top 11 scorers.

Warford was the program's only Black player in his freshman season of 1972-73. Larry Johnson and Merion Haskins came the next season, then Jack Givens and James Lee in 1974, then Truman Claytor and Dwane Casey in 1975.

"I'm sort of a patriarch," Warford said when I spoke to him in 2021.

Johnson, who said he signed with UK rather than Louisville because of Warford's presence, called him "my hero," and recalled their introduction. It came as Johnson moved into his UK dorm room as a wide-eyed freshman in 1973.

"He was there to greet me," Johnson said. "I was just impressed with how kind and generous that was. He didn't have to do that."

Givens called Warford "the big brother to all of us who came after him," and added that Warford was the "right person" to inspire acceptance of a fundamental change to Kentucky basketball.

"It needed to be someone who had a lot of confidence," Givens said. "Not just in his athletic ability, but confidence in who he was."

This "trailblazer," as Givens called the role Warford filled, also needed to balance having a defiant chip on his shoulder while being humble.

"You have to be able to pick and choose your battles," Givens said. "And you had to have a thick skin."

In interviews during 2020, Warford spoke of challenges he faced on and off the court as a UK student and basketball player.

"There were some people who didn't want you," he said. "They looked down on you like you were stupid. I tried to carry myself and make them see that there are intelligent African-Americans that can speak without using Ebonics, that understand social graces, and you can have a dialogue."

As for his social life, Warford said there were only about 14 Black coeds on the side of campus where he lived. He said he shared a girlfriend with another male Black student for a while. Later, he dated a White coed, which was not viewed favorably.

"It was like a gay marriage today," he said. "It was taboo, and you didn't want to have people who supported the university talk to you. And I did. I had a number of prominent folks talk to me about that, and told me I'd never play, and they'd get my scholarship, and all of that kind of stuff."

Warford said he turned to poetry to express feelings he kept hidden. He wrote about being "half-filled with hate." Another stanza said that "even a blind man can see that very few of you care."

Warford recalled a game his freshman season in which the crowd sang, "My Old Kentucky Home."

"There was a group of students that were singing," he said. "When they got to the part that says 'the darkies are gay,' they screamed it out really loud and looked at me, and laughed and had fun."

As he reflected on his four years as a UK student, Warford said, "For everyone who does something that hurts you, there's always been someone at Kentucky that's been able to pick us up."

Warford's big break as a basketball player came in 1971 when Drakesboro High School advanced to the 3rd Region finals. Howard Garfinkel, a nationally known evaluator of basketball prospects, happened to attend the game.

"He thought I was one of the quickest and best shooting guards he had seen," Warford said in a story posted on the Kentucky High School Athletic Association website in 2021. "I wound up on national scouting reports as one of the top sleepers in the Midwest."

Warford had committed to Austin Peay, where future UK assistant coach Leonard Hamilton was on the coaching staff. Praise from Garfinkel moved Kentucky's

Hall of Fame coach, Adolph Rupp, to send a friend from Owensboro, Donald "Quack" Butler, to appraise Warford.

When Butler came to a practice session, a teammate mistakenly told Warford that the visitor was Rupp. To which, Warford said he replied, "Adolph Rupp, what does he do?"

Warford laughed as he recalled his innocent question. "I was about as backward as you can get," he said.

Former *Herald-Leader* colleague Mike Fields wrote a story in 2019 previewing Warford's induction into KSHAA Hall of Fame. Warford recalled speaking to Butler after the game.

"Quack's question to me was, 'Could you play with 15 White boys?'" Warford told Fields. "I said, 'Well, can they play with me?'"

In 2018, Hall called Warford, Haskins and Johnson "three of the best kids I ever had."

Warford scored only 206 points in his four UK seasons. Hall suggested Warford's lack of glittering statistics was a plus.

"The feeling among the fans (and) a lot of people close to the program was that you had to be a superstar if it was a Black kid," Hall said. "I didn't see that. I just wanted kids that were of good character and could contribute."

Warford's father, Roland H. Warford, was a Pentecostal minister. His mother, Valencia Dean Warford, was a nurse's aide.

Of Hall's approach to recruiting, Warford said, "Knowing that my father was a preacher, (Hall) was very apt to mention that he was a regular church goer . . . Coach Hall was really nice. He said he tried to encourage the boys, and did not use (pause to suppress a giggle) profanity (laughs).

"So my mother was sold. She said he was a nice, God-fearing man."

Then Warford recalled his first practice as a freshman. The veteran players sat quietly awaiting a pre-practice meeting while the freshmen were "milling around, talking and laughing and excited," he said.

When Hall arrived, he smacked his hand against a metal locker to get the freshmen's attention, Warford said. "And yelled, 'horse shit. Get your butts in these seats.'"

Warford recalled another freshman, David Miller, saying Hall had told him he didn't cuss.

"I said, 'me, too,'" Warford said. "That was my introduction to Coach Hall the recruiter and Coach Hall the coach."

Growing up in the church led Warford to learn to play piano. As a UK student, he would play the grand piano that was on the 23rd floor of his dorm. His favorite songs to play included Bill Withers' "Lean on Me," the Miracles' "The Tracks of My Tears" and Creedence Clearwater Revival's "Proud Mary."

"Everybody loved Reggie," said Kevin Grevey, who joined the UK team a year before Warford. "Reggie was just one of those kinds of guys that people gravitated to. He was so friendly, kind, positive and happy all the time."

With time, Warford grew to appreciate his role as a Kentucky basketball pioneer. This hit home in his junior season when for the first time in program history all five UK players on a court were Black: Givens, Lee, Haskins, Johnson and Warford.

"I was the last one to get in the game," Warford said in a story posted on the KHSAA website. "I remember standing there at the scorer's table, realizing it was a big deal, a milestone."

After graduating with an Arts and Sciences degree, Warford earned a master's degree in education at Murray State. He got into coaching, which included serving as an assistant at Pittsburgh, Iowa State and Long Beach State. He was also head coach of the Harlem Globetrotters in 2003.

It was while an assistant coach at Pittsburgh that Warford won the United States Basketball Writers Association's Most Courageous Award for 1984. While on a recruiting trip to Lexington, he and Pitt Coach Roy Chipman rescued an elderly couple from a house fire.

The next day Warford saw his face on ESPN's "SportsCenter." His initial reaction was alarm.

"I said, oh, my goodness, I've been fired," he said. "Because that was the only time they showed you on SportsCenter. When you died or when you got fired."

ESPN was airing a report of the rescue from the fire.

Warford had to deal with major health issues in his last 20 years. He underwent a heart transplant in 2014 and a kidney transplant in 2017. He later developed a pulmonary condition that restricted his breathing. The muscles around his diaphragm atrophied. He needed to use a wheelchair and was on oxygen at night.

On the night before his kidney transplant, Warford called Hall. They exchanged I-love-you's.

"I'd love to hear him yell, 'Get a wall!' one more time," Warford said, "and then be able to do it."

Givens, the hero of UK's championship game victory over Duke in 1978, recalled how Warford mentored him. Even if Givens made shots, Warford encouraged him to keep trying to improve. Warford also interpreted scoldings Hall gave Givens as signs that the coach cared.

"It was a challenge," Givens said of the hardships Warford dealt with as a UK pioneer. "It would have been very easy for Reggie to go in and say, 'Hey, man, this is a whole lot more than what I bargained for. I'm out of here.'

"A lot of us wouldn't have had thick skin. So, he certainly was the right person. The significance of what he did probably has gone overlooked."

A form of immortality came in 2019 when Warford was inducted into the Kentucky High School Athletics Association Hall of Fame.

"The right thing to happen to him at the right time," said Jerry Hale, a teammate in three of Warford's four UK seasons. "It meant the world to him."

Warford's Kentucky career was in stark contrast to modern college basketball's here-today-gone-tomorrow model featuring the transfer portal. In his first three

UK seasons, he averaged 2.0, 2.0 and 3.6 minutes. Then as the team's lone senior, he averaged 22.0 minutes.

Two former teammates attributed Warford's patience to the importance he placed on integrating the Kentucky program.

"Reggie was a proud man, and it was important to him to be the first Black to play basketball for four years and graduate from the University of Kentucky," Hale wrote in a text message. "His decision aided Merion Haskins, Larry Johnson, James Lee, Jack Givens and others to feel comfortable attending the university."

Bret Bearup

Bret Bearup's death in May of 2018 led the Denver Nuggets to hold a celebration of life gathering in his honor. He had been working in the Nuggets' analytics department. His brother, Todd Bearup, who also played for Kentucky, said the family planned to scatter the former UK player's ashes in the Snake River in Idaho. The family considered that part of the country its home.

In early June of that year, former UK players and staffers gathered in Lexington to remember Bearup. Kenny Walker noted a difference from earlier gatherings that followed the deaths of such players as Melvin Turpin, Ed Davender and Charles Hurt.

"No tears tonight," Walker said with a smile.

About 100 people came to The Club at UK's Spindletop Hall. The stately mansion befitted a solemn occasion, I wrote, but laughter filled the wood-paneled Oak Room.

"I know Bret's here and loving seeing you and hearing you tell stories," his widow, Beth Ann, told the crowd. Then she added a note of caution, "Crazy PG stories," she advised.

One by one, people spoke of Bearup, who died suddenly at age 56 of a coronary attack.

"Bret was unusual," Bearup's UK coach, Joe B. Hall, said. Knowing laughter erupted.

"Bret kind of stood out in an intellectual way," Hall said. "Fun to be around. But he had a quirky side."

Bearup brought a dead chicken to Wildcat Lodge and put it under the bed of teammate Jim Master. "He thought that was funny," Master said as the crowd laughed. "I didn't see the humor."

Not that Master failed to appreciate Bearup's gift for lightening the mood.

Of any story involving Bearup, Master said, "Even if I heard it 44 times, I couldn't wait to hear it a 45th time."

Bearup dreamed of being a baseball player. He turned to basketball after being cut from a baseball team. A subsequent growth spurt made basketball a viable option.

Bearup tried to enhance his growth by taking melatonin and sleeping on an air mattress in the quiet of the basement because he thought a good night's sleep maximized the potential for growth.

As a high school senior, Bearup averaged 28 points and 17 rebounds. As a college player, he averaged 3.6 points and 2.7 rebounds.

"He could have been a great basketball player if he had focused (on basketball)," Hall told the gathering. "He was thinking way above athletics."

Rex Chapman, who lived with Bearup for five years in Denver after his UK career, said his friend made a decision once he realized he would not be a star player for Kentucky.

"I decided I'm just going to be a smart ass," Chapman recalled Bearup saying.

Master recalled a game in which Kentucky trailed LSU by double digits at halftime. Hall entered the locker room and said he needed to apologize to the team. This puzzled the players until Hall explained that he was apologizing "for putting Bret Bearup in the game."

Pat Madden, who attended UK Law School with Bearup, recalled a story. After benching Bearup, Hall asked him a sarcastic question: What team are you playing for?

To which, Bearup replied, "Well, right now, Coach, neither one."

Bearup's then 22-year-old son, Alex, recalled his father being invited years later by John Calipari to sit behind the Kentucky bench for a game. Bearup called the family to tell them to look for him on the game telecast.

Beth Ann's father had a needling response. "Tell Bret I've already seen him sit on the bench," Alex recalled his grandfather saying.

Once more Spindletop seemed like a comedy club as the people laughed. No doubt this pleased Beth Ann.

C.M. Newton

C.M. Newton, whose basketball legacy includes playing for one of Kentucky's national championship teams, later rescuing the UK program from national embarrassment and repeatedly opening doors for historically marginalized Black athletes and coaches, died in June of 2018. He was 88.

I need to credit Jim Host for spurring me a few weeks earlier to get the Newton obituary ready. I was driving from Elizabethtown to Lexington when Host called. I was and continue to be grateful.

C.M. Newton filled many roles in a basketball life that spanned more than a half century. He coached at Transylvania, Alabama and Vanderbilt. He was associate commissioner of the Southeastern Conference, Kentucky Director of Athletics, chair of the NCAA Rules Committee, chair of the NCAA Division I Men's Basketball Committee, president of USA Basketball, NIT Committee chair, USA Basketball representative at FIBA and inductee in the Naismith Memorial Basketball Hall of Fame.

"In anything to do with basketball, he was an ambassador," Kentucky Coach John Calipari said in February of 2018. "He is a basketball icon."

Yet, Newton was approachable. I remember a pointed question asked by another reporter: How did the cleanup effort of the Kentucky basketball program in the fall of 1989 compare with the Exxon Valdez oil spill in March of that year?

As I recall, Newton was not amused. But he did not scold the reporter.

Friends and associates described Newton as something of a paradox: an imposing presence because of a resume bursting with achievements. Yet, as former UK president David Roselle said, "kind of an aw-shucks kind of guy."

Newton brought credibility to each of his basketball roles.

"I don't know anyone more highly respected than C.M. of all the people I worked with in my 38 years at the NCAA," said Tom Jernstedt, the organization's longtime executive vice president.

Jernstedt recalled Newton's personal touch on display in Indianapolis for an NCAA meeting at the same time as "Grandfather's Day" at the elementary school attended by Jernstedt's youngest son.

Cole Jernstedt's grandfathers lived out of state and could not participate. Newton volunteered to go to Cole's school and act the grandfather part.

"And Cole still talks about that," Jernstedt said in 2018. "That's an example of his versatility. He's a man for all seasons."

Bill Hancock served as an NCAA liaison to the Division I Men's Basketball Committee for 16 years, six of which coincided with Newton's time on what's commonly referred to as the Selection Committee for the NCAA Tournament.

"I don't remember anyone walking into the room and having the respect of everyone in the room immediately to the extent that C.M. did," Hancock said.

In 1989, Kentucky had a dire need for the respect that Newton personified. The UK basketball program had been found in violation of NCAA rules.

After forcing the resignation of the basketball coaches and the athletic director, then UK president David Roselle convinced Newton to leave a successful coaching career and lead Kentucky's athletics department.

"Dr. Roselle convinced me that not only was I wanted as the athletic director, but that I was needed," Newton told *The Sporting News*. "It was the 'needed' part that really got to me because UK had been so good to me over the years."

Newton hired Rick Pitino as the new coach. Although Christian Laettner's famous buzzer-beating shot would defeat Kentucky in the famous Elite 8 game three years later, Kentucky was Kentucky again.

Roselle cited the credibility Newton brought to Kentucky basketball as a key to the resurrection. "One of the best hires I ever made," Roselle said.

Delany saw Newton as uniquely qualified to lead Kentucky's athletic department at that time.

"There probably was not another person in the country that could have put a period on the end of that sentence," Delany said. "Coaches, players, administrators and media people realized who he was and that as a very good man, in times of difficulty, that's what you want leading your program."

After retirement, Newton was named to the National Association of Collegiate Directors of Athletics Hall of Fame.

On several occasions in his career, Newton broke down racial barriers. He integrated the basketball programs at Transylvania, a small college in Lexington, and Alabama. Each decision was met with resistance.

According to author Andrew Maraniss, when Newton recruited Transylvania's first Black player, Jim Hurley, in 1965, Rupp told Newton he was "ruining basketball in Kentucky."

When Newton recruited Alabama's first Black player, Wendell Hudson, in 1969, someone set a cross on fire in Newton's front yard. It was only six years after the Alabama governor at the time, George Wallace, famously stood in the schoolhouse door and vowed to prevent Blacks from attending the University of Alabama.

On Dec. 28, 1973, Alabama had the SEC's first all-Black starting lineup: Ray Odums, T.R. Dunn, Charles Cleveland, Charles "Boonie" Russell and Leon Douglas.

"When you think about it, who would have the courage to do that?" Calipari said. " . . . You always wonder, if I were in a position like that, would I have the courage? People say to me, 'Yeah, you're progressive that way.'

"But it was a different time. It's a lot easier to be progressive today."

Later, as Vanderbilt coach, Newton orchestrated the school's long-overdue reconciliation with Perry Wallace, the first Black basketball player in the SEC.

Newton also hired Kentucky's first Black coaches in men's and women's basketball: Tubby Smith and Bernadette Locke-Mattox.

Newton declined to take bows for bringing about change.

"I get too much credit," he told Maraniss in 2016. "I was just very pragmatic."

In an email message, noted civil rights advocate Richard Lapchick wrote, "C.M. was a pioneer for using sport for racial equality in America. My own dad was given a lot of credit for helping to integrate the NBA. It was well deserved, but he did that in New York City."

Of Newton's actions in Kentucky, Alabama and Tennessee, Lapchick wrote, "He performed courageous acts when other White sports leaders stood on the sidelines. America is in C.M's debt."

Newton was a product of the South having been born in Rockwood, Tenn., and then growing up in Fort Lauderdale, Fla. He was self-deprecating about playing for Kentucky in the 1949-50 and 1950-51 seasons. The Wildcats won the national championship in 1951.

Newton liked to tell the story about Rupp taking him out of a preseason scrimmage and telling him, "You know what you remind me of? A Shetland Pony in a stud-horse parade."

Roselle recalled Newton downplaying his playing career at UK.

"He said he was a role player," Roselle said. "And I said, 'What do you mean by role player, C.M.?'

"And he said, 'well, on days of practice, I rolled the balls out for the other players.'"

That sense of humor helped lighten the mood when Newton became Kentucky's athletic director in the dark days of 1989.

Eddie Sutton

When Eddie Sutton died at age 84 in 2020, I wrote that his four seasons as Kentucky coach "showed that the combination of an acclaimed coach and an elite program does not guarantee success."

Sutton's 806 victories made him one of only 11 coaches to win 800 or more Division I men's college basketball games. He also became the first coach to lead four schools to the NCAA Tournament: Creighton, Arkansas, Kentucky and Oklahoma State.

Yet his coaching career had a yin and yang quality.

"The man is an alcoholic," one of his former players, Doug Gottlieb, said in 2017 for a planned documentary on Sutton. "The man is a great basketball coach. Those two things can coincide and be true."

Dwane Casey, an assistant on Sutton's staff, suggested that poor timing contributed to Sutton not being able to lead Kentucky to great success.

"It was almost a I'm-going-to-get-you mentality," Casey said of the media scrutiny and NCAA investigations at the time. "And I don't care what program you are, you have someone chasing after you 24/7, watching over your shoulder, you're going to make mistakes and stub your toe. I thought he was a victim of that more than anything else."

Sutton's biography in the 1988-89 media guide began with, "if his first three seasons are any indication, Sutton has met the challenge with flying colors."

But in October of 1988, the NCAA announced 18 charges of wrongdoing.

In his memoir, iconic radio play-by-play announcer Cawood Ledford wrote of the 1988-89 season, "the happiest moment of the season was when it was finally over. The program seemed to be in ashes."

After his second season as UK coach, Sutton sought treatment for his alcoholism at the Betty Ford Clinic. One of his sons, Sean Sutton, said that back pain contributed to his father's later relapse while coaching for Oklahoma State.

"I don't know what possessed him to buy a bottle of vodka and decide it was time to start drinking again," Sean Sutton said. "Because he had never done that ever at Oklahoma State.

"I love my dad. But sometimes with a lot of guys, the success he had, they think they're invincible and use poor judgment."

Christopher Hunt, the director of a documentary titled "EDDIE!," said the rise-and-fall nature of Sutton's career made for a riveting story.

"He was a hell of a coach who wasn't perfect," Hunt said.

Bill Keightley

Bill Keightley was the Kentucky basketball program's equipment manager from 1962 until his death in April of 2008 at age 81. As I wrote in the obituary, that span barely began to tell the story of his influence.

"Mr. Wildcat," as he was known, served as a father figure to generations of players, a confidant and companion to coaches, the spirit of the program and a beloved ambassador for UK.

"He is Kentucky basketball," Rex Chapman said.

Keightley died after falling off a bus that took him to the Cincinnati Reds' opening game of the season.

When reached by phone, Tubby Smith struggled to control his emotions.

"I don't know what to say," he said as he sniffled and paused. "There's nobody like him. Never has been. Never will be."

Marta McMackin, the longtime administrative assistant in the UK basketball office, said coaches retreated to the equipment room to be with Keightley and players sought his advice.

Smith said Keightley "had a way of making you forget all your cares and keep everything in perspective. He knew when to say, 'It's OK. It's time to move on.' You know how coaches are. We hold on to things."

The school retired a jersey in his honor, making Keightley only the second non-player or non-coach to be so honored. Cawood Ledford was the first.

Former UK Director of Athletics Larry Ivy released a statement: "You always hear that everyone can be replaced, but not this time."

"Almost Like We're Being Hunted"

Jacob Blake paralyzed after being shot seven times in the back. George Floyd dead because a Minneapolis policeman knelt on his neck for more than nine minutes. Breonna Taylor dead in Louisville. Rayshard Brooks dead. Eric Garner dead. Twelve-year-old Tamir Rice dead. Michael Brown dead. Trayvon Martin dead.

The ever-lengthening list of Black people killed or gravely injured unnerved Kentucky basketball player Keion Brooks, Jr.

"It's scary," he said during a teleconference in 2020. "Because I'm a Black male. And at times I feel like it's almost like we're being hunted."

This realization hit home for Brooks when he happened to catch his reflection on his cell phone. He noticed his haircut (the long twists were gone).

"I thought that, 'Wow, I kind of look like George Floyd right now," he said. "It scared me. Brought a couple tears in my eye. It really hit me and made me realize that could have been me. It could have been my brother or my teammate.

"Once I had that realization, it just made me want to do more to be able to do whatever I can to help."

A college sophomore at the time, Brooks was in a position to act. He was serving on three panels: The National Association of Basketball Coaches' Player Development Coalition, the Southeastern Conference Council on Racial Equality and Social Justice and UK's chapter of the Student Athletic Advisory Committee.

These panels seek to alert players that they have a platform and should use it, Brooks said before adding that one overriding message is that athletics is merely one facet of a person's life.

"The biggest thing to get across to everybody is just because you play a sport and represent your university, you also represent yourself as a human being," he said.

Brooks applauded the UK football team's decision not to practice one day earlier that fall to show support for efforts to fight social injustice and systemic racism.

When asked if the UK basketball team might take a similar stand, Brooks said, "We discussed some things that we want to do and we want to try to put forward to let people know we're not going to stand for these social injustices and to let people know that going through these things, they're not alone. We're with them."

Brooks acknowledged that there can be blowback from people who do not want players using their platforms to call for change.

A recent social media posting showing Kentucky Coach John Calipari following a call by the National Association of Basketball Coaches to inform and encourage players to vote drew sharp rebukes as well as support.

"I think people have a difficult time separating the athlete from the sport that they play," Brooks said. "Just because I represent Kentucky basketball and go out there and play at Rupp Arena, that does not mean I'm not a person that has morals, values, opinions and views on certain things. . . .We have strong views on topics just like the fans do."

Brooks put criticism of athletes' voicing opinions in the context of an effort to pigeonhole people as merely players of a sport. He suggested Black people can be marginalized as mere entertainers.

"We are just asked to go out there, entertain you for a couple hours," he said. "Go do a dunk, dribble between your legs, shoot a three and then go home and be quiet as we see our people shot and killed on TV every week.

"I don't get that. I don't see why they would think that way. That we're not going to get up and say something. But, I mean, I'm praying for them so that hopefully they can see change."

At that point, Brooks spoke of being wary.

"I'm not ignorant of the fact that . . . if I was to leave outside this bubble and be somewhere where I'm recognized as the Keion Brooks that plays for Kentucky, like there might be an officer waiting to make an example of me just because he had a bad day or something."

Players can get lost in their sport and not think of societal issues, Brooks said. He also said the ever-longer list of Black people killed or injured has changed his perspective on sports.

"Basketball is something I do," he said. "Not who I am. Once I leave the basketball court, I'm Keion Brooks Jr., a normal person just like anyone else. . . .

"Basketball is a game. But I'm talking about people losing their lives to violence that I don't ever grasp how that makes sense. . . . It really makes me realize this is bigger than basketball. This is a life issue. This is a social issue. And basketball can take a back seat to that."

The deaths of Black people and systemic racism put a story idea in my head. Were basketball heroes like Kentucky players immune from racism? I suspected not, but it seemed like a good story idea to bounce off former UK players.

While the status that comes with being a basketball hero can mitigate systemic racism, former Kentucky players said it didn't give them total immunity. Fred Cowan, who played for UK from 1977-78 through 1980-81, recalled how "that was just life" to be stopped by the police. "I didn't think I was worried," he said. "I didn't drink. I didn't smoke. Even my friends weren't allowed to bring drinks or marijuana in my car."

Then Cowan was in the passenger seat as UK teammate LaVon Williams drove from Kansas City to Denver. The speed limit was 55 mph. Cowan recalled Williams going about 60 when they saw the police lights and pulled to the shoulder of the road.

"As soon as the state trooper got out of the car, he pulled his gun on us," Cowan said. As Cowan recalled, the UK players tried to ease the tension by pleading, "We ain't doing nothing! "Then he started aiming at LaVon," Cowan recalled.

Cowan said he told his teammate to stay in the car. "All of a sudden, LaVon says, 'We play for the University of Kentucky! I'm LaVon Williams and he's Fred Cowan,'" Cowan said. "Believe it or not, you could kind of see him relax a little bit. And I really believe that's the only thing that saved our lives."

For the story in 2020, I spoke to Erik Daniels. He played at UK from 2000-01 through 2003-04. He was then coaching a girls' basketball team in neighboring Woodford County. After a game earlier that year, he returned to the school parking lot and discovered that someone had written the n-word on the back of his car. To make matters worse, his three oldest children were with him and first discovered what had been written on the car. "It kind of hurts because I had a lot of explaining to do to my children," Daniels said. At the time his children were 17 (Niyaune), 12 (Erik Jr.) and 11 (Eriyaune). "They don't understand why anyone would do that to their dad." Upon reflection, Daniels saw how the incident could teach his children "how to approach certain situations in life.

"Especially my son, being a Black male. When a police officer approaches the car, you have to be very cautious. Some of the things my dad taught me. When you get pulled over, just how to carry yourself being a Black male in America." Daniels, who is also the father of 22-month-old Eriyah, said his older children attended peaceful protests in Lexington. They made signs and wore T-shirts adorned with messages of support for protesters. "They like to be involved," he said. "They have a voice. They have friends that they talk about things with. I want them to know what's really going on."

Kenny Walker, an All-American for Kentucky in the 1980s, spoke of the difference made by being a basketball hero for an elite program like, say, Kentucky, Duke or North Carolina. There is much more acceptance.

"Let's not get it twisted," Walker said with a chuckle. "We will not get treated that way if we were just normal people that didn't play basketball." He chuckled again. "Maybe we were good people who just didn't have the talent to play basketball," Walker added. "We were going to try to see where life takes us. Would I be treated the same way? Nope. And I know that."

When asked how this made him feel, Walker said, "I'm torn. I know if I was just a regular person, I could be in the same position as any of these young Black men who have died over the years. I'm not going to shy away from that.

"But at the same time, I understand I was very good in basketball. . . . That's what separates us. I'm almost embarrassed."

In explaining the difference being a basketball hero can make, Sean Woods, one of UK's "Unforgettables," echoed a sentiment expressed at Muhammad Ali's 2016 memorial service in Louisville, which I covered for the *Herald-Leader*. A minister said Ali gave African-Americans a "sense of somebody-ness." The difference being a basketball hero can make for an African-American? "You're relevant," Woods said.

After completing his Kentucky career in 1981, Cowan lived and played basketball for 10 years in Japan. He remembered the decade as an eye-opening experience.

"I felt like a person living in Japan," he said. "The way I was treated wasn't because of my color."

Not being prejudged because of race?

"It'll blow your mind," Cowan said.

Cowan came to believe the Japanese were not free from bias. They did not like Koreans. But this ill feeling was not as stark and inescapable as Black and White.

One feeling of acceptance Cowan remembered came when the team returned to Japan from a game in another country. While teammates went to the customs desk for returning Japanese, he moved toward the line for foreigners.

"The whole team told me, no, you stay in line with us," Cowan said. "That kind of blew me away. You don't realize these things until you can see the difference. Because when you grow up in America, you get programmed. You know you're not supposed to do this. You're not supposed to go there."

When Cowan would return to the United States after each season, he tried to keep that feeling of acceptance he received from the Japanese as long as he could. He made a point of flying to the United States on Japanese airliners rather than American.

"I wanted to stay away from America, the prejudice, the way people look at you as long as I could," he said. "Because I knew if I flew United or Delta, as soon as I walked on the plane, I was a Black man. As long as I stayed in Japanese territory, I was a human being. I had no color."

When Erik Daniels played professionally in Europe, Asia and South America, he noticed a role reversal.

"Some of my Caucasian teammates from America felt a little different because they were usually the minority," he said. "They were usually the only White guy on the team from America.

"So they kind of understood or felt our pain a little bit because they didn't have the same support system that they normally would as far as seeing the same kind of faces or being around the same type of people."

A question came to mind while watching Minneapolis policeman Derek Chauvin brazenly keep a knee on Floyd's neck for more than nine minutes. If a sense of human decency couldn't prevent the killing, shouldn't the presence of a camera have inhibited Chauvin?

Not "if you don't care, if you feel like you've got the privilege," Walker said. "If you feel like you wear the badge. . . . Or maybe he was overcome with emotion and wasn't really thinking."

Whatever the case, Walker said he wondered why the three other police officers at the scene or an onlooker did not intervene.

"If I was one of those cops, I think I would have said, 'Hey, man, that's enough,'"

Walker said. "If I was one of the bystanders, I'm not sure I wouldn't have reacted myself and pushed (Chauvin) over and taken the chance of getting arrested or getting shot."

Before the 2020-21 season, Kentucky's basketball team posted a video on social media that had players calling for reforms that addressed racism. Players and Calipari wore T-shirts bearing the words Black Lives Matter.

Former UK players approved of the video because it showed that players also think, feel, lament, hope and despair.

"I love it,' Reggie Hanson said. "The problem with people when it comes to athletes is they don't look at them as people. They don't look at them as people who have problems."

As a certified life coach who aspires to work in the mental health services field, Hanson knew that players are not immune to human frailties and feelings. Having been a Kentucky player (1987-88 through 1990-91), he could see how this disconnect between player and person can be vivid at an elite program.

"I tell people this all the time: they look at what a player was ranked coming out of high school," he said. "He's, like, the top player in the country coming to Kentucky, the top program in the country. And they automatically assume this athlete is perfect. 'You're supposed to be great. Go entertain me.'"

When Brooks said that Black people in the United States could feel like "we're being hunted," this rang true for PJ Washington.

"I think it's crazy being able to feel like that just because of the color or our skin," he said. "It is outrageous to me. At the end of the day, we're all regular people. And we all want the same things in life. That's just happiness and being able to have respect from others."

Tony Delk, an All-American in 1995-96, found the police killing of Floyd particularly disturbing.

"As I watched that video, I was, like, man, if my mom was alive and here I am with somebody having a knee on my throat, and I'm screaming for my mom, and she can't do anything, she can't help her baby, she can't help her son, like, that's when it really, really hit home for me," Delk said. "And it took me a few days just to get over that. I felt for him."

Delk also saluted the UK players.

"Social media has given them a platform where people are listening," he said. "People are watching. People are waiting to tweet. So, it's a different platform in 2020 than it was back in 1992 when I first went to college.

"I commend this generation for what they're doing and they're speaking out and not accepting what's going on."

After watching – along with America – a policeman kill Floyd, John Pelphrey called one of his former Kentucky teammates, Sean Woods. The two are close friends who speak frequently. This time the conversation lasted about an hour.

"He feels embarrassed . . . ," Woods said. "John and I talked about it. How can we be this way?"

Pelphrey said he all but recoiled in horror when he saw the video of the policeman pressing his knee onto Floyd's neck.

"It made me feel awful," Pelphrey said. "It made me feel sick. It's inexcusable to treat another person that way. I got angry."

Pelphrey sought insight from Woods, who is Black.

"I don't completely understand what it's like to be Sean or my other teammates or my friends in how they might feel," Pelphrey said. "But I do understand my feeling, and, being a member of society, I know what right and wrong looks like."

Other former UK players, Black and White, also said they were sickened.

Jeff Sheppard struggled to find the words to describe his reaction.

"Speechless," he said. "Just horrified. It was awful."

Kevin Grevey, who ranks seventh on Kentucky's career scoring list (1,801 points), said he averted his eyes rather than watch the video more than once.

"I must have spoken to hundreds of people about that event," he said. "How aghast and disturbing and horrific it was. And I could only watch it once. I couldn't bear to see it again.

"I thought to myself, oh my God, on the heels of the other events that showed African-Americans being basically tortured or accosted or killed, I'm, like, oh my God, what is going on?"

In the aftermath of Floyd's death, protesters took to the streets of several American cities including Lexington and Louisville. There were reports of damage to stores and looting.

Former UK players spoke of misgivings about protests that were not peaceful. But they said that systemic racism lasting centuries made pent-up frustration boiling over understandable.

"Violence is kind of the frustration that comes about from it," Dwane Casey said. "I hope we don't get that all mixed up with what the real problem is.

"But (violence) is not the answer to cure the problem."

Walker, the program's second-leading scorer (2,080 points), saw the killing of Floyd as a potential tipping point.

"I'm not happy with the reaction, the rioting and the controversy," he said. "But I'm happy it is getting the attention that, you know, it needs. These things need to be addressed and talked about and put up to the light. And I think this incident is probably the straw that broke the camel's back."

Tyler Herro echoed that sentiment.

"Change is needed!" he tweeted. "I stand with people of color and support that everyone needs to be viewed the same. America is a melting pot and if we are all created equally, then we should be treated equally as well. Silence is a form of acceptance. And I will not stay silent."

Karl-Anthony Towns appeared in a video posted by the Minnesota Timberwolves.

In that 2020-21 season, Kentucky players and Calipari knelt during the playing of the National Anthem before a Jan. 11 game at Florida. Because of the coronavirus pandemic, I covered the game from home via television. The kneeling was not televised.

Brooks said that he, Davion Mintz and Olivier Sarr met and decided they wanted to "take a stand against what we're seeing in the world today."

Calipari said he learned about the players' desire to make a statement while the team rode a bus to Florida's O'Connell Center. He accepted the players' invitation to join in the silent protest.

"They care about this country, and all the other stuff," Calipari said. "They're trying to figure out life and making statements they think they have to make. . . . I'll support them if they want me to be there."

The players welcomed Calipari joining them in the preseason video and the statement made by kneeing.

"It's great to have the head man in charge backing you with everything you do," Brooks said.

Brooks also said the crowd that stormed the U.S. Capitol building five days earlier help inspire the UK players to stage a protest.

Not surprisingly, the players and Calipari kneeling during the National Anthem divided the Big Blue Nation. Messages of support and opposition were posted on social media.

Laurel County sheriff John Root and jailer Jamie Mosley held a "burning party" the next day in which UK memorabilia was destroyed. "I honestly can't believe a team from Kentucky (the Hillbilly State) took a knee to our National Anthem with the American Flag displayed," Root posted on Facebook.

Mosley posted, 'I back the real team in blue," presumably meaning the police.

Sarr said the Kentucky players expected less than 100-percent support.

"Well, you know, we understood our gesture would have consequences," Sarr said. "And that we just want people to understand. We knew some people would be mad or pissed at what we did.

"But we just want people to understand that it's just a peaceful way to protest in a way we can use our platform."

Freshman Isaiah Jackson said the objective was to "try to get through to everybody that we need equality just like everybody else.

"This is a great country. I feel like – and we feel like – minorities and stuff don't have equal rights like everybody else. That's what we're protesting, and that's why we kneel."

Neither the NCAA nor the Southeastern Conference had rules regarding conduct during the playing of the National Anthem.

Kentucky was not the first team to make such a symbolic protest.

Ole Miss players knelt during the Anthem before a game against Georgia on Feb. 23, 2019.

On that same day, a pro-Confederacy gathering protested on the Ole Miss campus and in Oxford in reaction to the school distancing itself from Confederate-themed history and symbols.

Sarr, who grew up in France, said that racism was not unique to the United States.

"You always have minorities that are being treated not as equal to other people," he said. "We are in a position to raise awareness, and that's all we're trying to do."

In his Facebook posting, Root criticized Calipari's support of the protest. "Until we get a real man to lead the Cats and a real team, you will not see me back in no UK junk," the Laurel County sheriff wrote. That presumably meant he would not wear clothing adorned with a UK logo or message.

Sarr expressed thanks for Calipari not only allowing the players to kneel at Florida, but to also kneel with them.

"Really powerful," Sarr said. "He took it with heart. He did it for us. . . . It's showing that we're all together on this."

The Kentucky team did not kneel again. Players and coaches stayed in the locker room during the playing of the National Anthem before home games the rest of the season.

When he entered the 2022 NBA Draft, Brooks said his social consciousness got positive feedback from NBA people

"In the interview process, they said they love the way I answer questions," he said. "They say it tells them I'm smart and I'm intelligent."

This brought to mind hearing Brooks say early in his college career that his father bounced questions off his young son in the hopes of preparing him for future interviews.

"My parents were very big on me being more than just an athlete (and) continuing to show people I have more to offer than putting the ball in the hoop," Brooks said. "So, I feel that has helped me as I go through this process."

Coincidentally, in terms of social awareness and racial equality, Kentucky played in arguably college basketball's most impactful game. That was the 1966 national championship game in which Texas Western played only Black players in beating an all-White Kentucky team. That game undermined an opinion held by many White people that Black players needed at least one White player on the court to lead them.

To mark the 50th anniversary of what has been called college basketball's version of the 1954 Supreme Court ruling in the Brown vs. Board of Education case that made school segregation illegal, *Herald-Leader* reporter Tom Eblen and I worked together on a story.

Players on both teams said they had only one thing on their minds that night at the University of Maryland's Cole Field House: winning a national championship.

"We actually didn't treat it any differently than we did any other game that we played all year," said David Lattin, who was Texas Western's center. "We didn't treat the guys from Kentucky any differently than we treated any other team. They didn't treat us any differently. No one said anything derogatory, you know. We were just 10 young men trying to win the game."

Blacks had been making inroads in basketball for years – except in the South.

San Francisco won the1955 NCAA Tournament with four Black players. So did Cincinnati in 1962 and Loyola of Chicago in 1963.

In his effort to enhance Texas Western's basketball profile, Coach Don Haskins recruited inner-city Black players from New York, Detroit and Gary, Ind.

Haskins decided to play only Black players in the championship game and used racial pride to motivate them.

"Right after the pre-game meal, like about three in the afternoon, he called all the Southern African-American players who were going to play in that game into my room and said, 'Adolph Rupp said at a press conference that five African-Americans couldn't beat his five White boys,'" Lattin recalled. "Then he said, 'Well, it's up to you.' Then he walked out of the room. He didn't say anything else about it."

A guard, Bobby Joe Hill, was Lattin's roommate.

After Haskins departed, Lattin said he asked Hill, "Do you really, really think he said that? And Bobby said, I don't know if he said it or not. But we're not going to lose."

Kentucky star Pat Riley said that Haskins made up the story about Rupp in an effort to motivate the Texas Western players.

"Adolph never said one word to us," Riley said. "I don't ever recall him ever saying one word (about) Black-White."

Kentucky guard Louie Dampier said race was not a factor in the game.

"It wasn't the first time we played against Black players," he said. "When we looked at the other end, that was just another team we wanted to beat."

Lattin remembered Kentucky's undersized big man, Thad Jaracz, saying "nice play" after his third dunk.

After the game, the coaches shook hands and Dampier made the unusual step of going to the opponent's locker room to offer congratulations.

"I had never done that before," Dampier said. "I don't know what motivated me. I just walked out of our dressing room and saw theirs just across the way. I wasn't happy and hand-slapping and all that. I just congratulated them. And Coach Haskins said, thank you."

Dampier added that after a radio station reported his visit, he received about 100 letters of appreciation from Texas Western fans.

Said teammate Larry Conley, "The only thing I was doing was playing for a national championship. That's all I cared about."

Media coverage was remembered as race neutral.

"At the time, it was not a big deal, especially for people in basketball," said Frank Deford, who wrote *Sports Illustrated*'s game story. "I mean, the Boston Celtics already were starting five Black guys. . . . Blacks were already dominating the NBA. Of course, all the Southern schools were White.

"The main point at the time was not the racial angle," Deford added. "It was much more the little team that nobody ever heard of beating the big royalty, and, oh, by the way, they started five Black guys. The race thing only took on significance in the later years."

Of course, a vast majority of Kentucky fans were White. But Black Kentuckians knew history was being made that night.

"A lot of people won't like to hear this, but we were rooting for Texas Western," said Porter G. Peeples, longtime president of the Urban League chapter in Lexington.

At the time he was a student at Southeast Community College preparing to transfer to UK the next fall.

"We identified with them," Peeples said of the Texas Western players. "African-Americans all across Kentucky identified with Texas Western."

Chester Grundy, then one of about 50 Black students at UK, said he and about eight friends gathered in a room in Holmes Hall to watch the game. They used a towel to seal the crack under the door so others in the dorm would have a harder time hearing them cheer for the Miners.

Kentucky Gov. Edward T. "Ned" Breathitt, who was then by law chairman of the UK Board of Trustees, pushed for the school's football and basketball teams to add Black players, said Don Mills, his press secretary.

Breathitt helped the football program recruit Nate Northington and Greg Page in 1966 to become the school's first Black scholarship players.

Kentucky would not have a Black basketball player until Tom Payne in the 1970-71 season. Rupp tried to recruit Wes Unseld and Butch Beard. Both went to Louisville instead.

"He just didn't make the effort that he should have," Mills said of Rupp. "I would say he was very lukewarm. The established community was very much opposed (to Black players), and he was aware of that."

In hindsight, many people believe the Texas Western-Kentucky game hastened the integration of college basketball, especially in the South.

"It was a watershed moment for integration, unbeknownst to us," Riley said. "I feel very proud of being part of that moment."

The players needed time to appreciate the historic nature of the game.

Heroes and Villains

With Kentucky basketball, it seems every dribble has the potential to be revered or reviled. So, there have been plenty of heroes and villains

Heroes are relatively easy to understand. The game-winning shot or clutch steal all but come with a form of immortality.

The New York Times quoted former *Herald-Leader* editor John Carroll as saying that villains are basically the flip side of the coin of worship.

"Villains are necessary when you feel that intensely about a program," said Carroll, who became a villain when the *Herald-Leader* published a Pulitzer Prize-winning investigation of the Kentucky program in 1985. "Good isn't enough. You need evil. As Gore Vidal said, 'It's not enough to succeed. Others must fail.'"

Here's a look at heroes and villains I wrote about.

HEROES

Princely performance

If Kentucky fans hadn't noticed the interlocking "U" and "K" that marked Rupp Arena's center court, Tayshaun Prince burned that decoration into their memory banks on Dec. 8, 2001.

Prince got so hot, his shooting eye got so keen, that after he made four three-pointers in less than two minutes, he stopped at the "U" to apply the coup de grace.

With his body language saying why not, he launched a three-point shot from the vicinity of center court. "The suburbs of trey-ville," UK radio commentator Mike Pratt said.

Like every other Prince shot in the game's first 15 minutes, it went in. The crowd roared as Prince led Kentucky to a 79-59 victory over North Carolina.

Why take a shot from near midcourt?

"Just because of the fact I hit the first four," Prince said after the game. "When you're in a groove like that, you feel you can hit it from anywhere."

In 2023, Prince needed no prodding to remember the game. He recalled making three-point shots in five straight UK possessions and seven straight overall.

He scored Kentucky's first 15 points, then added a sixth three-pointer with 12:37 left in the first half. That equaled his previous career high and gave him 18 of UK's first 20 points. The career-high seventh three-pointer came with 3:41 left in the first half.

When Prince missed his next shot, another three-point attempt, he smiled and clapped his hands as if to say a miss is possible.

The hosannas were plentiful in the postgame media sessions.

"Unbelievable," UK Coach Tubby Smith said. "I've never seen anybody do that. He was just possessed. Where he was shooting them from was unbelievable. If I was on the North Carolina bench, I'm thinking, 'What's going on?'"

Said North Carolina Coach Matt Doherty: "I don't remember a guy shooting the ball the way he did. He hit some ridiculous shots."

Smith made a telling remark when asked if he had asked Prince to take personal control of the game.

"Tayshaun's not that type of player to talk of taking over," Smith said. "That's not his demeanor. That's not him. He's one of the most unselfish players I've had the opportunity to coach."

I recall a team scrimmage early in Prince's Kentucky career. He played well. When I spoke casually with Smith, I suggested Prince could have scored 40 points if he'd wanted to. Smith agreed.

In 2023, Prince downplayed any notion of wanting to take a star turn against North Carolina.

"I was never the guy trying to score a lot of points or showcase my shooting ability," he said. "I was always a winning player, a team player."

Prince noted that when he went to the NBA, he sought to establish himself as a "defense-first player."

After the game in which he equaled his career-high of 31 points, Prince said his performance generated "a remarkable feeling. . . . to hit four or five shots to get the team going in a game like this, against North Carolina, that's something as a little kid you dream about."

Prince's first two three-pointers seemed rather ordinary – routine shots from just beyond the top of the key. Number three got a bit deeper in the right corner as he was challenged by UNC's Jason Capel. The fourth was a step-back move off the dribble over Will Johnson in front of the Tar Heels' bench.

And then came No. 5, a 27-footer from the edge of the "UK" logo at center court that brought a deafening roar from the stands.

"My ears started ringing after the fourth one," teammate Gerald Fitch said. "After the fifth, they were hurting."

After the fifth three-pointer, Prince looked over to the media row along the sideline with a facial expression that seemed to say, what do you think of that?

"I remember that," he said in 2023. "It's just one of those scenarios that nobody said anything. One of those times when you're in a rhythm. Obviously, the crowd is going crazy. It's one of those moment-type things that happen."

After the game, teammate Marquis Estill had a more ho-hum appraisal, albeit equally complimentary. "It didn't surprise me at all," he said. "He does that in practice all the time. Once he's feeling it, he'll pull up from anywhere."

In 2023, Prince said his shooting display had a history dating back to middle school.

Of his mother, Diane, he said, "she wasn't shocked by that game because she used to see it all the time. The only reason I pretty much did that (against North Carolina) was because it was just one of those games where one shot after the other went in. That's the reason I just kept letting it fly."

Triple-doubles

Although many Kentucky players were capable of posting a triple-double, only three managed to do it. I witnessed all three. Incidentally, none occurred at Rupp Arena.

The first came on Dec. 28, 1988. Freshman Chris Mills, who later was linked to the well-chronicled Emery Air Freight package mailed to his father that allegedly contained $1,000, scored 19 points, grabbed 10 rebounds and got credit for 10 assists in Kentucky's 85-77 victory over Austin Peay. In those days, UK played one home-away-from-home game in Louisville each season.

Three of Mills' assists came when Kentucky needed offensive production. Austin Peay had rallied from a 65-44 deficit to reduce the margin to 75-69 with 2:46 left.

"Chris played a whale of a game," UK Coach Eddie Sutton said after the game. "I don't know how long it's been since a player had a triple-double at Kentucky. It's been a while since I coached a player (to post one) at Arkansas, and I had great guards at Arkansas who never did that."

It could be argued that the second and third triple-doubles by Kentucky players deserved asterisks.

Another freshman, De'Aaron Fox, posted the second triple-double in Kentucky basketball history on Nov. 28, 2016. He had 14 points, 11 rebounds and 10 assists in a 115-69 victory over Arizona State in a game played in the Bahamas.

Or did he?

One of the assists was questioned, in part, because Monk dribbled twice and stutter-stepped before shooting.

After reviewing the play, it was announced the assist would not be removed.

"I didn't care," Fox said of this assist being questioned. "I'm not playing for stats."

Fox said he watched a replay and wondered, "how is this controversial?"

When asked whether he meant it was obvious his pass was or was not an assist, Fox said, "Clearly wasn't. But I'm not going to tell them to change it."

Because assists are more subjective than, say, points or rebounds, the NCAA did not recognize assists as an official statistic from 1953 until 1983.

J.D. Hamilton, who was an assistant director in charge of the NCAA department that governed men's basketball statistics, said, "people were not using the same playing field in giving assists to student-athletes."

The popularity of assists led the NCAA to begin keeping the stat in the 1983-84 season, Hamilton said. He likened this to the NCAA beginning to recognize blocked shots as a stat in the 1985-86 season.

The NCAA manual on statistics defined an assist as "when a player makes – in the judgment of a statistician – the principle pass contributing directly to a field goal."

Of the questionable assist credited to Fox, Hamilton said, "If there's two dribbles and a pump fake, then the player has created his own bucket."

For a game played in the Bahamas, personnel from the University of Central Florida compiled the statistics. Nate Blythe, an assistant director of athletic communications for UCF, was the person who credited Fox with an assist

Blythe did not return my calls seeking comment. He did not regularly work on the UCF stats crew, but he did fill in on occasion, sports information director Dan Forcella said.

The decision to award Fox with an assist was on Blythe's mind when he returned to UCF.

"He brought it up to me when he first got back from the Bahamas," Forcella said. "I said, 'oh, boy.'"

The third triple-double in Kentucky basketball history came almost exactly a month after the second. It, too, could be questioned.

On Dec. 29, 2016, Kentucky won 99-76 at Ole Miss. In that game, Isaiah Briscoe had 19 points, 10 rebounds and 11 assists.

In the final minutes of the game, teammate Derek Willis stepped to the foul line to shoot free throws while knowing Briscoe needed one more rebound for a triple-double.

In a somewhat subtle fashion, Willis signaled that he would intentionally miss the free throw to the side of the lane where Briscoe was stationed. Briscoe got the rebound to complete the triple-double.

Jeff Van Gundy, a former NBA coach who had moved to work as an analyst on game telecasts, happened to be watching the game.

"I was, like, is this really what the game has come down to now?" Van Gundy told me in a telephone conversation a few days after the game. "Really? We're going to miss on purpose so an individual gets one more rebound so that we validated that he played a really good game? I mean, I don't get it. I just don't."

Van Gundy was not being critical of the harmless subterfuge perpetrated by Willis and Briscoe as much as voicing unease with the growing importance placed on statistics. He called triple-doubles "the most over-talked-about thing in sports . . .

"You know, people say, oh, that's old school. No. To me, it's just stats-foolish, what we've become at times."

Van Gundy conceded that "numbers tell a story. But I think a lot of the fascination with the numbers now keeps you from actually looking with your eyes and appreciating the game for the beauty the game can bring out."

The setting of an effective screen. The pass that leads to the pass labeled an assist. Rotating on defense. Forcing an opponent to his off hand.

"Winning plays," Van Gundy said. "It's a highly nuanced game. Yet, we're trying to reduce it to sheer numbers."

VILLAINS

Going into the 2021 NCAA Tournament, I wrote a story about villains who supposedly tried to thwart Kentucky.

Yes, Kentucky had won eight national championships. But what about the 70-plus times Kentucky did not win the NCAA Tournament? And only four titles since 1958.

I returned to the theme of identifying villains for other stories.

Clearly, blame must be assigned, I facetiously wrote. Villains should be identified. They included:

COVID-19

More than once, John Calipari had said that Kentucky was on track to win the 2020 NCAA Tournament. Then, of course, the coronavirus was declared a pandemic in early March and the NCAA Tournament was canceled.

Referee John Higgins

After Kentucky lost to North Carolina 75-73 in the 2017 South Region finals, Calipari implied that the referees helped the Tar Heels win.

"You know, it's amazing that we were in that game where they practically fouled out my whole team," he said to begin his postgame news conference.

Later, he added, "I told (the UK players) at halftime, it is what it is. You've got to beat who's out there."

Some UK fans directed death threats at Higgins.

NCAA president Mark Emmert

Emmert acknowledged that he received threats from Kentucky fans after freshman Enes Kanter was ruled permanently ineligible in January of 2013.

When asked whether he could describe the nature of the threats, Emmert said with a smile, "I can't really quote without having them bleeped out."

Emmert said he and the NCAA took the threats seriously.

"We received enough communication that it was sufficient cause for people who worry about that to add additional security," he said.

Emmert noted how passionate fans add something valuable to the college sports experience.

"I certainly appreciate passionate fans," he said. "The last thing you want is fans that are not passionate about sports.

"But we have to be careful that they don't become the cause or the excuse for . . . repugnant behavior. That's true everywhere."

Christian Laettner

Does anything more really need to be said about the Laettner shot that crushed Kentucky's soul and gave Duke a 104-103 overtime victory in the 1992 East Region finals?

Earlier in the game, Laettner tapped a foot on the chest of a fallen Aminu Timberlake. The never-to-forgive Big Blue Nation still insists this was a "stomp."

When he came to Lexington for a charity game in 2011, Laettner acknowledged regret for the tap/stomp. "There was maybe too much adrenaline flowing, but it was a big mistake," he said.

Luke Maye

Maye made the jump shot in the final seconds that gave North Carolina the victory over Kentucky in the 2017 South Region finals (aka the John Higgins game).

In noting that he shared a uniform number with Maye, Laettner tweeted, "Luke, my son . . . may the force of the #32 be with you."

Then twisting the knife, Laettner added, #uncdownsthecats and #theshotlives.

Al McGuire

As Marquette coach in the 1960s and 1970s, McGuire led his team against Kentucky five times in NCAA tournaments. If Marquette winning two of those games was not insulting enough, McGuire's irreverence toward Adolph Rupp (and by extension Kentucky basketball) made him a villain.

Upon Rupp's death in 1977, sportswriter David Jantz of the *Milwaukee Journal Sentinel* spoke to McGuire, who recalled a news conference previewing the Kentucky-Marquette game in the 1971 Mideast Region.

Speaking first, Rupp turned to McGuire and, as Jantz described it, "said in his best Southern drawl, 'Now, son . . .'"

To which McGuire shot back, "If you're going to call me son, you better put me in the will."

On another occasion, friends urged Rupp to make amends with McGuire. So, Jantz wrote, Rupp called McGuire and said, "I know we've had our differences, but I just can't begin to tell you how great a coach you are."

To which, McGuire replied, "Then why don't you get off the line and put someone on who can?"

Rick Pitino

The former Kentucky coach made a startling transformation when he became Louisville coach in 2001. That made for an irresistible subplot when Louisville played at Kentucky in December, 2001.

Once the cheers for Pitino shook Rupp Arena, I wrote in the advance story on the game. Now silence would be truly golden.

I asked other coaches if they could envision coaching an archrival sometime in the future.

Lute Olson from Arizona to Arizona State?

"I don't think I'd get out of the city limits of Tucson if I said that," Olson said with a laugh.

Roy Williams from Kansas to Missouri?

"I don't think I can imagine that," he said after an initial laugh. "I think they'd probably shoot me. At both places."

Quin Snyder from Missouri to Kansas?

"Wow," he said. "I can't imagine that in my wildest dreams."

Two former Kentucky coaches – Eddie Sutton and Joe B. Hall – said for the 2001 story that they could not see themselves leading the Louisville program.

"I wouldn't accept that job if it was offered," said Sutton, who was then coaching at his alma mater, Oklahoma State. "That's a real tough situation."

I asked if Sutton could see himself someday as Oklahoma coach.

"That situation at Kentucky is a little different than me going to Oklahoma," he said. "The basketball tradition at Kentucky is so deep, there is a percentage of fans that would not be forgiving."

Hall said that after he retired as Kentucky coach he was approached by Tennessee and Vanderbilt to see if he had interest in their jobs.

"No way I could have taken a coaching job there," Hall said of being Louisville coach. "My family would have to move out of Central Kentucky."

Hall suggested that Pitino's New York roots made the move to Louisville easier.

"He's not from here," Hall said. "He doesn't feel that pressure."

Of course, Pitino did not move from Kentucky to Louisville. He was the Boston Celtics coach and leading light between the college coaching jobs.

Kelvin Sampson, then coaching at Oklahoma, saluted Pitino's can-do confidence.

"I always thought Rick had moxie and nerve," Sampson said. "When he took the Louisville job, that took courage. I respect him even more."

The NCAA

For Calipari, the announcement of seeding and bracketing came on Rejection Sunday. Almost annually, he rejected the NCAA Men's Basketball Committee's decisions regarding Kentucky's seed or "path" or playing sites.

I thought he was trying to inspire an us-against-them motivation for the UK players in early-round games.

Calipari wasn't the only Kentucky coach in my time to question NCAA decisions.

In 1986, Eddie Sutton bemoaned Kentucky having to play Alabama and LSU in the Southeast Region. It was the fourth time Kentucky played those teams that season.

After LSU won in the region finals, the NCAA amended the bracketing rules to prevent a repeat of such a bracket in the future.

Dean Smith

While beloved and/or respected throughout college basketball, the iconic North Carolina coach makes the list.

That's because he berated Kentucky big man Rick Robey during the championship game of the 1977 East Region. He objected to what he saw as Robey's roughhouse play.

If that wasn't bad enough, North Carolina beat Kentucky 79-72 by going to Smith's signature "four corners" stall in the final minutes. With no shot clock, UNC could retreat while UK wanted to compete.

Vaughn Wedeking

The little point guard for Jacksonville defiled any reasonable person's sense of basketball justice in the 1970 Mideast Region finals game against Kentucky. With Dan Issel not looking, he snuck up behind the UK star and took a quote-unquote charge near midcourt. It was Issel's fifth foul. Jacksonville won 106-100.

"The thing that sticks in my mind most is how much time there was left in the game," Issel said 51 years later. "I believe there was more than 10 minutes left."

Judging block/charge was ill-defined at the time. That Issel did not have the ball was irrelevant.

"The fact it took place at midcourt is what made it so hard to take," Issel said. "I was just running back down the court to the offensive end.

"It was a smart play on his part because if he gets called for blocking, that doesn't make much difference."

Wedeking, who died in 2009 at age 60, had no fouls in the game. Issel was one of four Kentucky players to foul out.

When asked if taking advantage of the rules in a sneaky way qualified as villainous, Issel chuckled and said, "he certainly is my villain."

John Wooden

John Wooden had the audacity to lead UCLA to 10 national championships in 12 years. That's put Kentucky in catch-up mode in terms of most NCAA Tournament titles for more than half a century.

Plus, the Wizard of Westwood had the temerity to announce on the eve of the 1975 national championship game that he would retire after UCLA played Kentucky. The Big Blue Nation was shocked – shocked – that an opposing coach would be willing to go to great lengths to gain an advantage.

Billy Packer

The CBS commentator was already perceived as biased in favor of the Atlantic Coast Conference (and, ipso facto, against Kentucky) when he further inflamed UK fans when from the network studio he questioned whether Patrick Sparks got away with a walk before being fouled and making game-winning free throws at the end of the Louisville game in 2004.

When he worked Kentucky's game against Kansas three weeks later, a fan held up a sign that read, "Hey, Packer, Sparks did walk (on water)."

When he entered Rupp Arena two weeks later to work Kentucky's game against LSU, fans chanted "Go home, Packer."

David Roselle

With the NCAA launching an investigation into the Kentucky program in 1988, school president David Roselle called for an internal and independent investigation into how closely the program followed NCAA rules. He appointed a sitting judge, James Park, to lead the investigation.

"I heard from a number of cowards in the state," Roselle told me years later. "They'd call and tell me what all was going to happen to me. I never took that all that seriously."

But, he added, he did report each threat to the police.

Me

Much to my surprise (true confession: and delight), Greg Bishop, then with *The New York Times*, did a story on me that was published during the week leading up to the 2012 Final Four.

The Times did offbeat stories on each of the Final Four teams.

It was interesting to be the subject of rather than the writer of the story. It gave me a better appreciation for the person responding to questions.

Bishop touched on the negative reaction my coverage could get from Kentucky fans. He noted an email I received earlier that season that read, "I can't wait for you to die, so I can urinate on your grave."

Message board postings included saying I was the Wildcats' "biggest enemy" and a "biased reporter who has an absolute vendetta against UK and Calipari."

That wasn't true. I just wanted to write good stories and keep readers informed as well as possible.

Still, a Lexington-based radio station playfully (?) aired the idea of taking a shot at me in Rupp Arena. I was not aware of this. But former *Herald-Leader* sports editor Gene Abell recalled that.

"We literally had a discussion," Abell said. The topic? "Do we need to talk to law enforcement?"

The Times' story included a quote from John Carroll, then editor of the *Herald-Leader.*

"If they gave a Pulitzer Prize for excellent beat writing under miserable conditions for a number of years, he should be the first to win."

"Best Marketing Mind of Any Coach"

There were no tornadoes interrupting Kentucky games during the 13 seasons I covered the program headed by John Calipari. But that was about the only exception to an ultra "newsy" span.

There were great highs: a national championship (2012), three other Final Four appearances (2011, 2014 and 2015), a record 38 straight victories to begin the 2014-15 season.

There were memorable lows: a first-round loss to 15-seeded Saint Peter's (2022), a 2012-13 season destined to conclude in the NIT first-round loss when Nerlens Noel tore an anterior cruciate ligament, the end of a streak of making a three-point shot at 1,047 games, a 34-point loss to Duke to begin the 2018-19 season.

There were memorable innovations: making so-called "one-and-done" players the foundation of teams, making platoons a substitution pattern in 2014-15.

There were surreal storylines: multiple ejections from games including having to be held back by players when Calipari appeared to want to accost referee Doug Sirmons, the coronavirus canceling the 2020 NCAA Tournament and then the pandemic disrupting preparation leading to Kentucky's 9-16 record the following season (fewest victories in a season since three in 1926-27).

All the while, Calipari commented on all this and more at news conferences, by tweeting, by posting on the UK Athletics website, by speaking on his weekly radio show, etc., etc.

Whew!

I led a Sunday Notebook in May of 2016 with a fan calling for an off switch on Calipari.

Reader Jack Taylor of Lexington sent me an email making that suggestion.

"Can Calipari SHUT UP for one day?" he wrote.

What prompted Taylor's question was Calipari's steady drumbeat of tweets, Internet postings and headline-making proclamations that spring.

Those included announcements about exhibition opponents for the next pre-season, a regular-season game against Hofstra and ESPN confirming a plan to air a "30 for 30" documentary on – who else? – Calipari.

Taylor's email suggested the previously unthinkable: there's a limit on Kentucky fans' interest in Kentucky basketball. And the emailer said there should be an off switch in the, ahem, offseason.

Taylor suggested that Calipari was "self-absorbed." But I suggested he could be merely a marketer with an excellent product with which to flex marketing muscles.

Jim Host, a Lexington-based businessman who over decades helped transform corporate sponsorships into partnerships with the NCAA, saluted Calipari's marketing ability.

"He's got the best marketing mind of any coach I've ever been around," Host said in 2023. "He could have run any major corporation or major business having to do with marketing and thought process.

"If something else is grabbing the spotlight, he has a great ability to come up with something that's going to grab the spotlight back."

Calipari has a degree in business marketing. To put it lightly, he has flexed his marketing muscles.

In 2020, Host wrote a memoir titled "Changing the Game: My Career in Collegiate Sports Marketing."

After Kentucky won the 2012 NCAA Tournament, Calipari called Host to ask him about an idea he had. Calipari was considering taking the championship trophy on a train tour of Kentucky.

"I said, I think that's a heck of an idea," Host recalled saying to Calipari. "Like a whistlestop presidential campaign?"

Yes, Calipari responded.

"I said my only advice is don't take it to Louisville," Host remembered saying. "Take it to Paducah. Take it to Pikeville and take it to outer regions of the state where they really, really care about Kentucky basketball.

"Which is what he did."

Host acknowledged that Calipari's marketing mind is ever spinning. That's a good thing, he said, even for Kentucky basketball, which seems never to be out of the spotlight.

"You have to constantly position the product," Host said. "If you don't, the light has a tendency to go out. And once it goes out, it's really difficult to get it back on again."

For a story in 2016, I spoke to William Sutton, who was teaching sports marketing at the University of South Florida. He likened Calipari to Bill Veeck, an irrepressible baseball owner and promoter in the mid-20th century who never let accepted propriety get in the way of a promotion. Veeck was the first to give away bats at games, which led to free balls, free pickles, free hot dogs, free lobsters, free ice cream and free tuxedo rentals. A Disco Demolition Night in Chicago led to a riot and a forfeiture of the game.

Sutton explained the thinking about promotions.

"Making people feel important and making them feel part of something," he said. "That's what Cal does."

Incidentally, Sutton shares the Pittsburgh area as a hometown with Calipari. He also arrived as a professor at UMass the same year Calipari came as coach. He watched Calipari go to dorms and off-campus bars to talk basketball, give away pizzas to students and promote his basketball program in other ways.

"He created a market for his product where there wasn't one," Sutton said.

In my reply to Taylor's email, I noted that Calipari had a degree in marketing from Clarion State in Pennsylvania.

"He must have been a Straight A student," Taylor quipped in a response.

The title of Chapter 11 of the book *Going Big Time*, which detailed how Calipari guided a UMass rise to basketball prominence in the 1990s, is a telling Calipari quote: "Anything You Do in Life is About Selling."

But Taylor wondered whether all the tub-thumping regarding Kentucky basketball was necessary. It was a well-known brand with zealous fans. Taylor likened UMass basketball, where Calipari got his start as a head coach, to Mr. Pibb. UK basketball was Coke.

"So there's no need to market the brand to this extent," Taylor said.

Sutton, who started a Sports and Entertainment Management program at South Florida, conceded that the UK basketball brand was well-established and probably didn't need market saturation.

"But I wouldn't say there's not a need for marketing," he said, "because it's always staying front and foremost. It's controlling the market. You own the market. You're No. 1 in the market. It's not letting No. 2 emerge."

Plus, ESPN posed a marketing challenge by airing many games featuring other high-profile teams.

"So he's got to maintain a position where he can keep people thinking of Kentucky first and foremost," Sutton said.

As a marketer, Calipari might go too far for some people. For instance, Kentucky played exhibition games in the Bahamas in 2014. These games were the first to be televised by the new SEC Network.

When the games drew high television ratings, Calipari proclaimed that college basketball should "own August."

Perhaps being a non-marketer, I immediately thought that baseball should own August.

When I asked Sutton about that Calipari comment, the marketing professor said, "I respect him, but I think he's a little bit over the top on that one. I think he jumped the shark with that statement."

Host disagreed in 2023.

"He is consistently coming up with thought processes like that," Host said, "because it's another way to get a few inches in the paper or get a blurb on TV. That constantly reminds people of Kentucky basketball. He's a master at that."

In 2023, Calipari said his comment was part of an effort to get college basketball to have a summer league. It would be like the NBA's summer league for draft picks and other prospective players.

Kentucky could play, say, Duke in Rupp Arena in August. Although a mere exhibition, the game would be televised and surely excite the Big Blue Nation.

Alas, Calipari said, rosters becoming ever more fluid by the transfer portal and Name Image and Likeness deals made such a summer league impractical.

When Kentucky was in the process of looking for a new coach in the spring of 2009, I was unaware of Calipari's background in marketing.

It didn't take long for Calipari to scratch his marketing itch. Five of his players were selected in the first round of the 2010 NBA Draft, which moved him to tell ESPN's Heather Cox that it was "the biggest day in the history of Kentucky's program. . . . the biggest day for the University of Kentucky."

When asked a few days afterward if it was the program's "biggest day" several former Kentucky players recoiled

"The dumbest thing I've ever heard," said Dan Issel, UK basketball's career scoring leader. He sounded more amused than annoyed as he added, "if the goal is to be a feeder team for the NBA, maybe that was the greatest day. I thought the goal was to win a national championship."

When I asked Issel in 2023 about questioning Calipari's draft night comment, he said, "I still feel the same way." He applauded the players advancing to the NBA, but added, "Winning at Kentucky, as a Kentucky fan, is a whole lot more important to me than how many players you put in the NBA."

When radio host Dan Patrick asked the next day if the draft surpassed national championships on Kentucky's biggest-day scale, Calipari hedged. "It depends on your reference." He added that his draft night comment might upset "the old guard."

I quoted skepticism voiced by several former players.

"For sure the championship is what everybody looks forward to," said Cotton Nash, an All-American in the 1960s.

Added Kyle Macy, who led Kentucky to the 1978 national championship: "The greatest day is whenever a program wins a national championship."

No question it was a historic day for Kentucky. No college team before or since produced five first-round picks in an NBA Draft. The five for Kentucky in 2010 were John Wall (first overall), DeMarcus Cousins (fifth), Patrick Patterson (14th), Eric Bledsoe (18th) and Daniel Orton (29th).

"(The draft) was special, but it doesn't top a championship," said Kevin Grevey, a UK star in the 1970s. Choosing his words carefully, Grevey added, "This is probably the greatest moment in John Calipari's history. It's a huge milestone for him."

In 2023, Calipari continued to insist the 2010 NBA Draft was the greatest day in Kentucky program history.

'It'll go down as never done before," he said. "And I know people are mad because they like winning the national championship. Well, we've won a bunch of them. Which one was the best? This has never never happened.

"I know some people would be upset, but I felt that way. And I still do today. That was one of the most special days and may never happen again in the history of our sport. And it happened here."

Macy wondered aloud if the 2010 NBA Draft served as a future recruiting pitch. Thus, Calipari laid it on thick.

Host agreed that Calipari's comment about the "greatest day" was a marketing tool.

"All he was doing was this is another example of his marketing capability of being singularly focused on recruiting the best talent he can find," Host said. "And by doing that, he will win. And he has won.

"He's got six years left (on the contract as of 2023)," Host added. "And I'm of the opinion he'll win one or two more championships before he's gone."

When I spoke to Issel in 2023, I asked him about interpreting Calipari's "greatest day" comment as a marketing strategy.

"Oh, for sure," Issel said. "I'll tell you what. If he doesn't start winning some important games pretty soon, he may have to fall back on (marketing as career change)."

Nash saw the 2010 draft as signaling an evolution in college basketball.

"When I played, it used to be a college sport," he said. "You stayed four years. You got a degree.

"Now, it's big business. It's motivated by money. Just a minor league for the NBA in a lot of cases."

In the case of Kentucky?

After a pause, Nash said, "I don't think intentionally."

As the 2010 NBA Draft suggested, Calipari did not always connect as a marketer. He swung and missed on occasion.

With Kentucky's dependance on so-called "one-and-done" players stirring sometimes negative comments early in his tenure, Calipari suggested a more uplifting term for players who used Kentucky as a launching pad to the NBA. In 2014, he suggested the label of "succeed-and-proceed" for these players.

Although UK players like Archie Goodwin and Daniel Orton proceeded to the NBA without great success in college, the label succeed-and-proceed was better than, say, fail-and-bail or null-and-void, I wrote.

But "one-and-done" stuck.

I came to think of Kentucky's dependence on so-called one-and-done players as selling recruits and their families what they wanted.

In 2023, I asked Tyler Ulis if there was a stigma attached to playing more than one season for Kentucky.

"It just is what it is," he said. "Your time will come. I didn't go one-and-done. I came back the next year with the mindset (of) I have to leave after this year.

"I feel expectations kind of hurt people at times if they don't live up to that hype, especially with today's media and social media."

Ulis said he did not use Twitter when he played for Kentucky in the 2014-15 and 2015-16 seasons. Now as a member of the staff, he said he advises players to stay off Twitter.

At the 2022 NBA Combine, Keion Brooks Jr., described his three Kentucky seasons as initially a learning experience, then dealing with adversity and then adapting to an enhanced role. He spoke of making long-lasting friendships.

With Kentucky synonymous with players entering the NBA Draft after only a season or two, Brooks was asked if there was a stigma attached to playing four seasons under Cal for UK.

"People probably do view it that way," he said. "That's not for me to be concerned with. My journey is different from anybody else's. So, I can't get into a game of comparing myself or trying to emulate what someone else did."

Host noted that Calipari saw being Kentucky coach as a position to be effective off the basketball court. The UK coach launched telethons to aid victims of an earthquake in Haiti and a hurricane in south Texas, plus promoted help efforts after tornadoes hit in Western Kentucky in late 2021 and flooding in Eastern Kentucky the next spring.

"He does love the place," UK Director of Athletics Mitch Barnhart said of Calipari in 2023. "He loves Lexington. And I think about things he's done for our communities. He's never once failed to respond to the call (for help). As a matter of fact, he's usually the first. And people have rallied around that."

Barnhart suggested a socially conscious coach who tries to help when disasters strike can be in a no-win situation.

"If you don't do it, they're saying why didn't you do it," he said. "And if you do it, they're questioning your motives. C'mon man! You can't have it both ways."

Marsha Poe, a retired postal worker who regularly participated in campouts for Big Blue Madness events, echoed that sentiment. To make the point, she said in 2023 that she had written Calipari letters several times.

"I've gotten, like, five little handwritten notes from him," she said.

On one occasion, Poe heard that Kentucky was considering ending the annual campout. She wrote to Calipari to appeal for it to continue.

"It wasn't long after that he said we're going to camp out again," she said of the response Calipari sent.

On another occasion, Calipari learned through a fellow church goer that the husband of Poe's friend had pancreatic cancer.

"Cal called him up and was talking to him," Poe said. "Then, two years later, Jerry was dying. Cal called him again."

Billy Gillispie did not embrace a public role outside of basketball for the Kentucky coach. But Calipari repeatedly said the job involved more than X-and-O thinking. He welcomed a public celebrity component.

I sensed that when I met him before his UMass team played at Kentucky on Dec. 4, 1991. The game came as a stopover on the UMass trip back home after playing in the Great Alaska Shootout.

I always tried to include the opponent's point of view in a story previewing an upcoming game. This usually consisted of a phone call with the coach.

But when I called Calipari, he invited me to his hotel room in downtown Lexington. This certainly helped the story.

UMass competed. Kentucky led only 46-41 at halftime. Surely fatigue factored in Kentucky pulling away in the second half to win 90-69.

That game was on my mind when Saint Peter's beat Kentucky in the first round of the 2022 NCAA Tournament. That's why I asked Calipari in the postgame news conference if he could accept that analogy. I meant it as a compliment to both Saint Peter's and UMass.

Joel Justus, who was on Kentucky's staff from 2014-15 through 2020-21, agreed with the suggestion that Calipari was a good fit for the job as Kentucky coach. That was the reason I suggested Calipari to Pratt.

"Absolutely," Justus said. "He's perfect. I don't know that there will ever be another more perfect coach for Kentucky than John Calipari."

Justus cited several reasons for why Calipari and Kentucky basketball were a good match.

"He has the confidence to coach great players," Justus said. "I think you have a lot of coaches who are scared to coach great players. They would be more comfortable coaching a great team of lesser players. Cal was much more into taking great talent and figuring out how to make them a team.

"And Cal is confident and he's very good at coaching great players with extreme talent, and giving them the blueprint on how to be successful."

A moment later, Justus offered another attribute.

"You have a lot of people who are process-driven folk," he said. "I think you have other people who are result-driven. Cal is the perfect combination of both.

"I don't know that there's ever been anyone as good as Cal. And I don't know that there ever will be."

Why Retire? It Was Time

I had been considering retirement for a few years before bowing out in the summer of 2022. It was sort of like when a coach says he'll evaluate whether it's time to retire once the season ends. I felt good and still enjoyed the reporting and writing.

Although readers enjoyed reminding me that I was aging, I was in denial. To quote Mark Twain, "Age is an issue of mind over matter. If you don't mind, it doesn't matter."

A sense of humor when interacting with coaches, players and other story subjects helped me continue. As George Bernard Shaw said, "you don't stop laughing when you grow old. You grow old when you stop laughing."

But I had to accept aging when I turned 70 in the summer of 2021. I kept working one more year in order to enjoy a final season and to make sure it was time to retire.

When I wrote my farewell story in the summer of 2022, it began with an anecdotal lead.

> Sahvir Wheeler and Lance Ware were Kentucky players at a Name, Image and Likeness event in Danville in the summer of 2021. But who was the third person sitting with them behind a baseline waiting for this Players First Satellite Pro Camp to begin?
>
> I approached this person and asked. His name was Jarvis Byrd. He said he had been on the Asbury University team the last two seasons and was transferring to play for Stillman College.
>
> When he said his father was former UK player Leroy Byrd, I said I covered Kentucky basketball when his father played.
>
> Jarvis' eyes widened in disbelief.
>
> Actually, my first season covering Kentucky basketball was 1981-82 (or two years before Jarvis' father, aka "Baby Magic," was a freshman).

From the beginning and through 41 seasons, I've felt fortunate to be reporting and writing about such a prestigious program.

But the changing nature of college basketball and the newspaper business helped me decide it was time to retire.

Although bylines tell the reader who wrote the story, the reporting and writing process is a product of collaboration. The newsroom was a place to bounce ideas off colleagues. The sports editor and/or a copy editor would read the story and make needed changes. Casual conversations could spark a story idea or bring a needed timeout in the process of putting a story together.

As Dorothy Parker said, "I hate writing. I love having written."

For me, that statement would need editing. I loved writing . . . or at least attempting to write. Completing the story brought relief and on occasion an urge to celebrate. Hence, newspaper bars were part of the learning process when I was a young man.

The Internet and social media changed the daily routine. Rather than almost always having the time to develop a story, the need to post a story on the website made for the feeling of working under a constant deadline. Sadly, copy editing suffered in this rush. I would regularly wince when reading my stories. For games, I had to work on a story as the action continued. I wrote about the first half at halftime, then used television timeouts to try to capture the second half. The deadline for this quick game story was minutes after the final buzzer.

When Joe B. Hall and Eddie Sutton were Kentucky's coaches, the media could attend practices. I remember going to "shootarounds" the day of a game.

I remember one such practice at Mississippi State. Sutton saw people in the stands asleep. He good-naturedly grumbled about believing his practices were interesting enough to keep onlookers awake, if not emotionally engaged.

In one Hall practice, the team worked on a box-and-one defense. A staffer asked reporters not to make this known to the public. As far as I know, no reporter did.

Rick Pitino brought change. Prior to him becoming coach in 1989, I could go to about any practice. Plus I could go to the UK basketball office anytime with a feeling there was at least a 50-50 chance of speaking to the coach.

One of the last practices I attended was at Rupp Arena. Pitino had the starters working on handling the full-court pressure applied by reserve players. I was sitting behind the baseline at the other end of the court.

With the starters struggling to not turn the ball over, Pitino blew his whistle to stop play. The first team big man was standing at about the foul line at my end of the court, thus not providing his teammates any help in handling the press. Pitino asked him if he was having a good time. I saw the big man shrug his shoulders.

To which, Pitino told him, "good, because we're getting fucked."

I laughed. A minute or so later, a manager came and told me the rest of practice was closed to the media.

Tubby Smith was more accessible. But since his time, it was rare to bounce questions off a Kentucky coach other than at a scheduled news conference.

In the first season or two covering Hall's teams, reporters could be invited to social gatherings while at the site of an away game. One such gathering came at the home of Sonny Smith, who was then Auburn's coach.

In 2023, Sam Bowie recalled the change from then to now when stories posted online can be written by who knows who.

"I remember you being in the locker rooms, being in the practices, being on the plane rides," Bowie told me. "Today, there's so much more delegating, much more anonymous recording. People won't put a name or a face to the report."

College basketball has changed what with the transfer portal and Name, Image and Likeness money. The former makes college basketball more like a pickup game. Who's got winners?

The NIL money distribution breathes life into something I heard said by Van Florence, who was a friend, sounding board and emissary for many Kentucky basketball coaches. He helped set up charity efforts for Pitino and Smith.

Florence, who was also the executive director of the UK Basketball Museum from 2000 to its closing in 2008, was in the hospital when I paid a visit. I remember him saying that fans think a school's athletic department is concerned with winning games.

But the primary concern is making money, Florence said.

Former Kentucky All-American Kenny Walker suggested that the use of the transfer portal should be restricted.

"I think you should only be allowed to do that one time. . . ," he said in 2023. "You can't run from competition and you can't run from adversity. 'I'm going to find a place where I can go to play.' That's great. But is (the portal) really good (at) teaching a kid a thing about discipline and working hard and fighting for a position on a team? Or are we just teaching them to give up and go someplace else?"

ESPN analyst Jay Bilas saw the transfer portal as increasing anxiety in college basketball.

"Players have always understood that talent is coming in behind them," he said. "But . . . players have a more difficult time wrapping their heads around an established player that is older than you could be coming in to compete with you.

"Everyone has feelings of insecurity. Fans years ago used to know what you have coming back. And the only variable was what good young players do we have coming in? Now, you might get the best player off an NCAA Tournament team from last year. . . . It's a different dynamic."

John Calipari has made Kentucky basketball synonymous with the one-and-done player.

Bowie, who spent five seasons with the Kentucky program, suggested that one-and-done weakens the player-fan bond. I had numerous fans say the same thing.

"In today's world, and you're a McDonald's All-American, and they're honest with you, their goal is to go to college one year and go to the league," Bowie said. "I can actually say I enjoyed being in college."

As for fans, "they tell me (one-and-done is) the thing they dislike so much," he added. "They felt I was part of their family because I was there for five years. It's hard for me to embrace the new signees because they're in and out, and I know they're doing what's best for their loved ones and their future. But there's something to be said about camaraderie and chemistry when you work together for four years.

"The game is more of a business today."

Walker said he considered leaving Kentucky for the NBA after his junior season. He had heard talk of him being a top 20 pick in the 1985 NBA Draft.

His parents and the newly arrived coach, Eddie Sutton, persuaded him to return for a senior season.

"I wish more parents would do this now," Walker said. "My parents (said), 'Kenny, we don't need you to go to the NBA and take care of us.' They were very happy that I was on track to get my degree."

Walker said he put a priority on getting a degree in communications. He also saw another reason to play for Kentucky as a senior.

"Maybe win a championship because that was what I was really wanting to do in college," he said.

The championship did not come, but Walker has no regrets.

"I'm glad I had good parents," he said in 2023, "because if they would have told me to do it, I would have done it. No question, I would have done it. But I think they wanted to make sure I was enjoying the experience. They didn't want to put any extra pressure on me. And I love my parents for that."

There was a change I enjoyed seeing. The sport had more parity, therefore more competitive games and more drama.

The 2023 NCAA Tournament had a Final Four that did not have a one-seed, two-seed nor three-seed for the first time since seeding began in 1979.

And 2023 was the second time in the last three NCAA tournaments that neither Kentucky, Duke, North Carolina nor Kansas advanced beyond the first week.

And Purdue became the second No. 1 seed to lose in the first round. Both times it happened came in the last five NCAA tournaments.

In the past three years, Purdue had lost to a No. 13, No. 15 and No. 16 seeds.

Kentucky had won only one NCAA Tournament game in that span. Or three fewer than Florida Atlantic.

None of the schools that had won the seven most recent national championships were in the 2023 Sweet 16.

Neither were any of the teams that won conference tournament titles in the Big Ten, ACC, Big East and Pac-12.

The top six winningest programs in college basketball history were also gone.

Conversely, Florida Atlantic, which had never won a NCAA Tournament game, advanced to the Final Four.

Former Kentucky player Scott Padgett, who has been coaching since 2009, endorsed the idea of greater parity.

"I think mid-majors are getting more athletic because they're taking more athletic kids from the high majors," he said in 2023. "High majors are taking more skilled players, but maybe not as athletic. Now the gap in athleticism isn't what it used to be, and I think they guard better and they can rebound better than they used to be able to against the high major (team)."

For example, Padgett cited a game from his Kentucky career: the 88-61 victory over Saint Louis in the 1998 NCAA Tournament.

"Larry Hughes was the best player on the floor," he said of a player for Saint Louis. "But if you look at us one through 10 and (Saint Louis) one through 10, it was a no-brainer. And we blew them out because we could focus a lot of attention on their one player."

Hughes made only four of 17 shots.

"Now (mid-major teams are) starting to have a couple more dudes that maybe they're not Larry Hughes, but they're more athletic and they can stay in the game longer," Padgett said. "The other thing is the longer they stay in it as a mid-major, the pressure goes up on the high major."

Former Arkansas Coach Nolan Richardson echoed the idea that parity is growing.

"I guarantee you a 16-seed ain't going to mean anything a couple years from now," he said in 2023. "The key is to get in the tournament. That's all. You don't care about numbers. Right now, everybody's saying he's the No. 1 seed. He's the No. 2 seed. I never thought about seed. I must have been crazy. I just tried to win."

Seeding used to mean something, Richardson said before adding, "now with NIL and all that, all the rules they have. One day you play for one school, the next day you play for another school. Shit. I guarantee you, hoss, it's a new venture out there."

With retirement came a flood of memories:

My second game on the beat saw Kentucky win 78-62 at Ohio State. Associate Coach Leonard Hamilton laughed when I asked a player if the game being televised inspired the team.

I had a lot to learn.

In April of 2021, I included NCAA Tournament memories in a Sunday Notes column.

Beginning in 1993, Kentucky had beaten Utah four times in the last 10 NCAA tournaments. UK and Utah were set to play a second-round game in 2003.

This led Utah Coach Rick Majerus to say during the day-before-the-game news conference, "When I die, they might as well bury me at the finish line at Churchill Downs so they can run over me again."

Kentucky's average margin of victory in those four victories over Utah was 18.5 points.

When a reporter suggested Kentucky was vulnerable in 2003, Majerus shot back, "Nobody's going to hold a telethon to help Kentucky get players."

The next day Kentucky beat Utah 74-54.

In the 1998-99 season, Kentucky went to Puerto Rico to play three games in the San Juan Shootout. A reporter from Italy's version of ESPN was there to work on a story about Kentucky basketball.

I agreed to speak with him. We had a pleasant conversation. When he asked me if I was a Kentucky fan, I said I wasn't.

This seemed to surprise him. So, I felt a need to briefly explain.

Kentucky had enough fans, I said.

He laughed.

During a conversation in the fall of 2007 about incoming freshman Alex Legion, his mother repeatedly made references to God.

The Almighty steered her son to the prestigious Detroit Country Day, a private school that produced such basketball stars as Chris Webber and Shane Battier. Then the Holy Spirit let it be known that Legion should transfer to prep powerhouse Oak Hill Academy for his senior year. Divine intervention brought him to Kentucky, a college he had not been considering.

"I had no clue Kentucky was a basketball school. No clue," Annette Legion said. "But God knew."

When asked about God's interest in her son, she quietly, almost as an aside, made a startling claim.

"Me being a prophet, He has truly ordered my son's steps," she said matter-of-factly.

Prophet? Did you say prophet? Like Isaiah and Ezekiel of the Old Testament?

"I'm a prophet," she said.

Later in our conversation, the player's mother looked into the basketball future.

"The Lord has shown me: they're going to the Final Four," she said of the 2007-08 Kentucky team before adding a qualifier, "providing they play together."

Was this prophecy? A prediction? Merely wishful thinking?

"I have spoken these things into existence," she said. "It's not by accident that my son is here and now the Final Four is in Michigan."

Such a triumphant return for Alex Legion, who grew up in suburban Detroit, would have to have come in 2009. That was when the Final Four was in Detroit.

But he transferred to Illinois during the first semester of his freshman year at Kentucky. And Kentucky lost to Marquette in the first round of the 2008 NCAA Tournament.

These factual missteps were well within the historical leeway given prophets, according to Ben Witherington, a New Testament professor at Asbury Seminary.

"Almost all prophecies of the ancient sort involved analogy, metaphor and indirectness," Witherington told me for the story. "You have to puzzle the meaning. Very seldom was it 'this is going to happen in the next five minutes, get ready.'"

Surely, Shaka Smart set a Final Four record in 2011 by quoting 19th century American poet Emily Dickinson one time.

When asked if it was possible for VCU or Butler to win the national championship with Kentucky and Connecticut also in the Final Four, Smart said, "I hope it's possible or we might as well go back to Richmond."

As reporters chuckled, Smart added, "Emily Dickinson said, 'Dwell in possibility.'"

Butler beat VCU 70-62 in one national semifinal game, while UConn beat Kentucky 56-55.

Then UConn beat Butler 53-41 in the championship game.

For several seasons, LSU had a live tiger in a cage-like facility outside its on-campus arena.

Before one Kentucky game at LSU, Mike the Tiger was wheeled into the Pete Maravich Assembly Center. As the cage was pulled around the court, LSU students chanted, "Let him loose, let him loose."

With the 1987 Pan Am Games in Indianapolis and the U.S. basketball team having a Kentucky flavor, I was assigned to cover the event. Rex Chapman played for the U.S. team coached by Denny Crum.

Led by Oscar Schmidt, Brazil beat the U.S. in the title game.

During an off day for basketball, I went to the diving competition. I wanted to see Greg Louganis compete.

Even to my untrained eye, Louganis stood out. He won gold medals in the three-meter springboard and 10-meter platform competitions.

Covering Kentucky provided opportunities for travel to exotic locales. As I once joked to a Zoom audience, that meant trips to Japan, Mexico and . . . Tennessee.

Three memories stand out from the 1986 summer trip to Japan and Hong Kong.

While in Tokyo, UK officials invited me to join them on a visit to a Japanese bathhouse. How many chances would I have to do this?

There were immersions in cold and hot baths, then a period of relaxation sipping beer and watching television.

Then came the massage.

When we returned to the hotel, I felt like I poured myself into the bed.

One evening on the trip, I felt I had a case of food poisoning. I called the front desk to ask to be connected to Walt McCombs, the team trainer. The man at the desk did not speak English fluently or understand what I was saying. I tried to tell him I wanted to leave a message for McCombs. The man at the desk asked me if I wanted a massage.

I ran into Walt the next morning and he gave me medicine.

Upon arriving in Hong Kong, the bus driver acted as a tourist guide on the ride from the airport to the hotel. At one point, he noted a high rise residence of at least 25 or 30 floors. Thousands of people lived in the building, he said.

This inspired a quip from Richard Madison, who said if someone farted in the building, hundreds of people would smell it.

During a trip to the Great Alaska Shootout, the UK traveling party was advised not to pet any moose that was on the Anchorage streets.

When it snowed almost 10 inches the day before my return home, I went to the front desk and asked if this might delay or cancel my flight the next morning. People at the front desk laughed. By Alaska standards, it was a mere dusting of snow.

Kentucky playing in the Maui Invitational was always a highlight of the season.

During one trip, the term "Polynesian Paralysis" was circulating. This meant teams from the mainland could lose a competitive edge in the sunny, 80-degree weather that featured a refreshing ocean breeze. There was a sensation of being removed from reality and whisked to another planet.

On the day before the basketball tournament began, then *Herald-Leader* columnist Johnny McGill and I were sitting in our hotel's open-air bar. The view included a swimming pool and the Pacific Ocean.

Johnny was working leisurely on his column and asked me if I thought the Kentucky team was susceptible to Polynesian Paralysis.

I replied, "Who cares?"

Johnny laughed.

I am thankful for the much-needed help others have given me.

Mike Connell, my last sports editor at the newspaper in Huntington, W.Va., the *Herald-Dispatch*, recommended me to his counterpart in Lexington. Mike Johnson, then the sports editor of the *Herald-Leader*, took a chance by hiring me. Gene Abell and Mat Graf followed Johnson as guiding lights.

John Carroll, whose resume included several Pulitzer Prizes, and his successor, Tim Kelly, set the tone for wanting objective journalism.

In a city and UK campus where everyone initially was a stranger, then columnist D.G. FitzMaurice was a willing guide. He provided a much-appreciated friendly welcome that included his infectious sense of humor and an introduction to Long Island tea.

I'm thankful to fellow staffers like Mike Fields, John Clay, Mark Story, Franklin Renfro, Mark Sonka, Jennifer Smith, Chip Cosby and the many others who gave me moral support and valued friendships.

They were all part of a newsroom camaraderie I will miss. Fellow media members who covered UK or other college basketball programs expanded this much appreciated bond.

The 2019 NCAA Tournament included an odd historical note.

Kentucky had won more NCAA Tournament games than any program. Kansas City had been the host city for more NCAA Tournament games than any other city.

Yet, Kentucky had never played a tournament game in Kansas City until 2019.

Another surprise came upon arrival. There was a comic-con convention being held at the media hotel.

On a drive to dinner one night, the Uber driver said he had given a ride to Spider-Man earlier in the evening.

That prompted a wise guy (blush) to ask, Spider-Man needs Uber?

A list of regrets must include how I angered Joe B. Hall on his 92nd birthday. This included a touch of irony involved that softened the self-incrimination and made me smile.

In retirement, Hall became a beloved figure. Whenever he appeared during games on the Rupp Arena video boards, fans would erupt in warm and enthusiastic applause.

When I heard that Kentucky planned to showcase Hall when he came to the game, I wondered what it would be like for a man in his 90s to be so warmly greeted. I thought it would make a sweet story.

So I called Joe and asked. He said the fans did not cheer him so warmly when he was Kentucky's coach. So, I thought, "he wants to go there." OK. I asked a few follow-up questions and wrote the story along that line.

When I saw Hall before the game, he let me know he was not happy with the story or me. I felt terrible. It seemed cruel to anger someone of that age.

A small consolation came in remembering that when he coached, Hall had accused me of steering him to say something he had not wanted to say.

This time I wished I had steered him to say how much he appreciated the upcoming ovation.

Hall attributed his longevity to heredity. He said he had a great-grandmother who lived to be 100. His mother reached 90, a brother 88.

I'll continue to watch Kentucky games. They are entertaining, plus I figure that Kentucky basketball will come up in casual conversation, so I'll want to have a sense of what people are talking about.

But my rooting interest in sports – yeah, we won!!! Or oh (expletive), we lost – has nearly disappeared.

A conversation with Dan Wann, the psychology professor at Murray State, came to mind when I retired. A year or two earlier, we had been just chatting after he responded to whatever questions I wanted to bounce off of him for an upcoming story.

I said my rooting interest in sports had diminished greatly. Wann then said, do you know what that indicates?

No, I said.

"Maturity," Wann said.

I laughed and said I couldn't wait to tell my wife that I had matured. She would be greatly surprised.

About the Author

Photo by Mark Cornelison

Beginning with the 1981-82 season, sportswriter Jerry Tipton covered the University of Kentucky men's basketball program for 41 years. This included nine Final Four appearances (1984, 1993, 1996, 1997, 1998, 2011, 2012, 2014 and 2015) and three national championships (1996, 1998 and 2012). He cherished the many chances to feel like he was writing the first draft of history. This included the 1983 "Dream Game" against Louisville, the so-called Christian Laettner game and Kentucky's 38-0 start to the 2014-15 season. Memorable "lows" in his time included the tornado that hit the 2008 Southeastern Conference Tournament, the historic loss to 15-seed Saint Peter's in his last game on the beat and the NCAA investigation that led to Eddie Sutton's firing.

Besides reporting on six basketball coaches (Joe B. Hall, Eddie Sutton, Rick Pitino, Tubby Smith, Billy Gillispie and John Calipari), Tipton's 41 years in the sports department of the *Lexington Herald-Leader* included covering UK's football team from 1981 through the 1986 season.

Before coming to Lexington, Tipton worked 10 years for the daily newspaper in Huntington, W.Va., the *Herald-Dispatch*. This time included two years as a part-timer while attending Marshall University and eight years full-time after graduating with a degree in journalism in 1973. During this time, he covered high school sports, bowling and Marshall's men's basketball team.

He was inducted into the Marshall University Journalism Hall of Fame in 2018, the Kentucky Journalism Hall of Fame in 2020 and the United States Basketball Writers Association Hall of Fame in 2005.

Tipton grew up in Hamtramck, Mich., which is one of two independent towns inside the Detroit city limits. He and his wife, Paula Anderson, live in Lexington. They have two sons, Stephen and Jackson.

Index

C

H

I

J

K

L

M

N

O

P

T

U

V

W

X

Y

Z